SOMEBODY TOLD ME...

Also by Danny Wallace

Awkward Situations for Men
Charlotte Street
Danny Wallace and the Centre of the Universe
Friends Like These
F*** You Very Much
Join Me
Random Acts of Kindness
What Not to Do and How to Do It
Who is Tom Ditto?
Yes Man

SOMEBODY TOLD ME...

ONE MAN'S UNEXPECTED JOURNEY DOWN THE RABBIT HOLE OF LIES, TROLLS AND CONSPIRACIES

DANNY WALLACE

EBURY
PRESS

Ebury Press, an imprint of Ebury Publishing
20 Vauxhall Bridge Road
London SW1V 2SA

Ebury Press is part of the Penguin Random House group of companies
whose addresses can be found at global.penguinrandomhouse.com

First published by Ebury Press in 2024

www.penguin.co.uk

A CIP catalogue record for this book is available from the British Library

Hardback ISBN 9781529931181
Trade paperback 9780091919054

Illustrations by Vyki Hendy

Printed and bound in Great Britain by Clays Ltd, Elcograf S.p.A.

The authorised representative in the EEA is Penguin Random House Ireland,
Morrison Chambers, 32 Nassau Street, Dublin D02 YH68.

Penguin Random House is committed to a sustainable future for
our business, our readers and our planet. This book is made
from Forest Stewardship Council® certified paper.

For Greta. This is all your fault.

Contents

Prologue

When she left us far too young in 2018, aged just 46, the Gorilla Foundation described the celebrated western lowland gorilla Koko as one who had 'touched the lives of millions as an ambassador for all gorillas'.

She was 'an icon', they said, and I remember those words in particular.

The experts continued: Koko was a vital figure 'in interspecies communication and also for people with empathy everywhere'.

* * *

Koko was a gorilla who did her job well and she knew it.

She never lacked self-confidence.

After apparently learning to understand more than 2,000 words in English as well as basic sign language, it's said she once proudly pointed at herself and declared herself 'Queen'.

She would just as acutely study the humans who would study her, in her state-of-the-art facility in the Santa Cruz mountains. And she would also play pranks on them.

Once, she tapped at a photo of a bird in a magazine, and then signed the words: 'THAT ME!'

The scientists were confused.

'UH, YOU'RE A BIRD?' they asked, apparently dumb-founded, and Koko nodded sensibly and claimed not just to be a bird, but a really GOOD bird, and she kept a straight face throughout.

The scientists were pretty sure she wasn't a bird – they were scientists, remember – and finally, Koko relented.

With a laugh, she said, 'GORILLA KOKO!'

This should have been a warning.

* * *

An ape with a fascination for human nipples (she once caused a sexual harassment case, later settled out of court, because members of staff felt obliged to show her their nipples), there is one reason above all that paints Koko as perhaps the most human-like gorilla of all time.

One day, in a furious fit of pique brought on by who knows what, so the apocryphal story goes, Koko used her giant muscles and immense animal rage to rip a heavy steel sink from the wall and toss it on the floor beside her.

It was hugely noisy, hugely messy, and the scientists were horrified.

What had happened to Koko? Why had she done such a random thing so violently?

Koko looked ashamed. She skulked in a corner. She knew she was in trouble.

The scientists stood over her, demanding answers.

And what they say happened next was a warning from history.

Because she acted on instinct. She did what a lot of us would have done in that situation. She did what more and more people these days do.

She lied.

She pointed at her playmate, All Ball.

And she said All Ball did it.

She said All Ball *ripped the sink from the wall and made the huge mess!*

This seemed unlikely.

Because her playmate All Ball was a very small kitten.

* * *

This is a book about lies.

Not lies like Koko's lie, which is so relatable because it is a tale of lies being almost in our DNA and reminds us of a million times when we've been in a similar position (maybe not ripping a sink off a wall) and blaming it on someone else (maybe not a kitten).

And it's not a book about our modern leaders or the ease with which even the most inept of them now lie and then lie about lying and then lie about that.

If that were the book I was writing it would have so many pages that you would already have broken both arms trying to open it.

It's about the more sophisticated lies; the lies that dance like blown dandelion seeds in the air around us every time we check our phones; the lies we are going to have to get used to as the seeds find the soil to settle into.

* * *

I'm only writing this sentence now because of an unexpected moment involving my dad and an old Chinese man by a lake: the sort of moment I'm sure that your own father

3

once had with an old Chinese man by a lake. It was a short, small moment that would lead me down the rabbit hole into a world of lies big and small, of conspiracies, trolls and grifters; lies which at a particular point in my life nearly made me question my own sanity.

And it meant that this would become a book about a new ecosystem of lies. How they infiltrate a relationship, how they can ruin your best moments, how they ruin whole lives.

It's about how this world of lies can affect our family, our street and our community. How lies can spread across a country, a continent and the world. How they take hold of our imaginations and make us feel both helpless and powerful, both meaningless and meaningful.

And it's a book about whether we are strong enough to beat those lies, because they can reach us wherever we are, leaping at us from our pockets and desks and living room walls, or in strange emails from old Chinese men.

* * *

Coming back to that idea of seeds I mentioned – the seeds for a lot of the very biggest lies we experience every day were planted centuries ago.

As one 'truther' we'll meet later puts it: 'The tree grew. And now the fruit is bearing. And check out the weather. It's perfect for producing the very worst fruit possible.'

That fruit can be swallowed by anyone.

I mean ... have you been keeping your eye on your grandma lately? Have you been calling her enough? You sure she's not spending too much time on YouTube? Is she talking fondly of dictators? Has she suddenly started quietly muttering in the

4

Aldi queue about the 'Jewish Space Lasers' she's heard are setting wildfires around the world to make sure everyone believes in climate change? Does she suspect Oprah is a demon?

Now anyone – your neighbour, your brother, you, me – can very easily become confused, consume lies disguised as the truth from internet forums or cable news monologues, or become a conspiracy theorist – or at least someone swayed by them. Your kid's teacher might well quietly believe that after a terrible car crash in 1966, Sir Paul McCartney was replaced in The Beatles by a body double who thankfully happened also to be great at bass guitar, singing Beatles songs, writing to the highest standard possible with John Lennon, and doing double thumbs-ups to order.

We even carry little liars with us. Our phones are happy to deceive us. With every real moment of shared humanity they bring – a text from a loved one, a birthday call for those who still stubbornly insist phones can be used for calling – they blink and flash and ding-ding to alert us to new sensational untruths written by unseen hands to tempt us back to the swipes and taps they gain such comfort from.

The words they display to us titillate, tease, bait us with a stream of *what if*, *could be* and *somebody told me*. They promise us the satisfaction of deep understanding and thrilling and seductive insight. They allow anyone, anywhere to reach through for a moment, into our real lives, and whisper to us anything at all to make us feel there is a point to things, that every story has a simple hero and a straightforward villain, and that only by taking its offered hand and climbing further inside can we really learn the truths that will give our lives the meaning we need.

And the question in among the believable and the unbelievable things that fly at us constantly, always there in the background waving helplessly at us from just behind the propaganda, is: what can we do to stop this?

Because it's got worse, hasn't it? You know it and I know it and neither of us like it. Lies are being weaponised and aimed right this way. The lies that find you in everyday life. That gnaw at you, beg for your time. The lies you let in, every time you hit *Like*, *Subscribe*, *Expand* or *Refresh*. The lies that are desperate for us, because we are the happy hosts of the parasites.

And we are living in a time when we are more susceptible to it than ever. The things imagined, and the things that are real.

So now, with everything I've just written in mind, can I ask you something?

— When did you personally notice that things had got really bad?

When did you notice that weather?

That weather, so perfect for the very worst fruit to grow?

Trust No One

In which I tell you how I found out about the
old Chinese man – and the messages that confused,
confounded, and made me set sail towards a
world of disinformation …

And we look at the day the world started
to believe *anything*.

What does it take for us to abandon our
smart, brilliant selves – and all because of
something somebody told us?

1

The Old Chinese Man

Spies, Lies and Chicken Thighs

My father died as winter faded.

You're not prepared for the strange things you have to do when something like that happens.

The paperwork.

The responsibility.

Your new position in the family as you are forced to accept a promotion you did not ask for and do not want.

It's your job to tell his grandchildren.

His friends. You have to call his sister and tell her. You have to make decisions on things you never talked about. You have to look through his phone, finding photos of the sea you never knew he'd taken. You have to go through drawers filled with old foreign coins or fountain pen ink or rechargeable batteries from the 1980s to see if you can find a book of passwords, and when you do you wonder why he chose such random passwords for everything. A hundred different ones.

Why is the broadband password for a 78-year-old man *DarthVaderBridgerton5*?

You have to answer questions you've never considered, like 'Would you like curtains with the coffin?' You have to whittle a broad and varied life down to two or three songs on a USB.

You have to look after your mum.

You have to read the last messages your adored father sent (Dad's was to someone on a customer queries team called Rory, thanking him for his very professional response to a question he'd sent and politely apologising for having wasted his time) and answer any emails that come in with the grim news and the reply they weren't expecting.

Emails like the one from the old Chinese man.

* * *

The old Chinese man was very, very shocked to learn our news.

I think more shocked than almost anyone we told.

And I was shocked by how shocked he was.

'We were very, <u>very</u> shocked to learn of the passing away of Professor Emeritus Ian Wallace, who passed away peacefully in his sleep on February 1st, 2021 at his home in Felixstowe, aged 78,' he wrote, touchingly.

And then he took a second, presumably.

And then he added:

Please restrain your grief!
Excessive mourning won't do any good.

I immediately laughed.

I'll admit, I found that an unusual response from a man I didn't at all know.

I was sure it came from a kind place, but it did feel a little like being told off for something you can't help. It would take a brave man to shout it at a funeral.

Also, the first part of his email featured a sentence lifted word-for-word from my dad's obituary, which I had written myself and which had only just run in the *Guardian*. It felt like reading a Wikipedia entry, or an essay by a student a little too reliant on copy-and-paste.

Still, it remained warming to see just how affected the old Chinese man was, given he was someone who had essentially met my dad for perhaps ten minutes or so, 12 whole years before, on the banks of the West Lake at Hangzhou, China, 6,000 miles away.

* * *

My dad had been walking, alone, as evening fell on an early November evening.

He'd been in China to deliver a series of academic lectures on East German writers, but his colleagues had all headed for their homes in the evenings. It seemed frowned upon to hang out with a Western colleague like Dad.

So my father ate another quiet meal, stretched, and took one more long but happy stroll before bed.

But this time, when he glanced behind him, he saw a man far behind.

The next time he turned around, a little further on, this old Chinese man was much closer. Dad smiled, and they started a conversation.

The man asked my dad to take a picture for him in front of the lake, then he gave my dad his email address. Pressed it into his hand. *Urged* him to get in touch when he returned home. They had *much* they could tell each other.

Opening up Dad's computer and looking through his emails, I found what I could of the rest of the correspondence between the two men, starting with the man's oddly formal starter:

This email is to test connection

And my dad's warmer reply:

It was a great pleasure to meet you and to talk to you as we walked along the West Lake! I shall send you some photographs as I promised. These will introduce you to my wife Trudy and also give you some idea of where we live, although I am sure you have already found it on the map as you said you would.

The man had indeed done that – he'd looked up the small coastal town of Clevedon in Somerset on the map, then soon heard from Dad all about me, my mum, my wife.

He'd even seen pictures of my firstborn.

* * *

After urging me to restrain my grief and excessive mourning, the old Chinese man softened, and kindly offered me his heartfelt condolences.

But then something weird happened.

He suddenly started to spell my dad's name wrong. He was no longer Ian. The name looked pasted in. There were new font colours involved.

'The news of Lan Wallace's passing away took us by surprise,' it said. 'His sudden death was totally unexpected.'

I was surprised, too, at the intensity of feeling about my father's passing.

Though at the same time it did start to sound like this man had done it himself. He might as well have added, 'It totally wasn't me!'

But instead he waxed long and lyrical about it:

Lan Wallace's passing has been like a dream.
We sometimes even don't believe it's true.
But it's true.

It's definitely true. I was there and I checked several times.

But I knew on some level that Lan must be a way of spelling Ian. A mistake not made in the earliest emails but which was creeping in now. The emails, though, kept up the strange, heightened intensity of feeling:

We must accept the reality.
We have lost one of our best friends.

OK.

I mean, 'best friends' may be stretching it.

This was my dad.

You've only lost a man you met for ten minutes by a lake in 2009.

You've lost a pen pal at most.

I wasn't sure how to handle it, as the old Chinese man wailed dramatically:

The reality can not be changed!
Let's cherish the memory of *Lan Wallace* forever.

I found them strange but funny, these emails.

Probably because I was depressingly well aware that the reality could not be changed.

But also because I was happy to find *anything* funny at the time.

I thought it was funny that the old Chinese man was claiming to be my dad's best friend. I could almost hear my dad's surprised flutter of laughter if I'd been able to tell him about it.

All I wanted to do was read these emails out loud to him, start calling him Lan, then grab him by the shoulders and shout 'Let us *cherish the memory of Lan Wallace forever*!'

And I wanted to giggle with my mum, and shout the words 'PLEASE RESTRAIN YOUR GRIEF! EXCESSIVE MOURNING WON'T DO ANY GOOD!'

You look for any moment of light when everything is dark.

But as I looked at these emails more, at first celebrating the innocence of them, I guess … I stopped smiling or laughing so much.

Because as I re-read them, I started to find them not just unusual to read, but even unusual to look at.

The strange hodgepodge of fonts and formatting, sometimes changing just for a name, sometimes halfway through a sentence.

The bizarre shifts in tone and topic.

Sections that I knew were copied and pasted, some written in a slightly different style.

And some very jarring indentations (which is the most middle-class complaint I've ever committed to paper).

Maybe some paragraphs had been put through Google Translate, for obvious reasons?

But all of these weird, emotive, intricate, intimate emails were so … *long.*

And then I noticed the thing that really set my spidey sense tingling.

Some of the errors or quirks you could put down to simple cultural differences, I think, perhaps differences in alphabets, but then I spotted something in his initial reply to our news that made me gulp and then forward it to my own email account.

Because this one detail from the old Chinese man felt so unusual, so *out of the ordinary*, that it took me from confusion to suspicion.

Part way through what felt like it was meant to be the old Chinese man's final email, there was this incredibly odd thing.

It was a *complete list of past correspondences with my dad.*

An accurate history of their email exchanges, offered up I don't know why.

Every message documented, timestamped, and every reply accounted for.

For example:

> We wrote to **IAN WALLACE** on 23-12-20 at 18:42 [CST],
> **IAN WALLACE** replied 24-12-20 at 13:22 [GMT].

Why?

Why was he doing this?

When was the last time *you* did this?

Who cares what exact time each email was sent?

And then – see if you can spot the *very unusual detail* which leaped out at me from this:

> We kept close contact, sending e-mails each other to exchange informations of every aspects.
>
> I checked that during the 12 years (2009-2020), totally I have sent 45 e-mails to **Mr.Ian Wallance** and he has sent us 34 e-mails.
>
> This is the last e-mail sent me from **Mr.Ian Wallance** (2020-12-24 04:35) (from Ian Wallace-34)

It's feeling less personal now, less warm.

And did you notice what I did?

Not the fact it reads like someone tidying up after a job's come to an end.

Not the fact it reads like a chore for a line manager.

Not the lack of care taken with his name to his family.

Not just more of the very accurate date and precise times no one needs to know.

Not just the confusion of 'I' and 'us'.

But *Ian Wallace-34.*

It was Dad's 34th reply. The old Chinese man had said as much.

But it had been *numbered*.

Do *you* number your emails? Do you keep them, and order them, and number them?

Doesn't this imply ... a *file* of some kind?

Organisation?

Like an easy way to reference evidence?

'Can you forward email 34?' – that sort of thing.

Oh, and always a curious shift in tone towards the end of the email, in which the old Chinese man went to great lengths to explain just how happy they were being Chinese citizens in a happy country where everyone was happy and now in 2021 Covid was totally under control, as proven by *incredibly* specific figures:

> As we ever told you, the epidemic situation in China always keeps very well.
>
> Till now, still each day there are only a very few new infected cases in whole country, and most cases of them are from other countries.
>
> But Chinese governments still always pay a great attention to prevent from its spread.
>
> 2,841,269,000 doses of vaccination have been inoculated in China.

In previous emails there'd also usually be a paragraph in which they'd demonstrate how normal their normal lives are.

We went to the Chrysanthemum Museum recently!

We enjoyed shellfish at the seaside with old school-friends!

And again, always these over the top and heartfelt reminders of my dad's importance to this man:

> May we forever remember Professor *Emeritus* _I. WALLACE_ and may he stay in our hearts.
> We were such close friends.

They were such close friends, him and 'I. Wallace'.

They were *good* friends.

They were *best* friends!

I started to wonder if he was maybe after some inheritance.

But I was also fascinated.

Because now something had opened up in me. It started with amusement, then noticing patterns, then questioning certain phrases.

I'd started to suspect something.

These emails did not read like emails.

How do you feel? Because I felt like they read like a *performance*.

They felt like someone reading out loud in a meeting.

The timestamps, the details, the *numbering*.

It was like making sure everyone on a team was all caught up and on the same page.

So obviously, I started to wonder who might have been bcc'd. Who else was in the room. Whether more than one person was writing them. Perhaps that's why there was this sense of 'let's get you caught up with the story so far' to them.

I may have been going mad – people do go mad in the thick of grief – but I was also feeling playful.

And I decided to send another note of my own to the old Chinese man, just to see.

How would he react?

What should I say?

So I thanked him for his wishes and told him my father had spoken fondly of him.

I paused a second before sending.

When he saw this, would things peter out?

Or, as I had been coming to suspect, would it be filed under *Danny Wallace-2*?

By *a Chinese spy*.

One closing a case?

Because, look – that's what all this felt like: a spy closing a case.

A spy saying, 'During the 12 years (2009-2020) totally **I have sent 45 emails to Mr.Ian Wallance and he has sent us 34 e-mails.** Here are the stats, the Wallace/Wallance contact is done, we can wrap this up.'

It didn't feel like something you'd send to someone's wife, someone's son – any more than telling them to restrict their excessive mourning or copy and paste an obituary.

No – to me, it felt like something you'd hurriedly tell your boss or put on record as a project comes to an end.

So, now I'd replied, would they ditch me or want to continue?

As it happens, they were surprised, delighted to hear from me.

They did reply.

And they wanted to remind me:

We suddenly lost a best friend, *Ian Wallace*.

And they had just … *one* request.
That request intrigued me.
They said that to honour my oddly italicised father, we should actually continue our correspondence.

We think in order to remember and think of *Ian Wallace* often, we and you should keep our close friendship following *Ian Wallace*.
We should keep contact *forever*.

Forever?!
So, deeply intrigued now, I wrote back, and said that yes, that would be great.
Just like they'd done with Dad, we could 'keep close contact and exchange information of every aspect'.
And I would be more than willing to keep contact.
Forever.

* * *

So look: the friends I shared my excited suspicions with were extremely polite, at least at first.
While yes, this old Chinese man *could* be someone initiating a spying scheme on my dad, they gently said, it was important I also explore the possibility that it was just some old man by a lake.

Just a guy who had initiated and maintained an email correspondence that lasted 12 years so that he might practise his English.

He *may* have been a Chinese spy, they reassured me with kind eyes … but again I should also remember to consider and maybe explore the idea that he was definitely *not* a Chinese spy.

Because why would a Chinese spy be emailing my dad? Why would a Chinese spy want to email me?

I could absolutely see all these points, but I also thought: why *wouldn't* a Chinese spy want to email me?

I mean, it would hardly be my first rodeo.

* * *

My family has a history with spies, propaganda and disinformation that opened my eyes to hidden possibilities everywhere from a young age.

Growing up, it seemed normal to me that, at times, family conversation might turn to who is or who might be a spy. My dad's work as a Professor of Modern Languages and his expertise in German literature was focused around the former East Germany, or the 'German Democratic Republic'.

The German Democratic Republic was not a republic, nor was it democratic. That just leaves German, and on that score at least it did very well. But it was a dictatorship, in which there was no freedom of movement, no division of powers and no free elections. It was a place of repression, paranoia, abductions and beatings.

My dad's colleagues described him as 'a pioneer with an international reputation' in two main areas of the GDR: the study of the GDR itself, and the study of those exiled from it. He wrote books, organised conferences, he taught, he researched, he set up journals, he travelled the world. Berlin, Los Angeles, Moscow, Belfast, everywhere.

He also laughed heartily when as a kid I'd splash him with water from the hosepipe, then chase me round the garden with a bucketful. He never even minded being woken from the big chair in the living room as the doorbell went, then having to answer the door to whatever 1980s double-glazing or Lipton teabag salesman it was, not realising as he talked sensibly to this complete stranger that I'd coloured the end of his nose a vibrant orange using the pollen from one of Mum's flowers.

Dad was handsome.

Sometimes he'd have Elvis hair, sometimes George Best.

He grew up without a dad in working-class post-war Carlisle, raised by a single mother working as a waitress in the Silver Grill bakery and restaurant, and on the production line at Carr's biscuit factory.

Dad earned his way into the local grammar school. Won all the awards. Fell in love with French and German. Won a scholarship to Oxford. Captained the football team, was a star at rugby and lacrosse and it shows in the pictures: confi-dent arms crossed over strong chest in black and white pictures where he's surrounded by young men who look surprised to have been picked for *anything*, let alone contact sports. Dad was gentle in personality but tough when it came to sports.

He was the boy who could barely afford to eat, living in a new world surrounded by those who'd never been hungry.

He met my mum, his wife, soon after. She'd just arrived off the bus in Oxford too, from Switzerland – a young, smart, funny, interested multilinguist born on Lake Constance who'd scored a job at the nearby Randolph Hotel.

Their team was born. Immediately inseparable. And within years as he started his work, he'd be travelling to East Berlin and the GDR, something that obviously required very special visas and permissions – permissions this young academic had somehow been granted.

There are sharp black and white pictures of him in East Germany. Wearing stylish clothes and black shades. Standing in front of Checkpoint Charlie, looking like he's probably concealing a weapon and knows how to rappel down the side of a building.

There's one of him I remember absolutely loving. This young man, before he was my dad at all, staring off into the distance, at the very beginning of his adult life, in front of the Brandenburg Gate.

Was he wearing Ray-Bans? Some safari suit maybe?

I don't know where it is anymore.

But do you know when it seems my dad met his first spy?

The day of my birth: 16 November 1976.

(It wasn't me; I'm not saying I was a spy baby.)

I'll explain.

* * *

So, this first spy.

The 'spy' in question was coming all the way over to the east-coast Scottish city of Dundee from Leipzig University as officially he wanted to get to know my dad and his areas of interest.

Maybe he could be of some help? Be a handy guy to know in Leipzig?

Dad couldn't meet with him that day because he was a bit busy in Ninewells Hospital suddenly being called Dad and being there for the woman he adored who'd just become Mum, but the very fact the East German man could travel to Dundee at all, *let alone* engage with a foreign academic like my German Studies lecturer dad, spoke volumes: this man called Dieter was a member of 'the Party', allowed out on a mission.

He'd been sent by the Stasi, the East German Ministry for Security, and he was a minder – a handler.

It would be Dieter who would 'look after' my dad on his first trips to East Germany, showing him around, 'keeping him safe', but also keeping a heavy eye on him.

Dad knew this, Mum says.

And despite knowing that one was most definitely spying on the other ... Dad and Dieter got on like a house on fire.

They became proper mates. Dieter was a *legend*.

Dieter and Dad ended up touring East Germany together.

They went hiking in the Saxon Switzerland mountains east of Dresden, they stopped at hostels for beer and chicken thighs, they probably wore little German hats and smoked little German pipes while they were doing it.

My mum tells me 'everybody *loved* Dieter' – not just a warming sentiment, but a great title for a 1980s East German sitcom.

But there remained a subtle atmosphere of danger around Dieter, and everybody who knew him – with his bottle-thick, heavy-rimmed glasses, long trench coat and brown cap, this man who walked and spoke extremely slowly but very interestingly – knew he had 'people' he talked to. And that was worrying.

One time, on a visit to East Berlin in 1980, Dad disappeared for a few days. Mum just couldn't got hold of him, or even Dieter, and she was dialling and redialling on the rotary phone in the hallway at home. She feared the worst, she told me: Dad had been due to meet with an East German writer in trouble with the authorities and there was talk of Dad smuggling a manuscript out of the country so that it might meet Western eyes.

Wait. Dad was a *smuggler*? This had never been mentioned before. If it had, I'd have forced Dad to come in and talk to my classmates about it on Careers Day.

Mum says she immediately assumed he'd been found out and arrested and was now chained up in some basement room somewhere in East Berlin by a couple of thugs with batons.

As it turned out, a man from the British Embassy sent to find him discovered him sweat-drenched and huddled in pain in the corner of his rented room in a phoneless university guesthouse, battling not the Stasi but a huge kidney stone.

Still.

It says a lot to me about that my mum's first thought was 'kidnapped, arrested and possibly beaten'. This was not what my friends' mums would have immediately thought if their other halves hadn't phoned them during a foreign business trip, which would be 'pissed and/or lost'. Or maybe 'chicken-thigh poisoning'.

* * *

Dad's work was always there, alive in the house. Books and papers everywhere. Weird, angry East German beat poetry played loudly from his study speakers as this gentle, kind Carlisle man made his notes about it.

And all of it enjoyed and pushed forward and supported by my Swiss mum, a woman with her own academic interests and who once, after arranging a trip behind the Iron Curtain for 30 totally normal but interested Loughborough people, received a medal in front of the Brandenburg Gate from stern uniformed East German officials for 'services to tourism'. It's genuinely the most communist-looking medal you've ever seen.

My point is, stuff like this was quite normal in our house. *I* liked *The A-Team* and *Knight Rider*, *they* liked East German literature and angry beat poetry.

Our house was often full of people speaking German – activists, writers, poets, playwrights, people dressed like extras from *The Lives of Others*, drinking yellow tins of 1980s Hofmeister beer or red wines so dark they already looked like hangovers.

I remember the famous East German novelist Erich Loest sitting at our kitchen table, a man in his 60s with hangdog features and knuckles wrapped round a pint glass, whose writing had seen him arrested for 'conspiracy against the government', and who was then sent to the brutal and overcrowded Bautzen political prison run by the terrifying Ministry for State Security.

That said, everyone's parents had a mate like that.

So naturally, there were people who wanted to know what was going on at these parties.

We're certain that our phone in Dundee was bugged. And we know that after Dad became a professor, one of his colleagues at a university in the 1980s turned out to be spying on him on the side, sending handwritten letters to her contacts about his activities and areas of interest.

And sometimes – sometimes! – unusual people from foreign lands would even turn up in *person*.

* * *

There was a very memorable spy called Frederick.

Frederick was absolutely *rubbish*.

He was a man who turned up in our lives pretending to be a twentysomething student, but whose first mistake was clearly being 47.

There was no Google, of course, and the East Germans had to just guess at what students in 1980s Britain wore. So, having been given a 'student' cover story, he turned up not in stonewashed jeans and a Live Aid T-shirt, but instead dressed like the Doctor out of *Doctor Who*, wearing some kind of long Oxbridge scarf and carrying a leather briefcase. He did not quite fit in at the student bar.

Frederick had been sent over so that he could secretly gain my parents' trust because this was his mission: to use the Wallaces to gain an invitation to a speech being made by a visiting East German – a high-ranking member of the Church who'd been invited to the town to make an important speech.

Frederick needed to know exactly what this man was going to say, and who he was hanging out with. In the last few years of the GDR, the Church helped in the push towards democracy, and ultimately the bringing down of the Wall. Church became a place where people could discuss human rights and freedom in a protected environment. The Church encouraged people to vote and made sure there were Church members at every polling station.

And so it was Frederick's assignment to inveigle his way into that exclusive event to find out what the Church was saying about the GDR in Loughborough.

And so, using all his spy craft, smooth-talking, fake background, accent work, disguise, Loughborough research and training, Frederick arrived and began his mission *impossible*: somehow to gain access to that very meeting.

He didn't realise it was actually a free event, totally open to the public. Mum told him he didn't even need a ticket and that everyone would actually be very happy he had come because he'd help make up the numbers.

He really hadn't needed to make quite so much effort.

After the event, during which he sat next to absolutely anyone who fancied turning up and learned precisely nothing, Frederick was in a sudden and grumpy hurry to leave – he secured a lift to the train station in someone's E-Reg cherry red Nissan Micra, but had to swing by the local cinema first, the Loughborough Curzon just opposite the Wimpy, because for some reason he had left all his suitcases there. (Knowing, presumably, it would be open late and allow him a quick getaway if the cops found out he'd tried to access a completely public and innocuous event publicised freely in the *Loughborough Echo* – his daring escape is still the most exciting thing about the Curzon.)

And so he disappeared, as quickly as he'd arrived.

I still miss him.

Loughborough's place at the heart of East German interests continued, thanks only to my parents.

Soon after, when my mum arranged for a group of East German students to travel over to the UK, I remember a trip to J Sainsbury's with her to pick up some melons for them. It was the 1980s and everyone was into melons and Parma ham as a starter. I can't tell you how much melon and Parma ham made its way to our house on Spinney Hill Drive.

The East Germans marvelled at the vast rolling hills of melons. Most spoke some English. If any of them had had proper access to Western films, it would have been quite fashionable at the time to have made a joke about Dolly Parton.

But they stared at the fruit and cooed sarcastically about how it must have been 'delivery day'; they thought we were showing off our temporarily full supermarket shelves to demonstrate the freedoms of the West. Their government seemed not to have mentioned to them that pretty much everywhere else in Western Europe had food whenever they fancied it.

And then – on 9 November 1989 – an *immense* moment.

I remember our living room. The tiny telly. The East Germans crowded around it.

The Berlin Wall had fallen.

And yet ... here's the thing about disinformation, lies, propaganda, conspiracy and control: at first, despite all the evidence right in front of their faces, delivered by Brian Hanrahan on the BBC, none of the remaining students believed the Wall had fallen.

I stood in the living room, a kid, listening to grown-ups passionately disagree in English and German. I remember these people standing around our small Matsui TV in our living room, shaking their heads and putting hands on hips.

This was disinformation, they said. Lies. Conspiracy.

Right in front of me, pointing accusingly, they claimed the BBC's footage of the people of East Germany rising up and taking literal hammers to the wall was 'Western propaganda'.

The East Germans were adamant: this was some kind of incredibly expensive *War of the Worlds* to for some reason make people like a 12-year-old boy in Leicestershire think a seismic event in Berlin had happened.

But it's the *BBC*, I wanted to tell them.

That, I think, was the first time I questioned what was true and what was false in the grown-up world, or wondered why grown-ups would even have questions about it.

Dieter, the handler, would have had a story for those guys – some explanation he could burp out between beer breaths, something his highers-up had invented .

I don't know if Dieter ever tried to properly turn my dad into a spy. It would have been much easier for Dieter if that had been a possibility.

I'm sure Dad must have been asked.

The temptations to 'help' have always been there, for some, for a particular *type* of academic: the money, the ego, the prestige, the contacts, the invitations to lecture and examine and perhaps even become a university vice chancellor with a free house, a fat contract and a chance at the House of Lords.

My dad didn't care about any of that. He cared about us, his work and Carlisle United, not necessarily in that order.

He'd never have done it, but the point is, I realise now he's gone that I'm not sure I ever got a straight answer about whether any or many people *tried* to turn him into a spy.

I did ask, but as so often happens, answers got lost in side-stories and details and things interesting to others become mundane to you – but I was missing my Dad-as-spy anecdote. Do you realise what a great anecdote a Dad-as-spy anecdote would be?

So now, with the emails from the old Chinese man – emails relentlessly recapping the story so far for the benefit of the room – I had the genuine feeling I was in the realm of bad spies again.

Frederick.

Dieter.

Bad information.

Lies. Propaganda. Eighties Paranoia, as prevalent then as video nasties, knock-off *A-Team* duvets and melon and ham.

Decades later, could it really be that someone was reaching out – reaching into my phone – who may also not have been who they said they were?

* * *

Of course I was jumping to wishful conclusions, yes, so let's consider why.

Total honesty: I had been beaten down by the past few years. I was tired, work was thinner, everything was more expensive. Then the sharp yet dull smack of grief. Unsurprising, on the agenda the second you're born, but shocking and all-consuming.

And all happening in a divided world sinking into madness and pandemics, with a side order of trolls, bots, conspiracy and the white noise of lies.

The sheer VOLUME of life of late.

At the same time I had watched friends of mine fade into translucent versions of themselves as they sent their first sneery tweets about how you can't trust the BBC or the *Washington Post* or the mainstream narratives – and then oil their own buttocks for a far more efficient slide into disinformation, retweeting clearly doctored propaganda clips or patently faked videos.

I realised that there were some things we no longer saw eye-to-eye on – including something as simple and obvious as the literal meaning of words. When out of nowhere, words like 'truth' or 'fact' meant something different to them than they did to me.

And I watched them happily making money out of what they knew was wrong.

I watched my whole country – a country I thought I knew pretty well – start to promote a different idea of itself, as if hypnotised to do so. It was no longer part of a global family. It had locked itself indoors and everyone else down their hallway was no longer a neighbour but an outsider. It was, I felt, taking an arrogant, combative approach to the world and one that no longer valued knowledge or learning but was instead suspicious of expertise and dismissive of intelligence.

The country was a paranoid hypochondriac, keen on all fronts to cling to the advice of quacks, not doctors. Certain it was being poisoned from the outside, despite all evidence that it had been nourished.

So the country withdrew further, becoming a curtain-twitcher, like that person locked indoors: an old lady in a top-floor flat with ideas above her station, standing nervously at her window making bitchy comments about the young people clinking glasses outside the modern Italian restaurant opposite, and feeling she'd won by bolting her doors shut and vowing revenge on them all by never venturing outside again.

And perhaps by osmosis, it had begun to make more sensible-minded people suspicious too. Suspicion was just going around, like a bug.

I think it bit me, too.

So with that suspicion in mind, and in that world of paranoia and uncertainty, I did what anyone would do to feel more secure when faced with weird emails from a random old Chinese man from your dad's past who you had, on the face of things, only really very limited proof might be a spy.

Your own research.

2

The Rabbit Hole

I Did My Own Research

I did not want to be an unwitting target of Chinese state contact.

I wanted to be a *witting* one.

And a quick and naive Google along the lines of 'Does China use citizens to spy on Westerners?' confirmed my suspicions.

Yes, historically China has actively encouraged everyday citizens to follow, spy on, engage with and provide tip-offs about foreigners.

Well, there you go.

Those citizens would be rewarded, either with cold hard cash, or with a 'spiritual' reward like a certificate and a good mark against their name. It was part of rallying the hearts of the people. Raising their morale by acknowledging that they were protecting their nation from the targets of their contact.

People like my dad.

And now me.

* * *

The more I thought about it, reading and re-reading the emails from the old Chinese man, the more amazing it seemed that techniques like friendly round-robin-style emails could not only still be in use outside of the suburbs of the 1980s, but that they could form a baseline above which the scale of propaganda and disinformation has become truly frightening.

People like this elderly Chinese man, I decided for myself, were presumably at the bottom of a disinformation and intelligence pyramid built on the work of thousands, which always leads to one person at the top.

Again, Dad never specifically told me that anyone had ever tried to recruit him properly – not the Stasi, MI6 or the KGB. There had been no formal approach I could remember, but then, he could also be quite oblivious to these things. He took people at their word. He may not have taken in their hints. He was the smartest man I'll ever know, but he would have made a terrible spy: he used to drive at half the speed limit and he didn't know how to wake up his phone, even though (as I would enthusiastically point out to him) there was only one button.

So when he started getting these emails from the kindly Chinese gentleman, I think he would have taken them at face value. He wouldn't have thought the changes in fonts or colours or style particularly odd. He wouldn't have wondered why every email started with a short briefing of where they were in the relationship.

Perhaps – on this and this alone – I saw more than he did?

* * *

There's a Chinese saying: *May you live in interesting times.*

It sounds like a compliment or a lovely blessing. It's actually a curse. It's saying, 'I hope your life is full of tumult and chaos.' And in recent years, in this country and every other, we have certainly been living in interesting times.

I had found it was hard to trust anything anymore.

One friend – Mark – told me in a pub near Charing Cross that while the emails were weird (I'd saved them to the photo reel on my phone by now), I was being weirder. It was the twenty-first century, he said. Wouldn't they just hack me or something? What was the point of sending laborious and wordy emails?

Well, I said. Disinformation is rife these days. So is propaganda. It struck my more paranoid side that we are knee-deep in something so similar to that Cold War landscape of lies, disinformation and covert operations, with clear skies clouded by an inability to trust what we see and hear. Mark just had to *open his eyes.*

The Chinese are very keen on befriending Western academics, I told him, having read one article. In China, academics are seen as revered thought leaders who shape the minds of the young. If they could find friendly academics who would say nice things about China to students, or in books, or on broadcasts, well, they would be useful assets, wouldn't they?

They were probably doing loads of it. It probably wasn't just my dad, or me.

Mark blinked at me.

Mark had questions.

Or, really, statements.

Why *you*?

It seemed a very slow way of doing things, Mark said.

Why didn't they just buy a TV channel like everyone else?

Mark was not prepared for the reading I'd been doing.

* * *

While at this point I felt it was vaguely possible I was being dragged into paranoia by the screaming insane asylum of social media and the rising tide of lies in everyday life, what if I was right, and this blatant approach was part of the 'Thousand Grains of Sand' system?

I'd only read about it the day before, but it made total sense to me.

The Chinese don't go for employing many spies professionally, I told Mark, as he gripped his pint glass a little harder and raised his eyebrows.

'They prefer to use the students they send abroad! The engineers helping set up new communications systems. The tourists that might happen to be holidaying in London anyway. The elderly approaching foreigners by lakes. The idea is to pick up as much information as possible – regardless of quality!'

The *grains of sand, Mark*!

A former FBI China analyst called Paul D. Moore came up with the phrase.

He said, 'If a beach were a target, the Russians would send in a sub, frogmen would steal ashore in the dark of night and collect several buckets of sand and take them back to Moscow. The US would send over satellites and produce reams of data.'

But ...

'The Chinese would send in a thousand tourists, each assigned to collect a single grain of sand. When they returned, they would be asked to shake out their towels. And they would end up knowing more than anyone else!'

Was my dad a grain of sand? Was I?

Mark just stared at me when I said that.

I needed more.

* * *

I have no idea if I'm allowed to use the name of the man I talked to next, because he's stopped answering my emails and there's no way to check.

Perhaps he thought he was talking to me 'on background' – happy to look at my story but now keen to keep out of it.

Perhaps I know too much?

If so, great: no one's ever thought that about me before.

I emailed him around this time after hearing him on the radio one day.

All I'll say, to remain safe, is that he was once about as high up in British intelligence as it's possible to be.

Like, if this were a James Bond film, he would be one of the men in suits with the power to get angry at Bond and tell him he had to come home now because he'd broken far too many rules. He was that high up.

And yes, I fully appreciate that it's weird I did this, but I'm someone who tends to think, Why not?

In my email I told him that I'd received some unusual emails from China I could do with his help in deciphering.

Incredibly, he too thought, Why not?

And so suddenly I found myself on a Zoom call with someone with vast experience of lies and spies. Far more than my friend Mark had.

He's educated. Very British. A man in his late 60s in a shirt and tie, with a certain cool swagger but an immediate seriousness about him too. More Ralph Fiennes than Bill Nighy.

In films he'd be called M; in Britain he'd be called C.

'This is the West Lake in Hangzhou by the sound of it,' he said immediately.

Well … yes. Yes, it was, I said, with a sense of rising excitement. I don't know how he'd managed to guess the actual lake given all I'd said was it happened by a lake.

'I wondered if it was maybe just a man keen to practise his English?' I tried, because I was in Shanghai for a week once in the 2000s. I had never been so stared at, but equally I remembered being cornered in a park full of pensioners by a man with one tooth. Everyone around us was doing Tai Chi as he started to talk to me. He had two sentences he knew well.

One was along the lines of: 'Did you know that when Neil Armstrong went to the moon, the one thing he could see on Earth was the Great Wall of China?!' which he exclaimed with delight, again and again.

Then I noticed that all the other pensioners had been drawn to us, slowly moving in and now surrounding me, as the man repeated his fact.

At this, my new contact laughs.

At some points in the recent past, he tells me, 'people were desperate for any chance to speak with a foreigner to practise their English. When I was in REDACTED as a REDACTED over there in the eighties, we used to learn to recognise the body language very quickly so you could run like hell before they could get hold of you.'

'But these emails,' I say. 'They feel like a performance of some kind. Like explaining the *story so far* for someone watching or to get the next person to email up to speed.'

The man smiles and nods me on.

'It feels like someone telling the story of a correspondence,' I say. 'This stuff about losing a best friend ... I mean, is approaching foreigners like this something people in a place like China normally do?'

He clasps his hands together.

'No, I don't think it is. I was slightly smiling when you started that narrative because within the Chinese Intelligence Services, "friend" and "good friend" are terms of art.'

'Terms of art?'

'In our world, they're basically slang for agents.'

I broke out in a slight sweat at this moment.

What did he mean, agents?

Was my dad an agent?

'Within the Chinese Intelligence Services, if you develop a "friend" or a "good friend" ... well, a *friend* is someone who looks like a good prospect. A "*good* friend" is someone who's swallowed the hook.'

OK.

Then what the hell is a '*best* friend'?

'Now I don't know whether that applies here or not,' he says. '[But] in the last few years until Xi Jinping we've seen a progressively greater emphasis on national security, and the concept of comprehensive security. There is now in China's National Security Education Day, when everybody is reminded of the importance of being on alert for the wiles of scheming foreigners who will do anything to steal China's secrets – and mandating the citizenry to be on alert and report anything to the competent authorities.'

* * *

China's National Security Education Day is a curious thing.

It's all sold as prioritising the safety of the Chinese people, thanks to the diligent and generous efforts of the Chinese Communist Party. People design posters, or hand out flyers, each of them reminding the people to be vigilant and cautious. Primary school children put on performances celebrating the ring of steel that surrounds the Chinese. Kids as young as three are taught national security law. Warnings are put out about perceived weaknesses, telling retired military personnel, 'frantic military amateurs', university students, teachers – *beware*: the West is targeting you. Foreign spies want your information. *Trust no one.* If you are someone who seeks an extravagant life, they will exploit that. If you are obsessed with the West, if you slander China, if you are an attention seeker, if you have low morals, they will use that.

And if you see something? Say something.

There's pride in reporting suspicious people.

Displays are put on to thrill the public – like dozens of police officers rappelling from a helicopter and shooting dead a pretend hostage-taker. The whole thing's lovely, wholesome fun and has never given a child a nightmare.

So I start to wonder whether the old Chinese man was someone who really had just taken it upon himself to strike up a conversation with my dad, presuming that despite his gentle demeanour he looked like a national security threat keen to bring down the Chinese government.

* * *

'Nowadays, because China is turning more inward, Chinese people are generally much more circumspect in their dealings with foreigners, particularly Westerners,' my contact told me. 'Those who are even remotely politically savvy are beginning to realise there could be more downside than upside in carrying on these kinds of contacts.'

Downsides? What could be the downsides to chatting with my dad?

'To use another term of art, they would at the very least expect to be invited in for a "cup of tea" ... which is code for being dragged down to the local police station to be given a thorough investigation and a warning to stop doing whatever it is they're doing.'

And then this man says something important.

'The fact this communication channel keeps going despite all that would also perhaps tend to indicate that this is *officially sanctioned.*'

Hang on. Did he just say what I thought he said?

That these emails had continued so long – and continue to this day – means that a Chinese state authority is *giving them the go-ahead*?

'The only communications I get now from China are ones that I know perfectly well to be officially sanctioned,' he says. 'I know – *they* know – that they're doing this because they're being *allowed* to, that there's a *reason* that it's state sanctioned.'

I think he's saying I'm right.

Take that, Mark!

But also: I am suddenly not sure how to feel about any of this.

'In my experience to date,' he continues, 'initiatives directed at foreigners are *not* the product of enthusiastic amateurs. But they can be. The Chinese Intelligence Services are getting astride what might have started out as a genuine relationship with no strings attached. And then seeking to exploit it.'

Wait, I think. The first email Dad received was so straight, so polite, so distant. All in one font. Quite dignified.

Three days ago, on Nov.6th, I was very glad to meet you by the West Lake in Hangzhou.

Simply there to 'test the email connection'.

So, what if? What if that was the only *real* email before someone else, some other department somewhere, took over the account?

Because after that, the tone changed completely from sober respect and a certain academic respect for grammar and syntax to an excitable puppy trying to convince you it loves you. All that was missing in the last few was love-heart-eyed emojis.

Suddenly it hit me very clearly – the difference between that first, respectful email, and the absolute shift in voice that occurred thereafter. It was like the difference between an email from a grandad and an email from a grandson. Part of the same family, but with very different ways of doing things. I wondered if my dad had noticed it too, but chosen to ignore it?

'Western academics are always seen as good targets. Professors teach students, don't they, and you never know, even if he is not useful he might serve as a useful conduit to others who might be. Also, there is a tendency to "mirror image", so in China senior academics are quite closely linked in with the policy elite, and I think there is a tendency to assume that this is the case in other societies too.'

Then he says something that worries me.

'But then *you*, by the same token – someone who's seen to be in journalism, broadcasting, the opinion-forming sector – similarly *might* be seen as a prospect worth pursuing.'

I could be a prospect?

And I suddenly remember their words.

Keep close contact. Forever.

Uh-oh. Was the old Chinese man fishing? Was I his (or their?) new 'best friend'? Had I already started? And what would now be expected of me?

'These things with the Chinese often develop quite slowly. I've seen examples where the Chinese have proceeded very slowly and with extreme circumspection, and other cases where – to quote a former boss of mine in a former career – they've whipped it out, slapped it on the table and said "what about it?"; so it's hard to judge what is going on here – but it would certainly make sense for you to take account of the possibility that this is not a real relationship. That it is being manipulated. Even if the end game is not immediately visible.'

Oh God. There's an *end game*?!

I'm suddenly not sure what my dad would make of all this. I think he'd laugh and think it was very interesting. But I also think he'd keep the communication going, just to be polite, and because it would be too awkward to say, 'Sorry, but is there an ulterior motive to all this?'

I think back to some of his replies to the old Chinese man. I'm sure he was confused by the affection this guy seemed to have for him. My dad was good at judging a mood and a tone. He would have seen how nice the man was being and just been nice back. It's why, in one of his final replies to the man, he writes, 'We hope you are well and we think of you every day.'

No he didn't. Of course he didn't. He was just trying to be as nice as the other guy.

'I think my dad would have found it slightly funny that this man was always calling him his best friend. It comes up again and again.'

'Well, the whole point of the word "friend" is that it's inherently innocuous,' says my contact. 'No one hearing that word would automatically go on the alert. So whether it was used deliberately or not is very, very hard to say. But it sounds to me, on the basis of what you've said, that there is more to this than meets the eye. *Somewhere* there is a string attached – even if it's not immediately apparent what that string is.'

Somewhere there is a string attached.

And now I'm on one end of it.

We think we and you should keep our valuable friend-ship following with Ian Wallace. We must go on with the close contact to you, the family of Mr. Ian Wallace as before!

And it strikes me suddenly that there are strings everywhere. Strings that make certain people dance the way other people want them to. Strings that can reach out of your screen and connect you to someone thousands of miles away, without ever meeting them or knowing truly who they are. Strings that aim to pull you in to worlds or thoughts you'd never considered before; perhaps that even want to make you dance, too.

Did someone somewhere now see me as a potential asset of the Chinese state?

'It's an interesting case,' says the man. 'It's an interesting topic, lies. One, unsurprisingly, I have a certain amount of experience in. Living a lie, learning to lie very fluently in what I believe to be a good cause …'

'There are lies everywhere, aren't there?' I realise.

* * *

While I felt vindicated (sorry for showing off, Mark), a further, and I think far more disturbing revelation was to come as I considered these emails and my reaction to them.

Because over the years, in various roles – as a presenter, a producer, a journalist – I have found myself in unusual situations meeting unusual people in possession of what we'll call fringe beliefs.

I have met those who work professionally in lies.

And I have met people who have been freely feeding lies, and people who have fallen hard for lies – some of which were convincing, and some of which really were not.

I've met whistle-blowers whose whistles turned out not to have a pea in them; I met a man in a forest who made a dubious claim he was involved with the Illuminati but then lost his nerve and quickly drove off. I've met 9/11 truthers, Lockerbie bombing truthers, people who claim to have the 'truth' about Princess Diana, people who don't believe the *Titanic* ever sank.

I've held in my hands what Reg Presley from the 1960s band The Troggs told me was some kind of alien technology that a man he met in a country pub had sold him late one night for many thousands of pounds.

I've been accosted by men in Roswell, New Mexico, and thought they were going to shout at me about Area 51 aliens, but instead they shouted at me about how cars can technically glide on potato oil and the government has been covering up electric battery technology since the late nineteenth century.

I've flown in a helicopter with a Second World War veteran looking for red-roofed barns and chicken coops arranged in the shape of swastikas that Dutch farmers apparently erected in 1940s Norfolk to guide in and welcome secret invading Nazis (we couldn't find any, though you might have better luck).

I've had dealings with various Flat Earthers in Yorkshire, members of a group that insists the world cannot be round, yet whose main website, I believe, used to boast of its many members 'around the globe'.

I've walked through the compound at Waco. (Did you know they call it Waco mainly because Waco was where all the journalists stayed? It should actually be named after neighbouring 'Elk', but Waco sounds a bit like Wacko and perhaps that fit better?)

I've been told to get lost by leather-gloved Scientology security guards in long winter coats in East Grinstead.

I've eaten sticky beef with Alex Jones in Texas.

I've been slated by Bigfoot truthers who called me a clown and said I didn't deserve to live because I thought their video of an unconvincing hairy Bigfoot in a wood looked a bit like a man in a hairy Bigfoot costume in a wood.

Once, on a conspiracy forum, someone investigated my background in case my career had been helped along by MI5 or the government and found it 'very curious' they 'could find no record of him before 1995'. I'm yet to explain how I managed to evade their detection, but it could be because I was quite busy being a schoolboy.

More recently, I've been labelled a lying 'remainer' and part of Britain's 'Project Fear' conspiracy, and a leftie member of the liberal media elite establishment who secretly decide on everything that happens over north London tofu nights organised by former Prime Minister Tony Blair, the chef Jamie Oliver and most of the world's leading scientists.

Far-right figurehead Tommy Robinson once put one of my tweets on a screen at an angry meeting, presumably as an example of a lying writer, but as I think my tweet involved complicated wordplay, none of his audience really understood it and no one got angry.

I am, then, what you might term 'lie aware'.

And yet here I now was, worried, because I suddenly thought I was being courted by the Chinese state so that ultimately I might become a Western champion of their aims.

What if it wasn't just me?

What if they were doing it to other low-to-mid-level entertainment figures across the country too?

Had they turned others? Had they got to Omid Djalili?

What was the plan? To slowly infiltrate my writing? My radio shows? To get to my friends? Or an audience?

To get to *you*?

And that was when it hit me.

Either I was 'a prospect worth pursuing' and now engaged in my own personal correspondence with unnamed secret intelligence agents from a hostile state, each of us ready to outwit the other in a daring game of cat and mouse ... them in some vast computer room in Shanghai, me sitting in my underpants in Britain ...

... or I was confused enough, confounded enough, beaten down by life enough ...

... sad enough ...

... not *feeling* enough ...

... *that I had just invented my own personal conspiracy theory.*

I couldn't be sure either way.

But I knew one thing.

It was everything the year 2020 had prepared me for.

3

May You Live in Interesting Times

2020 Vision and the Year the World Lost Its Mind

So: what if I had indeed invented my own personal family conspiracy theory?

And what if my only saving grace was that I was *just* self-aware enough to realise it?

I mean, sure, I join in with big and sometimes unusual ideas, but I also consider myself an independent thinker – just like everybody else on earth who thinks exactly like me.

But could you blame me for thinking that way? Consider the climate we've been in lately.

Didn't you also, in 2020 for example, find yourself more confused?

Swayed by ideas that in the cold light of day might seem ridiculous?

Perhaps sharing information – surprising, terrifying, revelatory information – that on reflection couldn't have been true? During lockdown here in the UK, I greatly enjoyed the national tradition of standing outside in my garden banging a pot as loudly as I could and listening to other pots being banged all over town so that nurses could hear us and feel better. It made me feel part of something. (But I used a wooden spoon and a Le Creuset saucepan, which I like to think made my thanks count a little more than most.)

Little did I know that this whole plot to reassure nurses was a terrible, cynical sham.

You see, when the British public came together at 8pm each Thursday night to bang their pots and applaud in genuinely heartfelt appreciation of the work of our frontline healthcare workers, some people knew what was really going on. Some people knew the *real* truth.

'Please stop clapping every Thursday,' a mysterious message circulating on WhatsApp groups around the country ended. Why?

Clapping is actually to cover up the sound of construction work being done to set up the 5G networks. Every week they need to test it but it makes a really loud buzzing noise for exactly 1 minute – the clapping is to cover it up.

In early 2020, didn't it feel like the whole world came together in a wholehearted, seismic rush of madness: one that knocked the planet and turned its spin to a wobble?

It was mad in the sense that there was a pandemic to deal with, and mad in the sense that in some people, it really did bring on a certain madness.

In the face of that pandemic, and with a mysterious disease sweeping the world, people were looking for answers, direction and, crucially, '*truth*' – no matter how true or not it was.

Disinformation and misinformation were rife. Conspiracy theories flourished and flapped their wings around the world like beautiful butterflies. Propaganda was back in full-fat fashion and a new disinformation era was born.

More people were infected by this disastrous school of thought than we've seen in living memory. Throw a few peanuts in any supermarket and sooner or later you'd hit someone who believed something they may well now be embarrassed to say out loud. People who had managed to go untouched by conspiracy or misinformation their entire lives suddenly found themselves believing the most incredible claims. And I use the word incredible in its purest form.

As a normal father-of-three, just trying to work out how we could get wine delivered in as many ways and as often as possible without someone breathing on us, I first noticed that collective madness when rumours began to circulate about the new 5G mobile phone networks that were being introduced at around the same time Covid struck.

A mast was installed not far from us.

A man delivering some shopping told me it looked like it was up to no good.

I laughed it off. But soon, the same thought he'd caught somewhere online spread far and wide. People who thought that it was just too convenient a coincidence, that phones were going to become more efficient at *exactly the same time that a new disease was appearing?!*

Yet lots of things happened around March 2020. Dua Lipa released the album *Future Nostalgia*, and no one seemed to think *that* was going to kill millions.

People in towns like mine and yours leaped on it. Theories about 5G began to pop up on Facebook, Twitter, NextDoor, YouTube, TikTok and Pinterest.

It was the upgraded radio waves from 5G masts that were altering people's bodies!

The beams were widening our pores, meaning the virus had more space to squeeze through!

Reaction was swift against our new, thin overlords.

First, an enemy virus mast was set on fire in Birmingham. I don't even know how you'd do that; presumably they're metal? I remember laughing at the oddness of it with Dad.

But the next day, two more masts were attacked in Liverpool.

More than a hundred masts were damaged or destroyed all over the country in the following month by groups of rabid anti-masters, with confused telecoms engineers in hard hats and yellow hi-vis vests singled out as evil Minions and abused on the streets.

More masts still were torched in the Netherlands, Ireland, Belgium and Cyprus. Some people embedded razor blades behind anti-5G posters or on the masts themselves in the hope of injuring mast workers.

The World Health Organization had to step in to point out that viruses don't spread on mobile networks, and Covid was also spreading in countries that didn't enjoy slightly faster download times in municipal town centres. Furthermore, 5G couldn't widen your pores and viruses don't need to squeeze into them anyway.

On breakfast television, noted British TV presenter Eamonn Holmes remained unconvinced by the science.

Now, Eamonn has been, to me at least, a very nice guy. My most treasured memory of him is once trouncing him in the head-to-head live final of a BBC One Saturday night quiz show, in which I was only marginally quicker to know the names of all the women in the pop group Girls Aloud.

He blamed my victory on his increasing age, but I knew it was down to a) talent, b) speed and c) a then improper interest in the pop group Girls Aloud.

Anyway, months later, by complete chance, I sat next to him in a cinema to watch the topic-relevant movie *Tinker Tailor Soldier Spy*, and he immediately fell asleep and snored on my shoulder like a drunk uncle at Christmas.

I didn't know what to do in this unique situation, so I acted like it was always happening with Eamonn Holmes.

However, a few years later he was suddenly awake – awake to the possible dangers of 5G regional phone mast technology.

'What I don't accept is mainstream media immediately slapping that down as not true when they don't know it's not true!' he broadcast to millions on ITV's *This Morning*, sternly. 'It's very easy to say it is not true, because it suits the state narrative.'

The mainstream media. The state narrative. I watched in disbelief as other television presenters of far lesser stature than Holmes started to ask their own questions based on very little research, buying into half-cocked theories or full-cocked conspiracies.

Hysteria was growing not in inches but speeding up in miles per hour.

* * *

Alistair Coleman felt it too.

It was absolute chaos, he tells me, as we peruse a kebab menu in a heatwave on a London street near BBC Broadcasting House.

He's gentle and funny and 57, which strikes me as a little old for kebabs, but never in his 34 years at the BBC had he witnessed anything like it – and this is a man who's been kidnapped at gunpoint and trapped in remote civil wars. A former technician turned author (his book, *Angry People in Local Newspapers*, is a collection of stories featuring people who are utterly furious at things like hedges or pies), he's now on the disinformation beat for the newly organised BBC Verify team.

When he started five years ago, there were three people charged with keeping their eye on lies, conspiracy and bad information for the BBC Monitoring department – a department originally set up in 1940 to help battle German war propaganda. Then those three people doubled to six. Now he's part of a team of more than 60, scouring for trends, talking points and disinformation spreaders. You have to recognise names and remember what other opinions they have; you have to be a relentless fact checker with a cracking memory.

We order the chicken shish.

* * *

The son of a professor of virology, Alistair's degree in Asian politics comes in handy for one focus of his work: Turkmenistan and its unusual dictator, the former dentist Gurbanguly Berdymukhamedov (I checked the spelling five times), who as well as writing strange books about horses, regularly has himself photoshopped into places he's never been in order to inspire and delight a nation.

But 2020 'saw everything change. There was just a huge explosion of disinformation, right from day one. People coming up with fake cures. I think one person overdosed on garlic. And of course the 5G theories, which is older than you think. Some of the same people were against 4G. Maybe even 3G. But they think 5G is an act of genocide.'

He checks his phone and then the towering pear trees that line Great Portland Street.

'I mean, I've got 5G here and there are no birds falling dead from the trees, which is what they said would happen.'

I can independently verify there were no birds falling dead from trees.

'It was easy for them to bring Covid and 5G together. 5G was "evil". There was daily debunking to do. It was relentless. Because people can hold multiple views. They'd say, the government want to control your mind, but they *also* want to kill you. And I have a whole list of genuine things various groups claimed were in the vaccine.'

He finds it on his phone and holds it up for me to read.

'They claimed the vaccine contains tiny tentacled creatures?'

He nods. I read on.

'Self-assembling nanoparticles. Magnets. Gayness?'

Also alien DNA, satanic sperm, 'Catholicism', eggs and a full working Bluetooth connection. It's certainly food for thought.

I look out at the street around us as we eat our fancy kebabs. Everything, these few quick years since the world seemed to convulse in paranoia and suspicion, seems back to normal. Construction workers, delivery vans, people Instagramming against unusual doors or holding sausage rolls or staring at phones.

But things *are* different.

There's a cost-of-living crisis. Rising interest rates. Inflation. Affluence is down, real families are struggling. All of which add fuel to the fire. Precisely the conditions that experts have long said can lead to some people thinking that powerful secret forces are plotting to impoverish them. To cull the poor and control the masses.

The very day I meet Alistair, a survey conducted by King's College London and the BBC is published. It shows that the 58 per cent of the UK public think belief in conspiracy theories is higher today than it was 20 years ago. It says the country is home to millions more conspiracy theorists than most people realise. And it claims that around a quarter of UK citizens think Covid was a hoax.

'What was it like in Turkmenistan?' I ask, for the first time in my entire life.

One word: propaganda.

'They claimed that they didn't have Covid. It just didn't exist in Turkmenistan somehow. They claim there's never been a single case, although they did say a virus was being brought into the country on dust storms.'

'On dust storms?'

'Yeah. So they sent up a load of anti-bac planes to fly around the city spraying stuff around.'

* * *

60

Similar craziness happened everywhere: on your street and mine. The messages people got in their own family circles, forwarded from concerned relatives, telling them to stay indoors in the evening because mass government aircraft would be circling the skies over Britain spraying dangerous chemicals onto the 'Covid virus gas clouds' that had drifted over from China.

Then came the solutions – the ways of protecting yourself with no vaccine yet in sight. Masks didn't work, even though doctors and dentists and surgeons had used them for years – no, masks were there to signify compliance and docility. So much so that one radio presenter cut some up live on air, against a backdrop of thousands dying each week and nurses really fancying some fresh, intact masks, saying, 'If we don't reject masks NOW they will be with us FOREVER!'* At least one on-air colleague resigned from the station in protest of his statement.

* * *

Across the world, bad information and outright lies kept coming.

Did you read it all? I did.

I read that in China, they said cups of tea would keep you safe. I drink about 60 a day, so I felt pretty good about that. Various Indian politicians claimed that drinking cow urine would help. On that they were alone. But drinking

---

* To even walk into that particular radio station building at the time, the anti-mask presenter in question would, according to those I've spoken to, have been required – on entry to his office and as a condition of his employment – to put on a mask.

cow urine and also wiping cow pats all over your body would cure you, they said – so long as the cows were very specifically from India, and also so long as you have absolutely no common sense whatsoever.

In March 2020, the All India Hindu Union put on what they called a 'cow urine drinking party', which was exactly what it sounds like and enjoyed by 200 people who don't understand the word 'enjoy'.

Leader of Belarus Viktor Lukashenko said you could keep Covid at bay by simply working hard, using a sauna and drinking pints of vodka.

In Iran, a famous cleric said Covid could be stopped by soaking a cotton wool ball in violet oil and 'applying' it to the anus, but this proved oddly unpopular.

Boris Johnson saw a video on YouTube that said if you blew a hair dryer up your nose it could kill Covid, and asked his scientists what they thought. Donald Trump wondered out loud whether anyone had thought injecting disinfectant inside the body might be a good idea? It went no further, but I've always thought a politician should lead by example.

The Mexican president, Andrés Obrador, didn't have much to contribute to the solution, so just carried prayer cards around, and a drawing of a six-leafed clover. He is not a scientist. And his drawing showed he's not an artist either.

At one point, the Pope was rumoured to have succumbed to the disease and been replaced in his duties by a hologram, something he denies to this day. Though I see right through that.

The French Ministry of Health had to release a statement which essentially said, 'Cocaine does not in fact protect against Covid', but I'm sure for some it was worth a go.

And so, exasperated experts like Alistair Coleman quite unbelievably found themselves having to say: hair dryers are not an effective treatment or preventative measure for this disease. No, nor lemons, chilli peppers or raw onions. No, eating ice cream won't do it either – a claim attributed falsely to UNICEF who had to literally come out and tell people that as far as they knew, ice cream would not cure the highly infectious respiratory disease Covid.

In an evil twist, fake posts proclaiming to be from Jeff Bezos urged Africans not to use 'the blue face masks made in America and Europe because these masks contain suicidal toxic'.

* * *

Then arrived the vaccine, to a global sigh of relief.

Science had done it, and this absolute marvel of human endeavour was celebrated for perhaps 15 seconds before people started shaking their heads and tutting.

So much damage had by now been done to our trust in objective truth, in experts, in governments, even in basic goodness and decency, that even that joyous moment was marred by a billion amateur virologists.

President Bolsonaro of Brazil said he wouldn't be taking it. You didn't know the side effects. It was all too new. 'If you turn into a crocodile,' he told his people, 'it's your problem.'

Because how else could you explain a vaccine so quickly? It was all engineered by the evil genius behind the Microsoft corporation – step one had been Clippy, step two a vicious and terrifying pandemic.

People doubted the vaccine before it even had a name. They believed it was too good to be true and would turn your arms into magnets.

They turned on doctors, because how come *doctors* seemed to know so much about medicine all of a sudden?

No, Bill Gates had planned this all along. Keep us in our homes, scare us, make us compliant, then force us to undergo a mass vaccination that as Alistair points out would either kill us, or make us do his bidding. Or kill us *and* make us do his bidding!

The vaccination wasn't even a medicine, it was a tiny microchip delivery system. The microchip would track us or record our data or know our bank accounts or political opinions or who we spoke to and what about, a bit like the phones we literally pay a monthly contract for and carry everywhere.

Jim Corr from the 1990s band The Corrs wondered innocently whether Bill Gates had unleashed the virus upon the world in order to promote his new Netflix documentary. Most people in marketing will suggest 'a viral video' in their first day on the job but this seemed an unlikely idea to have come up with at this time.

Everyone had a plan. Big Pharma had a plan, foreign enemies had a plan. The year 2020 was one of huge plots to cull the poor and control world population.

The New World Order, the Great Reset, the Mass Control Programme would begin on 8 December 2020, by chance the last birthday my dad would have, and for some reason the mighty powers of the shadowy elites decided the revolution would begin in the British city of … Coventry.

Of course Coventry.

The UK's 11th biggest city.

It seems obvious now that Bill Gates should choose to 'vaccinate' his first subject in the UK's 11th biggest city.

And the first person in Coventry and indeed the world that Bill Gates personally selected to be under his control?

To do his bidding, however evil, depraved or murderous?

What robotic Terminator did he unleash about the world?

What murderous vessel of poisonous controlled hatred had he hand selected?

Well, it was Mrs Margaret Keenan, a former local high-street jewellery shop keeper and long-retired grandmother of four, who would turn 91 the following week.

This was the ideal person to bring down humanity.

All would fear Mrs Margaret Keenan.

But we're still waiting.

* * *

Alistair Coleman thinks the reason he can do his job so well is that 'I'm cursed with a memory. I remember everything. Everything. I'm good at pub quizzes.'

He's particularly strong on 1990s bands. I ask him to name every member of The Boo Radleys and he does so with great flair.

But it's the fact that we're living in a time where 'everybody can do their own research to find their own version of the truth': that's the problem, he says. 'You have to remember that many people who hold these opinions hold them for very honest reasons. They aren't mad. They aren't idiots. They've arrived there logically. Even though their logic is faulty. And sometimes it's harmless, but other times ... well.'

You have to wonder, now things have calmed down a little, how people might be drawn to believing that smearing themselves in Indian cow pats might mitigate against a deadly virus.

But those 200 people at that urine-drinking party believed it would help them for many of the same reasons anyone might believe any work of disinformation.

Powerlessness is a huge factor, says Alistair as we finish our kebabs. We are each the star of our own film, and when there's a huge plot twist and we don't know why it's happened we suddenly start wondering if there's a secret director shaking things up. We yearn to make sense of things that don't make sense. It's obvious why they cast us – we're the best! – but was it to destroy our fledgling acting career? Why? We think there must be rhyme or reason to it and can't believe we can be impacted by random chance. There has to be a purpose behind what's happening; there has to be a plan. We seek ready-made solutions for problems that might not have any yet.

Wait. Is that like me?

So, risking it, I ask him, 'Do you think *any* of us might be susceptible to this? Like, if the climate is right or if we've been through struggle or grief or something? Could it happen to any of us?'

I'm thinking of the old Chinese man, obviously.

His answer: 'A lot of otherwise rational people have been led down dark alleyways in search of the "truth" of what's happening. And sometimes they settle on an easy answer to a difficult situation.'

Clinging to outlandish, sometimes crazed quarter-truths returns to us some sense of control, reduces our fear and helplessness, and if our trust in government, science or the media is depleted … and if there is almost anything else we can cling to …

Well, at least we have that.

* * *

That first year of assigning blame was for many of us a remarkable time for discovering unusual things about old school friends. Distant cousins. Aunties. Parents. It wasn't just happening on our airwaves; it was happening around our dinner tables.

They turned from people posting Facebook videos of themselves baking soda bread to people who were 'just putting it out there' or 'just asking questions'. They did their 'own research', as Alistair points out. They began to quote statistical evidence from foreign countries like they were reading out the football results. Human Rights Watch had to warn governments that 'racism and physical attacks on Asians' were spreading along with Covid, while Chinese-run businesses were being attacked globally and suspicions about the Chinese government were spread by people who'd never given them a second thought before.

And after talking with Alistair, I have to challenge myself: while I have absolutely never been anti-Chinese, would I have been as suspicious of those emails my dad received if they'd been from closer to Belgium than Beijing? Would I immediately have thought, This friendly octogenarian Belgian man my dad met by a chocolate and/or lace factory is clearly spying to increase the international influence of the Benelux regions?

So maybe on some level I *was* guilty of similar prejudice.

Elsewhere, everyone, suddenly, was an amateur epidemiologist, somehow finding 'evidence' on home-made podcasts or in blog replies inexplicably overlooked by every single one of the world's leading scientists.

And just as worryingly: anyone who disagreed with them was an immediate enemy, a 'sheeple', believing 'facts', someone too lazy to know it was all out there, you just have to read this or that obscure blog from this or that totally unknown academic.

* * *

See – and call me biased, but it's based on experience – this is what I've always found from my time with conspiracy theorists or those with unusual beliefs: they can't simply, clearly and convincingly explain their theories.

Instead they talk quickly and in footnotes.

I tell you, hanging out with conspiracy theorists on a regular basis is merely to accept the position of listener. No question you ask is unanswerable. No rebuttal cuts through. Talking with a conspiracy theorist can be exhausting and overwhelming. Often you get the sense that they pity you. That they think you are stupid.

I've learned through spending time with them that the obsessive's greatest tool is the reference. You're constantly being told to read things, watch things, look up obscure unverified things, and of course that classic: 'do your own research'. If you don't know precisely what they claim they know for sure, you for sure know nothing. It's an endless conversation made up of unutterably tiny references. A protective shield no one else can possibly own, an unpublished book no one else can ever have read. A narrative you can never question.

What was interesting during Covid was that – as Alistair pointed out – many of the people we watched develop these ideas and punt them out weren't in any way stupid people. Some in fact were professors, leaders in their fields.

And I suppose that makes sense. Very often these were people who enjoyed thinking, enjoyed analysing, enjoyed feeling they knew something others didn't and could talk for hours on the subject. When you can link one piece of bad information to another with apparent ease, it's easy to feel it has the ring of truth, when it's still just bad information.

There is an instinct in some people to look for simple answers to complex situations and to find those answers far too easily. All in pursuit of an existential yearning to feel safe. And there is an instinct in some to home in on topics that very few people in their audiences are experts in – science, medicine, geopolitics – meaning those theories are hard to debunk and easier to believe.

Often that instinct accelerates quickly.

I mean, in a mere matter of months I went from listening to a trusted and fairly left-leaning name on the radio talking about the few benefits of a pretty middle-class lockdown – his time with the children, less pollution, 'nature healing', hearing the birds sing in his garden, how lucky he *was* to have a garden – to furious and unhinged right-wing rants about Dr Anthony Fauci and how Joe Biden stole the US election using dodgy election machines.

And yet, although I said 2020 was quite the year and a real one-off for blindly grasping for mad answers to a new question, on reflection it was entirely predictable – if you use the benefit of hindsight and that 2020 vision.

Turns out, we'd been preparing for this moment for a long time.

Because way before Covid, in the 1800s, when cholera hit, vast amounts of people unable to deal with the horrifying concept of a pandemic began to deny that cholera even existed at all. They turned on the doctors, accusing them of making up the whole thing so that they could steal body parts and cull the poor. 'Cholera is not real!' they yelled in 1832 at riots in Liverpool.

When Russian flu hit, rumours began to circulate about what the real reason for such widespread sickness must be. It couldn't be the new railways and transport routes making it far easier for ill people to get around. No – and get this – people started to talk about … *the new telegraph poles* that were being introduced at around the same time.

It was just too convenient a coincidence that electricity was going to become more efficient at exactly the same time that a new disease appeared.

Yet lots of things happened around January 1890. Old Mrs McCormick released her new song on phonograph cylinder ('An Irishman's Perplexity') and no one blamed that.

But the *New York Herald* was 'only asking questions' when it reminded people that 'the disease has raged chiefly in towns where the electric light is in common use'.

Now that you think about it, the same could be said of Covid, and almost any disease of the electrical era.

It was suggested that the reason for this was nothing like our own 5G lies of the modern era. It wasn't that telegraph poles were widening our pores so the virus could squeeze in. No, it was microbes feasting on underwater telegraph cables and then transmitting themselves down the line while producing flu.

Do you know what happened? People began attacking telegraph poles. They began abusing telegraph workers on the street. Somewhere in rural nineteenth-century Ireland, Eamonn Holmes's distant relative turned to his wife and said, 'It's very easy to say it is not true because it suits the state narrative.'

No one knew what to do when it turned out that chopping down wooden telegraph poles didn't stop the flu. Doctors started suggesting maybe brandy would work, and if not brandy, then oysters?

Then, when Spanish flu arrived almost exactly a century before Covid, there grew very quickly a huge distrust of aspirin and a growing wariness of doctors.

Doctors seemed very keen to prescribe aspirin.

Wait. What if the flu was actually *caused* by aspirin? Just asking questions. I mean, what if aspirin had flu *in* it, and that was why they were so keen to give it to you? Aspirin was, after all, produced by the German company Bayer. It could be a German plot. Or a plot by Big Pharma, by foreign enemies, by doctors, by experts, a plot to ... *cull the poor and control the masses.*

* * *

So why, now, do so many of us continue to believe things that are demonstrably untrue?

Well, most obviously there's the speed at which they can now reach so many of us at once over the internet, where even the weakest concepts can find an audience. It doesn't matter if you can't convince your fellow villagers anymore – you've got the world at your fingertips.

And there's consistency too. Often, those spreading nonsense can't stop spreading it once they've started. Their identity and self-worth relies on it. They've built for themselves a vast brick wall of bizarre ideas. They're stuck behind it. Removing a brick means weakening the wall, destroying everything they believe to be true, and exposing them once again to the chaos of the real world.

People aren't willing to destroy themselves that way.

And often it's because, look, some terrible things definitely have happened in the world. Unbelievable things that sound like conspiracy but have been shown to be true.

Like, it's true that in 1932, a 40-year experiment called The Tuskegee Study began, in which 600 Black men in one Alabama county were unwittingly given syphilis just to see what would happen.

It's true that in the 1980s, both Exxon and Shell knew all about climate change and what their operations were likely to do to the planet and the people trying to live on it. They knew in the 1980s – the companies themselves did studies on it – yet according to the Yale Program on Climate Change Communication in 2022, 22 per cent of Americans are 'doubtful' or 'dismissive' that global warming is even happening.

And it's true that in the 1950s the CIA undertook bizarre and unethical experiments on US citizens in which they secretly gave them LSD in order to see if they could then control their minds.

That all these things happened only serves to shorten the jump you have to take to get to the idea that Hillary Clinton is a satanic sex trafficker who drinks the blood of children to maintain her youthful glow, or, sickeningly, that school shootings are in fact 'false-flag' operations undertaken by the US government or shadowy groups. Something a 2022 YouGov poll suggests is believed by a staggering 18 per cent of Americans. Something discussed and debated in actual living rooms.

* * *

Alistair is quite worn down by having to point out the truth all the time.

He and his colleagues are regularly sent horrible or threatening emails.

He received another just a few days before we met.

Intimidatingly, people have been known to turn up outside the BBC unannounced requesting 'a word' with his colleagues.

It's far worse, predictably, if you're a woman who dares question the largely nutty male-driven narratives. His colleague, the disinformation expert Marianna Spring, who he's been sitting next to in the office this week, is the target of an estimated *80 per cent of the entirety of online abuse* received by BBC journalists.

But it's tough work for anyone. Alistair had to take four months off work after the first horrific imagery began to surface from the war in Ukraine – imagine sifting through the worst deeds imaginable trying to work out whether they're real, faked, or from another conflict in history entirely. It's a puzzle no one wants to have to solve.

While little in comparison, I was not untouched by the disinformation during Covid, I tell him.

When Dad passed away, he had by chance only recently had his first vaccine. And I knew what would happen if I told people that. I knew the conclusion *some* people would leap to, despite the medical evidence and the reports and the experts.

But that said, it was of course certainly something I wondered myself, because you just would.

But that's all I did: wonder.

More strongly, I could not bear, in my grief, the strengthening walls of disinformation rising outside. And the private fury I found while being told the experts were lying to me was compounded by the uselessness of the people telling me that.

Because I *knew* some of those people.

I had met or worked with some of those I watched succumb to and bow down before the growing madness.

The actors low on work who'd found a way to a new and bigger stage than ever before. The bad comics who found new audiences as they mocked those sticking to the rules and revelled in the feedback – a sound they'd never heard before, a laughter unfamiliar.

The estranged husbands and divorcing wives doing their own research in their flats during lockdown.

The former pop stars suddenly low on attention and rich in unsupervised free time.

The bland radio personalities let go from their duties and perhaps going through personal traumas who found an audience and a confidence that grew with each lie they told.

The people emboldened by misguided self-importance, the doctors who'd bought their degrees off the internet, the politicians who'd never bothered the front benches. The columnists who'd never had an opinion they weren't told to have. The school dad at my door who said, 'Yeah, but do you actually *know anyone* who actually *got it*?'

Quite apart from Covid, there was another sort of global sickness brewing that continues to this day.

It made me want to zoom in. Right in.

It can affect anyone – including me, including you – but what happens when it affects a whole country?

Or when it poisons a community?

Or a single street?

Or one house?

Or a double *bed*?

Family Lies

In which we meet a husband living with lies,
a grieving son accused of spreading them, and a
pop star whose family is blind to the truth.

Also: poisonous swans.

4

'You'll See'

When Bad Information Divides a Relationship

These days, we're probably more aware than ever of our friends and neighbours' beliefs.

Isn't that weird?

I certainly never really cared how my neighbours voted before, or what their opinion was on basic medical matters. I didn't care what papers they read. But over the last decade people all over the world have come to surreptitiously take real note of what our friends, colleagues and neighbours think so that we can take that great human delight in judging them. Judging them hard. Beliefs become gossip: who they follow online, what they listen to in the car, what absolute drainpipe they think 'talks a lot of sense actually!'

Perhaps it's because in more innocent days – when we all watched the same TV programmes on a Saturday night, when we all got ready for school listening to the same person on the radio – there was an inherent belief in community and that those around us shared the same reality and had at least similar sets of values.

So imagine if the beliefs of anyone who lives near you might now be so out there and the reality they occupy so radically different that you just don't know how to handle them?

Information that you would bat away has reached through their screen and for some reason appealed to them, excited them, delighted them in a way that you think could never happen to you. You have now nothing in common.

Like if you find out that someone in your life – someone you trust, who you work with, who you assume thinks like you do – reveals that they believe the theories of one of Britain's most prominent and early conspiracy theorists – David Icke, say – and that they too now think the King's a lizard?

The King's a lizard!

Now, you know the King is not a lizard because common sense tells you that he is not a lizard; people aren't lizards, there's no evidence he's a lizard, and if the King was a lizard you're pretty sure you'd have noticed by now. It would have been in the newspapers. You'd have seen the King feeding on mice, or shedding his skin, or using sentences like 'I'm the King and I'm a lizard'.

So that's one thing, but knowing your colleague is either convinced or even simply considering an idea like that would be a shock. It means he or she is living in a different reality from you and perhaps everyone else in your life.

You can't say 'Agree to disagree'; you can't even meet them halfway. You can't say, 'Well, maybe the King is a *bit* lizardy,' without walking away from the conversation shaken, and thinking, My colleague thinks the King is a lizard.

It could be any belief, of course – any crazed theory, any thrilling falsehood, anything somebody told you.

But now imagine it's not your colleague who believes it, but the person you share your bed with.

* * *

Ben loves Heidi very much. That's the first thing he wants you to know.

They're the bedfellows I want to tell you about.

I believe Ben when he tells me he's loved Heidi for more than 25 years, after they met in that café in east London on that sun-kissed afternoon, and spent the rest of the day playing table football and laughing and sipping ciders.

Together they raised two beautiful children, who are teenagers now, and they all live in a nice house in a normal town somewhere outside the capital.

They're in their late 40s, but look younger. They wear band T-shirts and Vans and look like the kind of people who prefer vinyl and took their kids to Glastonbury first chance they got.

Everything was always so easy between them, but now Ben and Heidi have their differences.

See, Heidi's always been the happy-go-lucky, carefree but sensible one, while Ben claims he spent much of his 20s experimenting with psychedelic drugs and amusing himself by watching intense documentaries about UFOs or Bigfoot and having lively chats with his mate Johnny about whether advertisers used subliminal messaging to rot our brains and make us buy more Diet Coke.

Heidi got a bit fed up of Ben's mate Johnny after a while.

She'd sigh when Ben started talking about some new thing he'd learned off Johnny, and say 'You're starting to sound like Johnny' – that was when Ben knew to shut up.

The closest Heidi got to any of this fantasy stuff was when she was growing up. She'd been a self-described nerd – her bookshelves heaved with Pratchett and Gollums and Potters – but she had no spiritual beliefs or any real interest in them. She wasn't into science or politics or how the world works. She was a gentle atheist taking life as it came.

So if you had to bet on anyone in this relationship falling down a rabbit hole, you'd bet on old Psychedelics Ben, right?

'By the time I started to get alarmed, it was already too late, I think,' he says.

* * *

Heidi runs her own small business from home. It's always gone well, she has regular clients and she's very capable. But when she started to miss deadlines, Ben noticed, because it just wasn't like her. And then there was the phone.

'She was never someone who relied on her phone. She didn't have a smartphone for years, and when she got one she barely remembered to take it out with her. But then one day she installed TikTok.'

TikTok is a social media app not without controversy. It's highly addictive. It pays attention to things you like, notices how long you spend on them, and then offers you a million other things just like it. The dopamine hit is intense. Short, fast videos begin to give you exactly what you're interested in, constantly.

Which is fine if you're into greenhouse or gardening videos, or perhaps power-washing videos in which wholesome men and women clean patios or garage doors with impressive results.

It is less fine if you're a teenage boy and find yourself empowered by misogynists keen to tell you how to treat women badly. It is less fine if you are open – even just a hairline crack – to the idea of scientists creating vaccines specifically to make us drop dead in 18–24 months.

A recent study by the French foundation Reboot, which promotes critical thinking in young people, found that 17 per cent of young people who use TikTok for an hour or more a day wouldn't or couldn't 'definitively say that the earth is round'.

Soon, Ben noticed that Heidi was waking up earlier, while he dozed. Getting up, heading for the sofa downstairs, spending a good 90 minutes on her phone while everyone else was asleep. She would still be staring at TikTok when Ben got up. Every time she watched one video, another popped up just like it. Soon, she started asking him unusual, deep questions. Like whether he believed in life after death. Or alien abductions. Ben tells me, earnestly and with a tremor in his voice, that he began to notice more and more Amazon vans parking up outside across the days, delivering more and more weird books on a range of unusual topics. Heidi joined some societies dedicated to New Age beliefs and past-life regressions, which she'd never shown any interest in before. She befriended a local woman called Pauline, 'who was whatever you wanted her to be – psychic, tarot reader, yoga teacher, whatever'.

Heidi had been embarrassed at first. She told Ben, laughing, that she just found this New Age stuff interesting, but that if she ever bought a crystal, he had her full permission to shoot her.

A month later she bought a crystal.

'She didn't see what had happened – she was like, "This crystal will protect me!"'

Ben had been in hospital around this time. He'd caught Covid and it had taken its toll. Heidi wasn't allowed to be in the hospital when he was there. She had more time on her hands and Ben had more on his mind. When he realised what was happening, he knew he couldn't demand she delete TikTok from her phone. In any case, she was locked in the cycle of addictive behaviour it thrives on. So instead he told her something he'd heard from Johnny: that TikTok was actually a spy app developed by the Chinese government to harvest your data and take pictures of you when you weren't looking. She did her own research and immediately deleted the app.

But it didn't stop her finding new information. Websites. Forums. YouTube. Pauline.

By then, 'she was in too deep. She immersed herself in these worlds completely. And we started to argue. And she'd get really upset with me because I wouldn't believe her or I disagreed with what she was saying.'

For someone who had always been quite a left-leaning, liberal person, Heidi was suddenly coming up with some unusually potent right-wing viewpoints. A lot of it from a very American angle.

She'd started paying attention to the QAnon movement online – the hugely powerful and influential conspiracy group started on right-wing message boards in 2017 by someone called Q who claimed to have top-secret government clearance.

Based largely on this single claim, Q's followers now think Hollywood celebrities run the world while harvesting life-extending chemicals from the blood of trafficked children, all of which is being secretly battled by Donald Trump and his sidekick, John F. Kennedy Junior, who faked his own death in a plane crash in 1999 so that he could bide his time before joining the then-playboy hotel magnate in a global fight against international paedos.

If it sounds like a new phenomenon, it really isn't.

At its centre, in among all the noise and chaos that whips and whirls around it, is a plain old anti-Semitic trope that you can find almost anywhere from the Middle Ages on: that a group of evil Jews is plotting to take over the world. Of course, they're called globalists at the moment, or bankers, or 'Manhattan lawyers' or 'Hollywood elites'.

In recent years, QAnon has become so powerful it is knocking on the door of the mainstream – enough to rival some major religions. A Public Religion Research Institute (PRRI) report shows that one in five Americans say they agree with this base level QAnon statement: 'There is a storm coming soon that will sweep away the elites in power and restore the rightful leaders.'

When it comes to those people who mainly watch and trust the far-right cable news channels like Newsmax and Fox News, a chilling 40 per cent of them agree with this: 'The government, media and financial worlds in the US are controlled by a group of Satan-worshipping paedophiles who run a global child sex trafficking operation.'

The same report ('The Persistence of QAnon in the Post-Trump Era'), based on a random sample of nearly 20,000 people, suggests that at its peak, 17 per cent of Americans believed in QAnon. That's around 54 million people at least sympathetic to the idea that popular actor and typewriter enthusiast Tom Hanks was recently arrested by the US military in Milan, executed, and then replaced with a clone.

* * *

What QAnon represents, I think, is a very strange shift in the world of conspiracy theories that relies on the speed and efficiency that the internet has brought us. It is not a world in which people have to dissect painstakingly researched nuggets of real information and attempt to link them together to provide a convincing narrative.

Instead, often they simply see 'clues' everywhere.

According to the *New York Times*, when the Alabama State football team gave then President Donald Trump a football top with the number 17 on and he held it up for the cameras, QAnon took it as a signal that he was on their side – because Q is the 17th letter of the alphabet. Never mind that it was 2017 and in 2015 they'd given Barack Obama a shirt with 15 on it.

Often, Q organisers just need to say something utterly, palpably unbelievable and untrue and then rely on their audience to drink it in and spread the word. Evidence does not need to be presented; no one needs to be truly convinced because they're predisposed to be. Lies like this avoid the traditional gatekeepers – the editors or the heads of department or the fact-checkers. You can simply say that Tom Hanks was executed and replaced with a clone and away you go – millions will start to discuss it using their own secret knowledge as if they're involved in some kind of peer-reviewed study.

If it's not immediately shot down, it is believed, spread, and within moments the lie can have found its way to a loved one near you.

And it's a problem, because QAnon followers believe *hard*. That same PRRI report suggests that 18 per cent believe that violence may be necessary to get America back on track. Because 69 per cent of them think that Joe Biden stole the election.

And lies like this are now widely accepted as fact by adherents all over the world. Tens of millions of believers, drawn in at first by memes, or posts in otherwise innocent Facebook wellness groups, or that first intriguing TikTok video before the second, and the third, and the deluge that automatically, coldly follows.

* * *

It was all a lot for Heidi to take in, but according to what Ben is telling me, she'd quietly decided Donald Trump was a misunderstood genius who was being hounded by the Deep State.

She was certain of monumental government cover-ups.

The Ukraine war was not Putin's fault; he was trying his best.

She believed that yes, children probably were being sacrificed by the US government and had to be saved.

She became paranoid and distrustful as she wallowed in wider-ranging disinformation, propaganda and conspiracy.

She believed that anything the mainstream media told you was a lie – always believe the opposite.

She no longer tolerated trans people – 'she became *massively* anti-trans', which Ben found painful as they have a trans friend.

She thought racism was a left-wing trait. She believed there were extra-terrestrials being held secretly in Roswell, New Mexico, and became particularly obsessed with further alien cover-ups – from basic abductions of farmers in Nebraskan fields to the existence of human Super Soldiers training on Mars to fight the evil galactic empire that threatens all humanity.

It was all spilling over, from websites, speeches and books – a constant stream of theories, cascading into and out of her: this is unusual, because most truthers tend to stick to one lane.

Instead, Heidi was drowning in connected and unconnected worlds, and Ben was struggling to keep up. He could still see her, standing right there in front of him in the kitchen or as they held hands – the real Heidi was behind the eyes in the calmer moments, but Ben assures me he was not used to this type of conversation coming from the woman he does the Tesco shop with, watches box sets with, raised children with. And as the rivers of plausible and implausible lies mixed together, Heidi didn't like it when Ben doubted her or asked probing questions.

'She'd say something very matter-of-factly, like, "Of course the Earth is actually hollow and there are giant mega-cities down there and everyone knows about it."'

What she was referring to is the 'Hollow Earth' theory – the idea that there is an internal earth hidden deep beneath our feet, lit by its own sun. It is home, say some, to 12-foot-tall aliens who never catch colds and live alongside escaped Nazis and a group of lost eleventh-century Vikings in immortal bliss.

I'm saying nothing; I urge you to make up your own mind.

Sometimes – only sometimes – Ben says he would get angry with her. But she'd dig her heels in. 'She'd read a book about these underground mega-cities and be like, "Why would they lie about it? Why would they *make something like this up?*"'

Heidi has never been someone who's wanted to admit she was wrong about something, Ben says. I take him at his word, but he thinks that feeling small has a lot to do with what happened to her. Small, powerless, lost, insignificant. The same way many of us felt in lockdown. The same way many people feel all the time.

He says he thinks that his wife's many-months-long descent into what most of us might deem the objectively preposterous world of QAnon was a massive shortcut to a feeling of finally getting ahead of something. For someone who had largely ignored politics, history and science for most of her life, she felt she had a lot of catching up to do. But rather than school, university, lectures or hard graft, couldn't you achieve that same level of learning by watching 50 YouTube videos on vaccines?

'Her strongest belief is always whatever book she read last,' says Ben, quietly and with regret. 'It's much easier to forget everything you already knew about the world if you didn't really know that much to begin with'.

I don't think he's being mean about Heidi. I do think he is very frustrated and sad and finding his way through a wildly unexpected chapter in their story.

It's a story that has played out in other living rooms and kitchens all over the world, to the point where the EU

Academy now offers a course on 'How to deal with conspiracy narratives in relationships'. Fathers, mothers, siblings, cousins – those who become more isolated, then hyper-focused on 'truths' only they can see. The effects on a family can be devastating and wide-reaching. It's not just who you lose, but who you might lose next. The parents terrified their partner will radicalise their kids. The brothers who no longer speak, their children kept apart. The grandkids no longer allowed to see their grandparents.

Ben says he just wants his wife back. But Heidi has been swept up not just by lies that scare her, but by something just as dangerous: lies that excite her.

Her belief in disinformation, propaganda and QAnon conspiracy has actively made Heidi's life 100 per cent more exciting.

As Ben put it: 'Where real life is nuanced, messy and confusing, Q provides the plot of a Hollywood movie, where we all know who the heroes are, and we know who the evil bad guys are, and we know what needs to be done to save the world. It's a thrilling, mammoth struggle to save the country, world, universe.'

To Heidi, this isn't just about belief. It's about existential threats. She believes she is involved in a rebel alliance armed with special knowledge ready to take on great evil. She once described herself as a 'renegade hero'.

The only reason Ben is able to talk to me today is because Heidi is away. She is at a conference in the south of France. For many years there have been rumours that Adolf Hitler found a UFO in Antarctica and his scientists used it to fly to Mars, where they set up a secret space programme and began kidnapping members of the public and reprogramming them into super soldiers and killing machines. These space Nazis were then sent to fight aliens on different planets, including their main enemies: vampires, zombies and lizard people. Heidi will be listening to lectures from experts, former super soldiers turned whistle-blowers, and making new contacts in the resistance. Other renegade heroes. All while Ben's at home watching *Bargain Hunt*.

'She says "you'll see" a lot,' he says. 'She says when all this comes out, "*you'll see* that I was right".'

If it sounds exhausting for Ben, it is.

'There have been dark days where I'm thinking, how can we live ... you know, how can we be a husband and wife if we actually live in completely separate realities?'

* * *

Dr Daniel Jolley is a social psychologist with a joyous laugh, who's made a name for himself in the study of conspiracy theories: something that was derided or mocked 20 years ago but which now is necessary to the point of vital.

He is Jolley by name and by the time his academic career is over he will be absolutely delighted that writers have stopped saying 'and he's jolly by nature'. But he is; he's very jolly, and he should just accept that.

We meet up by a lake at the University of Nottingham, where I buy him a cup of tea and explain what Ben's been telling me.

Daniel is not surprised that TikTok has played a part in Heidi's story. He loves TikTok himself. He loves Twitter, too, though it embarrassed him recently. He saw a picture of the Pope that had been doing the rounds. The Pope in a huge white P Diddy-style puffer jacket, looking like an arctic rapper. He loved it. He didn't realise it was a fake. So when a journalist phoned him up and asked to have a chat about the fake images of the Pope that had been going around, he probably would have had more credibility with her if he hadn't immediately gone, 'WHAT? That's FAKE?!'

I fell for it too. Someone reading this right now is blushing, because they did too.

And it proves Daniel's point, when he talks about the sheer threat posed by social media, and TikTok in particular.

'It's just so powerful. So, so powerful. Someone can very quickly find themselves locked in to TikTok for hours, watching video after video.'

He says that Heidi has to be careful. And that Ben has to be gentle. Because just like Ben said, they're in different realities right now.

Daniel says Ben might need to ask his wife, 'What do these ideas offer you? Why? This idea that the elite are out to get you – what does that offer you right now? Do you feel you have no power sometimes? Can we focus on the things we do have power over? It's really about trying to get the other person to think very clearly about things. Trying to think through the evidence that they're being exposed to in their other world ...'

* * *

Heidi doesn't discuss her beliefs with her friends anymore, not even the gentler friends or the gentler beliefs. They laughed her out of the room the last time she tried and she found it humiliating and sad. Ben can't really talk to many friends either, because they're all mutual and he wants to protect her. She doesn't post her beliefs on social media. And 'she does have times where she's kind of bursting into tears, going, "I'm so confused, I just don't know." There are a lot of people in these communities who talk online about this "journey of awakening". They've lost friends, spouses, family members who don't want to talk about it anymore. It's not easy for them.'

There are moments of clear-eyed reality that surface sometimes. When Heidi can see herself through other's eyes, or when she hears the sentence she's just spoken out loud. 'Just so you know, I am fully aware of how mad this sounds,' she once told Ben.

But how do people get there? How do they get to the sentence they say to their friends one day that ruins everything?

'If you immediately come out and say to someone, "I believe that there are galactic federations plotting to overtake Earth", it sounds absolutely nuts,' says Ben. 'But to her it's not. Because it's been incremental. Starts small, builds and builds, and then you have a version of reality which is so far removed from reality that to any person who hasn't had that incremental education it seems totally absurd.'

Ben has read up on marriages like his online.

He thinks the advice given to people in his situation is too extreme.

'They're all like, get a divorce lawyer now! Get out of the house! Leave her!'

But that's not easy when there's real and deep love involved.

'And kids, of course. I should tell you something actually, which really did hurt me. A few months ago, she said

"I wish I'd known all this stuff earlier, and then we could have brought the children up completely differently." She didn't say it to be malicious. But all these wonderful memories we have of bringing up our kids – she was like, "I wish all that didn't happen and we'd done it all differently". Or that's how it felt to me.'

And while Heidi is similarly hurt that Ben won't go along with her stories – he feels that just as keenly. Why won't she listen to *him*? Why doesn't she trust him enough to believe him when he says there really can't be giant mega-cities operating in a hollowed-out earth?

He thinks she mentioned the kids because lately, well, they've been questioning her too. They've been raised on science. Raised to be independent thinkers. They sound savvy. 'They laugh at her, basically,' he sighs. 'And that must be frustrating. I feel sorry for her. If you truly believe that stuff, you must have an awful lot of frustration as well.'

* * *

Dr Sophia Moskalenko is a psychologist, specialising in the psychology of radicalisation, in mass psychology and in conspiracy theories, among other subjects. She works at the University of Pennsylvania, and when I tell her about Ben and Heidi, she's sad but not surprised. Her work means she's often contacted by those who are losing or have lost someone to the world of conspiracy – QAnon in particular.

'And some of these were quite dramatic stories where, for example, college students were kicked out of their parents' homes, because the parents were anti-vaccination, and the college students would get vaccinated. And so that was the end of that. Or where a mother refused to wear a mask during the pandemic, and the people at home felt unsafe because of her beliefs, and that caused a lot of trauma and rift. This woman – I think it was in the *New York Times* – she said that she was spending so much time researching QAnon that she was neglecting her three children and basically not providing meals for them, because that would take her away from the screen ...'

Interestingly, she says that in her research, she's found that it's the women who are more likely to be the ones in the relationship to fall for QAnon. She says it often started with 'wellness' websites devoted to seemingly harmless New Age thinking. Yoga, kale, meditation, crystals, those pedicures where they get fish to nibble the dead skin off your feet. The kind of places with a natural suspicion of man-made vaccines. People open to different ideas, let's say. And as people found these QAnon ideas and themselves going deeper, there is the natural human reaction to want to share with your group this special knowledge that sets you apart. It was the idea that QAnon was out to rescue children from satanic paedophiles that most appealed to so many. It became a rescue mission 'that reverberated through a lot of online spaces frequented by women ... by stay-at-home moms or the parenting-as-lifestyle people'.

And with more time on their hands during lockdowns, 'It all fell on very fertile ground. It fell on a public opinion that was already highly sceptical of the government and the elites. There had already been so many sex scandals in Hollywood, the Me Too movement, crimes that were covered up for decades, including abuse of minors. Sex scandals in the White

House too. It all played in to QAnon, these cover-ups. It did not fall on rocky ground.'

Often, she says, it's the partners and families of those with these beliefs who suffer longest. 'They can get PTSD. More anxiety. It presents an almost completely new kind of danger [to people]. What beliefs like this do is chip away at trust. First within families. But also trust in institutions, trust in democracy, trust in science and trust in medicine. And it is so prevalent here in the US. They spread these narratives prolifically. And there's, like, tens of millions who believe it, even by the lowest estimates. So I think you're looking, in this particular family you mention, at a microcosm of that.'

She says that for the families of people lost to the rabbit holes, it's almost akin to a type of grief, though one with no closure. 'You're definitely losing a person. Not in the same sense as death, but in some ways it could be even more devastating. I know that sounds strange, but when someone is able to be with you but refuses to be, that can be even more painful than losing them to, God forbid, a car accident. It is not just a loss; it's also a rejection.'

* * *

Ben's waiting for Heidi to come home. From the south of France, but also from wherever else she's disappeared to.

He has given up trying to challenge her or debunk her theories. There's no point, and it's cruel. Once, his tactic in an argument was to say, 'Well, let's tell all your friends, and see what they make of it!' – but he wouldn't ever do that. He doesn't want to shame Heidi. He wants to be there 'when she wakes up'. For now, he will simply listen, then maybe ask her *why* she believes something. Or what piece of evidence it would take for her to believe the opposite. He sees hope sometimes. 'But then she'll ruin it by reading a book that's supposed to be about the banking system, but which is actually just a huge manifesto about why the Jews are bad.'

He is trying to be calmer. He is patient, non-patronising, careful and supportive. He listens.

He worries about picking her up from the airport, though. Maybe she'll return not believing in Nazi space soldiers. Or maybe she'll return with bags and bags of new books.

Ben wasn't sure whether to speak to me about all this. I'd reached out after finding a short statement he'd posted on an internet forum; a kind of howl of rage and sadness into the void at his situation. But then he said he imagined a future where Heidi – the old Heidi – is back. And he imagined her reading this book, and as she is finishing this chapter, as she is reading the same words you are right now, he watches her and waits, and then he leans over from next to her and nudges her and says 'that's about us'.

So that she saw that it was hard.

But so that she can see that he tried.

That he's still here for her.

And most of all, because if that happens, that might mean she was back.

* * *

The positive side of Ben and Heidi's story so far is not just the bond and the love they share despite occupying one house but two different worlds. It's also that Heidi can sense she is convincing no one. While this is isolating, she has a supportive partner. For others, the danger comes in the sense of community they find, where lies are no longer questioned, but escalated and amplified in a sort of frenzy to show not just who is right, but who is the *rightest*.

It's there, in that world, that you'll find the people so sure that they have special knowledge and that you must be so wilfully blind to it that you must be pretending, and they will expose you for it. They will actively seek you out – sometimes when you are at your very weakest – and you will know their righteous rage.

This was something the next man I'd meet found out in spades. He faced an almost invisible army that was nowhere yet everywhere.

It's the story of Francis versus the World.

5

Going Viral

How the Worst News Can Attract the Worst People

Francis Goncalves is a man who one day found himself accused of being a liar.

Not just a liar, actually, but that day, when he was at his lowest, he was accused of being a crisis actor.

Crisis actors do exist, just not in the way the term has become popularised and weaponised in recent years. They're supposed to be an actor so short of work they take up gigs playing dead bodies in fabricated news stories designed to instil fear in a population.

In reality, a crisis actor is usually a student or volunteer, paid to take part in emergency drills to help train first responders or the army.

Francis was accused of being the first type.

Someone who might pretend to be a wounded soldier in a conflict not actually taking place. Or the victim of a staged mass shooting. Or a witness to a fake war crime.

The idea is that they lend pre-planned scenes authenticity when played out on television or online.

What's unclear is where you can hire these crisis actors, or how they ever get more than one gig.

I don't know if they have crisis agents who take 15 per cent of their crisis work fees.

I don't know if crisis actors can do a crisis so well that they then go on to bigger things.

I've never watched a witness to a bombing or an earthquake and thought, Wait – is that the guy who played the Soup Nazi in *Seinfeld*?

Of course, there are definitely people who take part in propaganda videos. Some recent footage of Vladimir Putin visiting a military base, a boat, a church, does seem to show the same woman enjoying roles as a soldier, sailor and carol singer. But was she an actor? Or a bodyguard? Spotting a clue – a small truth in the lie – does much to make people think a bigger story is happening, and forums and YouTube monologues immediately drum up huge rage against innocent people who find themselves abused and humiliated by sometimes hundreds or thousands of people.

It's how Alex Jones, a man we will get to later on, is set to lose an unthinkable amount of money that he doesn't have after accusing some of the small children killed by a gunman who attacked Sandy Hook Elementary School in the state of Connecticut, USA, of being crisis actors. The lunacy of such a claim was matched only by its blatant cynicism and absolute lack of human compassion.

But I can tell you that Francis Goncalves is not a crisis actor.

I can tell you that he's a friendly and open restaurant manager who lives in Cardiff, Wales, and is a man who did not deserve what happened to him.

* * *

He brings his partner Caitlin with him when we meet at my hotel, in a city battered by rain.

Smokers stand outside the NCP Car Park opposite, just by the Mexican restaurant that advertises proudly on its wall that it serves 'unauthentic food'.

There's a room off to one side in this place, with an honesty bar. It's dark out. Wind batters the plastic seats on the terrace, and cushions lift and flap intermittently. It's cosy in here and you can pick your own bottles of Spanish wine, and it turns out Caitlin is a sommelier, which I only discover after I've already offered to pay for that wine, and which will make me question just how honest with this honesty bar I want to be.

As she chooses a bottle and I psychically will her away from the expensive end, I realise why Francis brought her. He's been scared about this. It's exposing. His eyes dart around, he wipes his forehead with his sleeve. He'd said he wanted to meet somewhere people wouldn't see him. People have been out to get him. His world has been made smaller in a lot of ways.

Despite him living in Wales and the others in Portugal, Francis describes the Goncalves family as 'small and close'.

Both he and his brother, Shaul, had one aim in life: to get to a point through hard work where they could take care of everyone else. That ambition and graft had allowed them to lose sight of each other for a while, to lose that close bond for a moment. Maybe that's why he hadn't paid too much attention to what Shaul had been watching online.

But not just Shaul, because this part of his story began when he noticed that his parents were showing a lot of interest in similar videos online.

'My parents … well, they'd been pulled into conspiracies in the past. My mother had suffered from clinical paranoia for many years.'

Shaul, a fit and work-obsessed 40-year-old teetotaller with a plant-based diet, had been extremely slowly drawn in too, watching seemingly harmless videos of passionate and convincing people pontificating eloquently about what was really going on in the world. Alex Jones of InfoWars. The comedian Russell Brand. Former *Fear Factor* host Joe Rogan.

They talked often, and Francis would have lively but polite conversations about Covid with his family. It was playful but forthright. Same as a lot of families. He'd toy gently with his parents, Basil and Charmagne, 73 and 65.

'We would have normal discussions about where Covid was coming from. What the ideas were. Interesting conversations, the type you'd condone across the board, because you've got to allow people to question things.'

His dad, his mum, his brother – they were all questioning things. It didn't start out badly. They were just asking questions and doing their own research.

'But then all of a sudden it turned.'

It turned when Francis had the vaccine, as soon as it was available to him. His parents were appalled. They couldn't believe what he'd done. Didn't he realise? Hadn't he heard?

'It started more from my father's side. There would be almost a nasty attack on the ideas I was putting forward. [I was saying], you know, you need to take a step back from the YouTube videos, and actually listen to people who do this for a living, not just some doctor running a blog where he's talking absolute rubbish. Sure as hell not anti-vaxxers and propagandists. But you could see it from his point of view. He was the protector of the family.'

But Francis became really concerned when his mother messaged him about it all. She had some strong opinions. Ones Francis thought were based on lies.

'We had an argument. We didn't speak properly for about a week.'

But the very next time they did, 'Mum said she wasn't feeling very well. And then she put the phone down on the bed and [I could hear her] dozing off. And I didn't know what was happening. So I phoned my father, and he said they were really ill.'

Panicked, he phoned Shaul, also in Lisbon. And Shaul said, 'I have to tell you something. We've all got Covid.'

Basil, Charmagne and Shaul were, as you might have suspected, unvaccinated. Basil had been to the hospital for kidney stones a day or two earlier. It's possible he picked up Covid there. Two days later – a Saturday – everyone met up for a regular, cosy family dinner at Shaul's.

By Monday, it had hit them.

'My father went to ICU first. My mother followed. My brother stayed at home. On the Saturday I texted him and I remember him saying his mucus had turned from green to brown. I said, that's blood in your phlegm. That's pneumonia. Go to the hospital. Go now. And he said he phoned through but someone told him it was normal and he'd get better. I don't know if that's true. Maybe he was just too busy to get sick.'

Francis kept texting, phoning, FaceTiming. His brother looked 'greyish blue'. Francis had to find a way to get to

Portugal from Cardiff at a time when travel was restricted. For his parents, for his brother.

'And about one o'clock in the morning I received a phone call. And his heart had given way. And that was the moment I broke.'

He stares, eyes filled with tears. Caitlin stares too, at the wall behind me.

Francis clears his throat, tries to settle himself.

'The unfairness of it,' I say.

Caitlin squeezes his hand, there for him, the reason she came, then rubs his arm.

'It is unfair. It's incredibly unfair. I think unfairness is one of the most undervalued words you come across. It is unfair, when he had so much to give.'

He takes a breath.

'And it just spiralled from there.'

By the Tuesday, his father was in a very critical state.

He died that afternoon.

After leaping through every legal and medical hoop forced on him, Francis arrived at the hospital in Lisbon. Caitlin couldn't join him; her South African passport made things harder. And it was noisy in the hospital, confusing, chaotic: everything we remember from the TV. Francis was terrified; he knew his mother had underlying health conditions.

'I had to find my mum. I didn't know where she was. I was standing downstairs and my aunt managed to call a doctor saying "please let him in". And they took me through to the Covid ward and the one doctor pulled me aside and said, "Look, I'm not going to lie to you. She's in a very bad state. She's in ICU. She's face down. And some of what you're going to see is not pleasant." I had to wait half an hour. I was wearing basically a hazmat suit. And as I walked in I could see a nurse was just finishing up my mum's hair. And what they had done was try and make her look respectable. And I really do appreciate that. But that was when I realised: this wasn't going to turn right. And the next afternoon she passed away.'

Francis lost everyone in a week – the people he'd grown up with, laughed with, eaten with, played with, bickered with, the people he wanted to look after, the ones at the family table – all gone in seven days. An unbearable weight he somehow was forced to bear. He lost more people in a week than many do in decades. That's what unfair means.

'And that's when you think, What do I do with this? Am I just going to move on with my life, or can I do something to help people? I was numb. Completely numb. Ninety-nine per cent of me was screaming. One per cent was holding it together. I wanted to kick some common sense into the situation.'

Francis found himself eye-deep in grief, alone, and responsible for arranging everything that happens after a death. Hospitals. Paperwork. Attorneys. Funeral homes.

A week after his mother passed away, on a lonely Sunday, he buried all three members of his family next to each other, at Lisbon's Alto de São João cemetery, in the separate and cordoned-off Covid-related deaths section. The people at the cemetery told him they'd never before had three bodies brought in together from the same family.

Caitlin was there for him on the end of the phone, but this was a man bereft.

And then he did what some people – people who saw not a pandemic but a global plot to control the masses – were very keen for him not to do.

He started telling his story. Using social media. Starting a Facebook group. Contacting the press. And reading the science. The actual science, not the pseudoscience. Urging people to get vaccinated. Begging them. Maybe part-therapy, but despair too, and certainly anger. He became combative. He felt he'd lost so much that there was almost nothing else to lose. He felt rage. He warned critics not to come into his physical world. And he had nothing but venom for the people who had lied to his once small and close family.

'How much money have people made spreading fear online from Covid alone?' he says. 'All of this stuff … "Does anyone know anyone who has actually died of Covid? Genuine question!" All that stuff. And it was just a matter of pushing through a few days, just to raise awareness that Covid is real, it is not a joke, it is not just a cold; we all need to stop referring to it as that.'

Wales Online ran the story. It soon spread. You would think it a story that would garner nothing but sympathy. Sadly, the world doesn't work that way.

The *Daily Mail* was typically gentle with its headline: 'Covid Wipes Out Anti-Vaxxer Family'. Eyes swivelled towards Francis. People declared him an attention seeker. Mistaken. A propagandist. A liar. Many called him a crisis actor. Paid to push the vaccine narrative.

'People were after me. There were some horrible comments. Immediately it turned. I still haven't read the comments under the original piece on Wales Online. Even to this day.'

'They were horrific,' says Caitlin, who had.

They were indeed horrific. Most have since been cleaned up and thrown away by Wales Online, leaving only those that scraped by on technical grounds.

Look them up on Facebook – new accounts, no friends, and no posts other than about this story!!

I don't believe this for one bit, they probably died of food poisoning and its being used as more scare tactics

Don't respect lies and fake stories, nothing in the records of deaths

And of Francis: 'He's looking very smug for the photo Don't you think? Would anyone consider he may be a well paid Crisis Actor? Nothing would surprise me tbh.'

※ ※ ※

This crisis actor thing.

Paul is a former US cop who tells me he fell hard for the crisis actor idea.

We found each other online, danced around one another, then got talking. He checked out the other posts I'd made on the website in question to make sure I wasn't a force for evil. Thankfully, those posts were largely saying what a nice cheese the hard-to-find Baron Bigod brie is, and how it really is a very high-quality British version of a French classic, and then perhaps reacting politely to people telling me what other similar cheeses I might try, so I don't think he saw me as some kind of threatening left-wing radical.

Crisis acting just made sense to Paul, he says, starting from 2016 onwards. He thought governments worldwide *would* employ a bunch of roving disaster-minstrels performing their self-tapes and auditioning at various sites of awful national trauma.

I asked him what it would have been like to meet him – Crisis Paul – in 2016.

'I would likely warn you not to meet me in 2016. I was lost, angry, suffering from ongoing PTSD, depression and mood swings. The 2016 me has a hair-trigger temperament, is easily angered, and suffering from ongoing mental health battles.'

I asked him what I might have liked about him.

'I would say you'd probably like that I was still compassionate and as kind as I could be. I was and still am very outspoken against any forms of abuse.'

But it was 2017, at Christmas, when he found himself completely hooked on the crisis actor idea, thanks to posts he found via – them again! – QAnon.

'The crisis actors narrative is a way to cope with horrible events. [Some people] can't possibly entertain the idea that natural disasters, mass killings, genocide, and pandemics occur naturally or as a result of individual choices. Blaming "actors" is a way for them to not take responsibility for their own [denial]. It's always an "all-powerful elite enemy" instead of humans themselves. They are always the victims instead.'

And when it comes to the people who accused Francis of being a crisis actor, he says, 'Yes, it makes sense. They would always have accused him of being a crisis actor or a Deep State plant. Easier to call him a puppet. It's very evil stuff.'

It's also weirdly understandable. Wouldn't we rather pretend the images we see or even imagine can't be real – but the result of people trying to trick us, prosthetics, and Hollywood tricks? In a 2022 'Truth under attack' survey from King's College London, 14 per cent of people in the UK said it was definitely or probably true that 'the Manchester Arena attack involved "crisis actors" who pretended to be injured or killed – people were not really killed or injured'. That's one in seven people. You know seven people. Which one of them is it?

People who believe ideas like this tend to be more right-wing. In America, that means they tend to feel more tenderly towards gun ownership. Saying school shootings don't happen makes it a lot easier to justify the AK-47 under your bed.

Alex Jones claimed that the US government staged the 2012 Sandy Hook massacre using crisis actors in order to take away the guns of everyday Americans. A lie. Sickening and horrific. Twenty kids died that day, along with six members of staff, in a shooting carried out by a deranged 20-year-old man. Those are the facts.

Yet Jones insisted for years on his InfoWars show that it was all staged – staged, despite the evidence, despite the witnesses, despite the families. Their suffering was already unimaginable, but now he condemned them to even more unthinkable pain.

He was finally taken to court. Relatives of some of the victims testified that because of his lies, many of them had been threatened or harassed by 'truthers'. One parent testified that conspiracy theorists had urinated on his seven-year-old son's grave. One woman received rape threats.

He was ordered to pay nearly $1 billion in damages, then a further $473 million in damages. I watched the trial in fascination and horror. Because I'd spent a little time in America with Alex Jones. He gave me a dollar with his phone number on it. He should probably have kept that dollar.

Paul the cop got out of that place just in time. 'I went very far into the conspiracy world. I got so far until I reached the real truth, which was that QAnon is just a repackaged trope of all the old stuff. The same manifestos Hitler and the Nazis used to justify the Holocaust.'

But he got out. Paul the cop got out before it was too late.

* * *

The rumours about Francis – if you can call them rumours – weren't just online, and they didn't stop at insults. There were people in the real world who slowly began to take things even further.

'I was threatened. I was threatened by a guy from Italy. And I was threatened right here in the UK.'

'Why do you think they were so angry with you?' I ask.

'There was just a huge number of people telling me "The vaccine has already killed millions. Far more than Covid. You are just killing people." There were so many.'

'Also just a lot of random people calling you a twat,' says Caitlin, and we all paused, then laughed.

More threats followed. More name-calling. More accusations of lying from unusual accounts with strange grasps of English and similar grammar.

Perhaps spurred on by this, people started actually turning up at São João cemetery in Portugal to 'do their own research'. More than once. Armed with cameras, looking for the graves, searching for the names, sure that just as Covid was of course fictional, so was the Goncalves family.

Francis says that part of the conspiracist's trick is that 'it doesn't have to be true, just say it with confidence. And look in any industry and you've got this. You have a waiter who's not a sommelier. Ask the waiter about a bottle of red and you'll believe whatever they say if they say it with confidence, when they don't know it from a bar of soap.'

'It's true,' says Caitlin, holding up her glass.

Francis set up a Facebook group to combat disinformation, and you can imagine how well that went down. Grief can propel us into finding out everything we can on a subject. It can send us crazy, or it can ignite in us a search for truth. Some learn everything they can about a disease, a treatment. Francis too was reading every scientific paper he could find. Looking for facts, not opinions masquerading as them.

'I used to be a lawyer,' says Caitlin, 'and half the stuff Francis tells me goes over my head.'

I now realise that as a sommelier and lawyer, not only can Caitlin beat you in any argument, she can drink you under the table while she does it.

'You look at things very differently when something like this happens,' says Francis. 'You become different. You act on your true north. You don't become flexible anymore. You know what's right and what's wrong. I'm not going to tell you your food was terrible, you don't need to know that. But if someone tells me you're going to hell because you don't believe in Jesus Christ, I'll tell them they're speaking absolute rubbish. I'm religious, Catholic, I pray, when I was younger I was going to become a Catholic priest. But I will speak up and tell you you're talking absolute trash if you say that.'

I start to wonder who Francis blames for compounding his grief. I know it's not the everyday people who've found themselves down the same rabbit holes his father fell into. It's the rabbits themselves, isn't it? The ones doing the digging.

'You have these people online … and all they do is plant a seed. Now, do you think they make much money through people subscribing $3 a month? Absolutely. Do they make money from engagement? Absolutely. Will some of the people clicking be trying to shut them down? Sure, they don't care, it's all more money. But there is a moment. That moment someone thinks "Should I really get my child vaccinated?" They have sown the seed. And that moment can cost a life. Just for more viewers. It really is that simple.'

* * *

Dr Bharat Pankhania is driven mad by things like this. He calls Francis's story 'a tragedy', and he says he's had enough.

He's a smart, passionate senior clinical lecturer at Exeter Medical School who in the spring of 2023 was invited onto the TV channel GB News to have a one-on-one chat with the former actor turned anti-vaccine campaigner Laurence Fox.

If Pankhania hadn't had white hair already, he soon would have had.

GB News is a channel that has been found to promote untrue narratives and has been subject of many investigations by OFCOM. Over the years its main stars have tended to be cut-price adverts against divorce, mid-life crises or general breakdown.

And as the show began, it was clear to Dr Pankhania that this was not to be a one-on-one chat at all, and instead a panel discussion in which his facts would be 'balanced' by some random other guest's opinions.

He felt he was a victim of 'an absolute ambush', and as the former actor Laurence Fox – all louche and cocky – blithely welcomed him to what he described as a show and asked for his thoughts on a report he wasn't aware he'd be speaking about, a shocked Pankhania said, 'I sometimes wonder why you exist, to be honest with you.'

Now Fox looked like he'd woken up, startled, as Pankhania continued, 'A lot of these things that you spew out, that are worrisome to people, are not verified; not factual.'

He went on, 'You just have your own agenda, that's what I think. You are just spewing out your biased views. That's how I feel about you.'

If I may add a little something here, there is pride to be taken in turning down the approaches of a TV channel which actively plays fast and loose with truth. I have myself received several invites from various producers, the first of which I responded to with the words, 'No disrespect to you personally, but I would rather set my balls on fire.'

* * *

When I talk to him from his office in Bath (where he is also deputy mayor), Pankhania says, 'I am an examiner and when I examine students and the students give me a bullshit answer, I get really, really angry because I say, look, you either know or you don't know, but you can't make it up. [...] But I find, you know, as a scientist, we are not media trained and the opposition who are interviewing us can cut us off at the drop of a hat. So when you are being interviewed with their lies, you need to be so nimble to get your word in if you wish to attack those lies.'

See, science is hard. Calling science wrong is easy. In times of confusion and calamity, clinging to a lie as you flounder in a sea of confusion is like clinging to a lifeboat.

'All their lies go along the lines of: if it's believable, say it. If you say it, it will have traction. Because people believe a believable lie.'

Pankhania regularly suffers violent condemnation and racist abuse from those who wish he'd shut up with his facts and evidence so that they can listen to the comforting and believable lies unencumbered. 'I believe I am a good scientist, an honest scientist with no agenda. You know, I had one just a couple of days ago, telling me I ought to be in prison for promoting the vaccines. I'm here to save all lives, irrespective of your political or other leanings.'

I ask him if he thinks the people who deliver these long monologues on TV about Covid vaccines damaging women in order to bring society to its knees, for example, really believe what they say. Or whether it's a bandwagon which can lend them a quick authority they never earned and an audience they never had. He doesn't know for sure. But he knows they're effective, these broadcasts, these videos, these people: he's suffered the result of disinformation himself. There are people once close to him he can no longer speak to, who believe the monologues from strangers over evidence from a friend – a literal expert in the field.

'There are dark forces at play,' he says, sounding for a moment like a man about to concoct a conspiracy theory of his own. 'Because if they can sow those seeds of doubt and discontent and dissatisfaction, then we have a divided nation. And when we have a divided nation fighting each other, they can get their dark agenda forward, whatever that dark agenda is.'

* * *

Francis is shaken as we finish our evening together. He's going to take Caitlin for some food. They're starting their own restaurant in Cardiff soon. He tells me the concept but asks for my silence. Not just for business reasons, but because, I think, he could do without an internet pile-on. I can tell he's relieved our chat is over.

'You know, this idea that Covid is a government conspiracy to kill people,' I say, standing up. 'I mean, why Covid? Is malaria? Was Russian flu? What about avian flu? It's just this one, is it? There are thousands of other things out there killing people, but it's just this one?'

He smiles.

'I bumped into a guy I knew. And he said to me – what if all these people, these people that are anti-vax. These people who say Covid is not real, who say you shouldn't wear a mask or social distance. What if it's *those* people?'

'How do you mean?' I say.

'Well, what if those people urging you *not* to take Covid seriously – what if *they* are part of a hidden movement to bring down the world population? What if *they* are the New World Order and that by urging us to not get vaccinated it is part of some grand plan to kill us all off?'

I think about it.

'It's genuinely more convincing than Bill Gates pumping microchips through tiny syringes.'

He smiles again.

'And that's how easy it is to develop a conspiracy theory. You just have to press a button or two. And it is very, very frightening to see how easily a person can be pulled in. Just say it with confidence.'

'Whether you believe it or not?'

He nods. Whether you believe it or not.

And for a second, imagine being on the other side of that.

Imagine *knowing* something is true, seeing it right there in front of you – and being told you are wrong, feeling gaslit, being assured by trusted loved ones that you must have lost your mind.

And I realise in that moment that I happen to know some-one who's been going through exactly that experience.

And so that's where we go next.

6

Information War

When You're Told What's Definitely Happening is Not Happening

When she was shaken awake at four in the morning on 24 February 2021, the Ukrainian pop star and operatic diva Kamaliya Zahoor couldn't work out if she was dreaming at first.

But the windows of her Kyiv mansion had indeed been rattling from an explosion.

Then another – BOOM.

Now her walls started to shake.

The phone calls started moments later.

Friends, relatives, they were all telling her: the city was under attack.

She was confused. This wasn't possible. It was supposed to be a bluff. Everyone said so. The Russians would never invade.

Then another explosion. Not far away.

Her husband, the Pakistani steel billionaire Mohammed Zahoor (known simply as Zahoor), had been right to get the kids out of the country. He'd felt so silly doing it. He worried people would think him a coward. But they had a house in London and twins to protect.

She watched from her window as rockets rained down on Ukraine – rockets she could feel in her bones as she fled to the basement.

Kamaliya had no idea what to do.

* * *

Kamaliya is a big deal in her native Ukraine.

She's a pop star (six albums) who in happier days even performed at the Kremlin for Vladimir Putin, alongside her old friend Volodymyr Zelenskyy – though that was when he was a comedian. She's also a TV star (*Dancing with the Stars* in Ukraine and the Fox reality show *Meet the Russians* in the UK). She's a former Miss South Ukraine, and she was the proud winner of Mrs World 2008.

She's starred in films (in *Mantera*, she plays scientific genius Dr Natasya Pushkin who has designed a robot glove that can turn a motorbike into body armour) and her music videos do great business online (the video for 'I'm Alive', in which Kamaliya has a car accident and then meets a magic horse which transports her back to Roman times, has been viewed 45 million times – and there are only 44 million people in Ukraine).

She's been painted as a little silly in the past, a little flashy. All blonde hair and long nails. Someone who bathes in champagne and is constantly surrounded by little dogs.

I mean, the last bit is true.

I know, because I've been in that Kyiv mansion with her. I saw all the dogs. One of them wore earrings. I remember

Cliff, Bertie and the one that sat on a tiny velvet cushion whose name was Guy Ritchie, though because of Kamaliya's accent I spent most of the day thinking they had a dog called Gay Ritchie.

I remember the expensive imported gold wallpaper, the karaoke machine and the falcon that lived in the hallway, chained to a stand. I remember the fat white cat with the completely shaved body who looked incredibly pissed off about it.

But Kamaliya is not in fact silly. She's an activist, an ally, a gay-rights campaigner. She was born in eastern Siberia, a military kid who at nine years old watched the black cloud of Chernobyl spread across the blue sky above her. She spent time in hospital, fighting off lymphoma years later, perhaps as a result. She feared she'd never have children. But she worked hard. Her star rose. She met her husband, the self-made man from Pakistan, and they travelled the world.

I spent a few days with the Zahoors in Ukraine in 2014 when they were making a bid for UK stardom equal to that which they enjoy in Ukraine and in some parts of Europe. I was profiling them for a magazine, so I went to a Kyiv nightclub with them, all heads turning towards her as we walked through a security gate which had a sign very specifically banning any and all use of hand grenades in the club.

I slept in their pool house, next to where they kept the vicious guard dogs and near a giant mural of Kamaliya standing like a goddess while Zahoor folds his arms by a yacht.

They flew me in one of their jets to a fish restaurant in Odesa, we stood on the Potemkin Steps together, and they shared their love of Ukraine.

Kamaliya is wide-eyed, likeable, sincere, open.

And she was not expecting to have to flee to her basement.

'My friends started to call me,' she says, 'K – they start war. The rockets are bombing us. Russian rockets bombing us. I say – I can't believe it. Maybe it's some terrorist?'

* * *

We're sitting at their incredibly long dinner table at their house in Hampstead, west London. It's an opulent place they've owned since 1996, the kind with snugs and ante-chambers and extra rooms that they've run out of purposes for, so they just put chairs in.

On the table in front of us, next to a bowl of sugared fennel seeds she will pick at, is Kamaliya's phone.

The phone lights up every few seconds, with every new alert. It looks like you'd imagine a phone looks when someone's sent a particularly successful tweet – or a particularly bad one.

But these aren't shares or likes, she tells me.

Her phone does this every time a missile is fired at Ukraine. She wants to feel what it's like still to be there.

'So I'm standing just in my night clothes,' she says. 'So I start to watch the live channels. The presenters and the normal people making videos and photos in real life. I look at Instagram. And when I speak with a friend, I heard a BOOM outside – and then I heard it on his phone too. And we hide in the basement, and for a whole day we watch what is happening.'

It was an objectively real war zone. So Kamaliya was confused when she saw people were being less than sympathetic. She was confused when people said it wasn't really happening, or if it was, it was for the right reasons.

'So I started doing my "lives". I go on Facebook, Instagram, TikTok, everywhere. And I try and open the eyes of everyone out there.'

She wanted to tell Putin to stop. She wanted to tell Russians to stop. She wanted to tell everyone what was happening: her family, her friends and in her position as a trusted celebrity – her fans.

She didn't get the reaction she expected.

'Russian people were telling me – but you are doing this. Your soldiers are doing this. Your soldiers are hitting your buildings. But I was watching rockets fly over my house! I saw Russian jets fly over my house!'

They had an answer for everything. Any footage they saw – even that which Kamaliya filmed herself – was 'fake' or 'a montage' or 'from a Hollywood film'. Photos were photoshopped. Stories were made up. Witnesses were liars.

'She felt like she was talking to walls,' says Zahoor, next to her. 'The propaganda had prepared the Russian people. They were ready to believe anything. And then the lie changed. Her own family in Russia were telling her, "Kamaliya, you just have to wait a little bit, because we are going to free you from these Nazis and then we will all live together, and all will be well."'

Kamaliya laughs but her eyes don't join in.

'And I say, "What Nazis?!"'

So either the Ukrainian government was destroying its own city, or the streets of Kyiv were suddenly filled with Nazis, all goose-stepping about the place, and Russia had to save the Ukrainian people.

Zahoor takes a moment and sighs.

'I am amazed they could have put this into the brains of the Russian people.'

* * *

It's no coincidence that many of Kamaliya's fiercest fan-critics were younger.

The propaganda surrounding the invasion of Ukraine is interesting because there was a greater focus on persuading Russia's youth that the things that were definitely happening were definitely not happening. Or that the things that they could see were definitely happening were actually happening for a whole different set of reasons.

The minds of the youth had to be captured, guided and controlled because Vladimir Putin was worried they were too internet-savvy. They could use secret apps or websites to get around Russian news. They could WhatsApp their friends in the West. They could stream people like Kamaliya on Facebook. They could see past Putin's claim that he was 'compelled' to invade Ukraine because of 'the tragedy' of a planned genocide against Russian speakers in the country.

Vast numbers of young Russian influencers were given the same scripts to read, which they performed almost verbatim and which flooded the internet. Thousands of photos and videos appeared of attractive young Russians proudly displaying the Z symbol in apparent support of the war against the evil Nazis in Ukraine. State-run television ran constant propaganda programming – a mix of surprise, outrage and anger – that would make Fox News blush and then perhaps take some very detailed notes.

Meanwhile, younger kids still in school were given lessons on the 'genocide against Russians' and what the West was now doing to poison their minds. One governor said, 'The West has declared a real information war against our country that openly allows for pouring of dirt on our Russians, our army and everything that is connected with Russia.'

It's not a new tactic. Lenin once said, 'Give me four years to teach the children and the seed I have sown will never be uprooted.'

In 2022 it became a crime in Russia for journalists to describe the war in any way that displeased the Russian government. Repeat the lie, accentuate our victimhood, or spend 15 years in jail.

At the heart of lies like these is that if they're believed they produce fury, a sense of injustice, and ultimately fanaticism.

And on impressionable minds, they did. Thousands of Russian teens became obsessed with the war. And obsessive. They'd litter their VK (a sort of Russian Facebook) pages with violent rhetoric and anti-Ukrainian sentiment. Ukrainians were 'pigs', 'sons of bitches', 'less than human' for what was going on in, er, Ukraine. Everyone's a Nazi. The Ukrainians are Nazis. NATO are Nazis. The US President is a fascist.

They weren't just wrong, they were violently wrong – and they were ready to be violent.

* * *

Kamaliya stayed in Kyiv as long as she could, an influencer desperately trying to influence.

'When people didn't believe me, I'm saying – ask people. Ask anyone. Ask your friends. Ask Ukrainians. Don't watch

Russian TV, watch international TV. Look at Facebook. TikTok. It can't be that everyone is liars!'

'People we *knew*, people started to say,' says Zahoor, 'that this war was faked by the Americans, who want the Slav brothers to kill each other so that the Americans can come and take their lands.'

I frown.

'Who told them that?'

'Some astrologers,' says Zahoor.

Wait.

'*Astrologers?*'

* * *

Every country has its own version of those using lies to pad their wallets – unserious chancers, cynical manipulators, out-and-out conscience-free grifters. But after Covid and as the Ukraine war began, a particular and peculiarly Russian version really hit its stride.

Russians have found comfort in astrology in a big way before, and also in a time of confusion. In the late 1980s and early 1990s, as the world changed and more people turned their backs on communism, what were they supposed to turn to for guidance instead? In the grand tradition of people embracing cults, conspiracies, religions, essential oils-based pyramid schemes or right-wing YouTube channels, these Russians needed reassurance, guidance and the sense that all the uncontrollable chaos was part of some grand cosmic plan.

The *Great Soviet Encyclopaedia* at the time defined astrology as a 'false science', but nevertheless, suddenly you couldn't move for astrologers in Moscow: whether mysterious women wearing unusual scarves, or men with long beards cosplaying sci-fi scientists. Star charts and complicated celestial bodies were rising and falling all over the place. If he'd played his cards right, Russell Grant could have taken Red Square in the 1980s. The Moscow Academy of Astrology was founded in 1990. On its first day, 2,000 people applied to join. But as things settled down and Russians found their place in a new world, they found it less necessary to seek help from men with long neckbeards or unusual be-scarved women.

I remember as a kid being fascinated by Nostradamus – the sixteenth-century astrologer and claimed prophet whose book foretold great wars and disasters, and which would bring for every generation worried about life on earth an eerie dark comfort. A quick glance at how he thought the times around 2023 would go tells of war, the rising of an antichrist, fish boiling in the seas, parched fields, economic meltdown and food shortages, and a great red hail that falls across the lands. Though he also mentions an uptick in cannibalism, so take what you like from that.

In the last couple of years, belief in astrology has come back in a big way, and not just in Russia. In America, astrology apps brought in more than $40 million for their creators in one year alone. Nowadays, more people know their star sign than their blood type.

I phone a friend in Moscow – a radio journalist called Sasha – and he is not surprised by Zahoor mentioning astrology as a key player in where people get their information.

'They charge something like six thousand roubles [£55] and they tell you any old shit,' says Sasha. 'Whatever you need for your comfort. Like "Yes, I can see the stars, they say Russia will rise again like the mighty bear," or "Yes, your son will be fine, you can sleep well, he is protected by Mars," or whatever.'

In the first week of the Ukraine war, searches on Russia's Yandex search engine for 'astrologer' more than doubled. New schools of astrology were founded. Politicians and priests flocked to them. On television and radio, stars were consulted and new stars were born.

Astrologers made some bold claims and took some big swings. One claimed that she had a star chart which absolutely proved that it was the United States of America that had invaded Ukraine.

'My mother say to me,' says Kamaliya, 'oh, the astrologers told the Americans that soon their land will be underwater so they need to find some new land. She saw it probably on Russian TV. Also people believed that the Ukrainians are somehow filling the mosquitos and sending poisoned mosquitos to Russia.'

'How do you tell the mosquitos what to do?' I ask.

'Yes!' says Zahoor. 'Or when to come back?'

'And these mosquitos were told to go to Russia?' I ask, just in case I've misunderstood.

'And the swans,' says Zahoor. 'Ukraine was said to have swans as well.'

'Poison swans?'

'Yes. From bio labs. Half the Russian people talk about bio labs in Ukraine where the Americans and Ukrainians were not only inventing Covid together but experimenting on mosquitos and filling them with poison to send over the border. I mean, you could have just flown them into Moscow. Or just thrown the swans out of the aeroplane.'

'Maybe the stupider the lie, the more willing people are to believe it?' I say, thinking about what Sasha in Moscow told me.

'Absolutely. This exactly.'

* * *

Faced with this kind of opposition, and with Russia increasing its aggression, Zahoor convinced Kamaliya to stop trying to convince people online and get out of Kyiv.

'I said, what are you doing in the basement that you can't do here but better? We can help from here in London. But they will come, they will kill you, they will rape you. But she wanted to stay. She wanted to fight.'

She couldn't take Cliff, Bertie, Guy Ritchie, the falcon, the shaved cat or the dog who wore earrings. But she did what she could, slamming a suitcase into the back of a snarling Ford Raptor and taking friends with babies on a six-hour journey that took four days. She reached the bridge she needed. She watched rockets destroy it in front of her with cars still on it. She spent her time driving other people – mothers and babies – to the border, until she felt ready to leave herself. She headed for Budapest, where she'd meet Zahoor. She drove herself through Europe for the first time. She was used to being driven. Now she was more driven than ever.

* * *

The plan was to help stop the lies and expose the truth.

Because imagine something devastating happening to you. Something reported worldwide and with irrefutable evidence. Imagine having your own evidence, but having that evidence rejected or scoffed at because not even your own family will believe you.

Not because they are gaslighting you – but because they simply don't, *can't*, believe you.

Around half of Ukrainians have family somewhere in Russia. That's more than 20 million people. But later, as Russia banned Facebook and Twitter in early 2022 in order to control the narrative, access to on-the-ground information became limited.

Kamaliya's own aunt – with whom she had always shared a close bond – told her, 'President Putin is very nice. And soon he will even come to Berlin.'

It sounds lovely; sometimes we all deserve a nice city break. But that's not what she meant. What she meant was that once Russia had taken Ukraine, the rest of Europe would be next, and Kamaliya had to understand that this was all for the best and out of the goodness of Putin's heart. She wasn't to believe in CNN or the BBC. She had to put her faith in Vladimir.

There was a strange calmness to Kamaliya's aunt. No real sympathy. A sense of 'Why are you panicking? Why are you making a big deal out of this?'

Kamaliya wanted to save her aunt from the bad information, but her aunt was having none of it. She kept talking about Ukrainian Nazis and how the country needed to be saved. She implied that Kamaliya was stupid or naive. That it was in fact Kamaliya believing bad information. That she hadn't seen what she'd definitely seen, because it was impossible. Russian TV had explained it all to her. It made Kamaliya feel desperate, frustrated, outraged and helpless, and it was happening to millions of other Ukrainians at the same time. Huge rifts were opening up in once close homes as the fundamentals of what was objectively true and what was objectively not came into question on confused phone calls and some *very* awkward family group chats.

'I understand they're zombies,' says Kamaliya. 'From the propaganda and more. But my aunt, she's not stupid. She have a high education, she work with international companies, she moved a lot around the world. She was an interpreter, and a master of sports.'

'But when she said that to you, what happened?'

'She died for me,' says Kamaliya, meaning that she was dead to her. 'I won't ever speak to her again.'

Her eyes fall. The thought hangs heavy in the room.

'And if she apologises one day, and says she was wrong, and begs you?'

'I don't know the answer to this,' says Kamaliya. 'Because such a lot of people died because of such stupid ideas. And she was not the only one in my family. She has son, daughter, husband … they are all as one. All believe the same thing. So all are gone. It was difficult to put all those relationships behind. But I can't imagine what they should do for forgiveness. How should they wash all those sins?'

This situation has been repeated with countless families during the war. They tell me about a Ukrainian woman they met at the school gates the other day, who said sadly and with tears in her eyes, 'I'm not going to talk to my mother ever again. Never again.' They don't need to tell me why.

Zahoor says every family has experienced something similar – maybe with relations, almost certainly with friends.

'Fathers, mothers, sisters, brothers – everybody. All torn apart by the lies. The propaganda.'

Torn apart too by confusion. Part of the Russian tactic, it became clear, was also simply to confuse. Fake 'fact-checking' organisations were set up specifically to denounce the truth. Political influencers were employed to amplify absolute nonsense. They faked images, they released 'secret' fake documents. More vast rooms full of people tapped away on keyboards to flood social media or find targets to take down. Normal people's heads must have been spinning around, not knowing what to believe, so it became easier for them just to accept one particular narrative.

In an email, the journalist Sasha asked me whether I'd seen the website Papa Believe.

For a moment I was worried that Papa Believe was the rather on-the-nose name of a popular astrologer. But it's a website built from desperation and necessity as a tool for Ukrainian relatives who have found themselves bewildered by their relations' willingness to believe propaganda and lack of curiosity.

'Call your loved ones in Russia,' it implores. 'They were being lied to for over 20 years. They are tired and very scared. Help them. Tell the truth.'

It's a website that provides the facts that counter every standard talking point that Russian families were being fed by state TV and which they would throw at their Ukrainian relatives.

So when your uncle in St Petersburg yells, 'The Ukrainians *begged* Putin to save them from Nazism!', you click on the relevant statement and say, 'If that's true, then why aren't

Ukrainians fleeing to Russia?' and because they hadn't thought of that in quite such coolheaded terms, you quietly take it from there.

There are recordings of calls between families divided by lies. Like a painful conversation between a father in Russia and a son in Ukraine, in which Dad has swallowed the propaganda and Son gently explains what he sees with his own eyes in his own life.

The gulf between them is vast and exposed by the restraint they show in their patient silences. Yet in those eight minutes, a slow uneasy progress is made, and while Dad isn't ready to change his mind entirely, he concedes just a little ground.

'Well, I told you everything,' says Son.

'I sincerely understand your feelings,' says Dad.

Above all, Papa Believe begs for compassion towards the Russians. It urges you not to raise your voice, not to talk sharply, not to end the call dramatically.

'You speak the truth,' it tells Ukrainians. 'You don't have to be nervous.'

Kamaliya too knows her family aren't bad people. They grew up in a time in which it was just accepted fact that the West was out to get them and that the only people they could truly trust were their leaders. Russian propaganda is of course incredibly effective at shaping public opinion. Of creating fear of others while casting the Russian people as the brave heroes. Those unbelievable things you're hearing – those big, simple, unbelievable lies – they become far more credible if you tell yourself there must be a reason behind it, that someone or something in authority must know what they're doing – whether that's a president or Saturn moving into Pisces. Those messages drown out all the good information – which is suddenly far harder to find – and play to people's emotional needs – comfort, reassurance, safety, righteousness. They're getting rid of Nazis – even if there's no evidence those Nazis exist. And the constant bombardment of the same messages makes it more believable and creates an Us versus Them. You can't be the oppressor, you are the liberator, and the victim. You can't be the baddie here. The influence of and pressure from your family or your social group make you feel that if you think critically or independently, you're an oddball. The way Kamaliya's family in Russia must have thought she was an oddball. Why didn't she just admit there were Nazis everywhere? Because if everyone else believes it, well, it must be true.

'Also, they are *scared* to believe [the truth],' says Zahoor. 'Because in Moscow they have Stalin syndrome. They think if they touch the internet and go to Google and try to put in the words "Ukraine Russian War …"'

'Their door will get kicked down?'

'It is easier to watch the TV and absorb whatever is told to them.'

* * *

Kamaliya hasn't spoken Russian since 24 February 2021. She has stopped singing any songs in Russian – only Ukrainian. She has been back to Kyiv to literally pick up bricks and pave broken walkways. For months, the Zahoors housed 16 refugees in their London home, moving all their own things into one bedroom which they shared with their young twins.

Their house in Kyiv is still standing. But they cannot believe the madness that has engulfed them. The death and destruction, of course. But also the madness of the narratives that surround it.

They're yet to find many Nazis in Kyiv. Every country has nationalists, of course, including Russia and Ukraine. In the 2019 elections, the combined vote of the various far-right parties in Ukraine came to 2.15 per cent. No one's found any Ukrainian bio labs creating Covid either. No one's spotted a poisonous mosquito, and the number of poisonous swan attacks remains mercifully at zero. America remains very much not underwater.

But Kamaliya and countless others like her have lost family nevertheless. Loved ones who think she's either swallowed the lies or is a liar herself. People who think that one day she'll realise all this was for the best. Perhaps because often the truth is far scarier than the lie, and it's those lies – spilling out of screens all over the world – that spell success for propagandists.

For this is the golden rule we've discovered in the last couple of chapters: it doesn't have to be genius; it doesn't even have to be clever.

It just has to be loud, and it just has to confuse, and it can come from anyone. Those who are convinced, and those who are paid to convince.

But who would do that? I wonder – and how do I meet them?

The Believers

In which we meet a man who spent 15 years believing
I was his enemy, a guy who thinks his town is being
targeted by shadowy forces, and we consider who
might take these movements further.

7

Building a Brand

You Can't Say Anything These Days
(But You Can for Money!)

You are a middle-aged white man whose career has seen better days.

Bear with me, this will make more sense in a moment.

We'll call you Simon.

Maybe you're a low-level stand-up comedian whose stuff never really cut through. You managed to host a few TV shows in your time, so you've got a name, but there are no more book deals, all the corporate events dried up during Covid, and there's nothing that sets you apart anymore. You're fed up of parents at the school gates saying 'So, anything coming up soon?' and having to say, 'Oh yes, some very exciting stuff in the pipeline!'

It's not your fault. Industries change. Unremarkable straight white men had it easy for a long time. And you can hardly say 'all my jobs are going to young non-binary-identifying Black and Asian women or people with ADHD or something', can you?

137

You quite like it when you hear the American comics saying it on podcasts though.

So you're relieved when you get some cover work on a right-leaning news and talk radio station, even though the listeners absolutely hate you. You get abuse on the texts. They say you're boring. You sound like a libtard. You feel a hot flush of shame as you read the screen, refreshing too quickly for your liking, and you lose confidence.

Later that week your producer, Yolanda, says, 'Simon, it's probably better if you take a harder stance.' You're relieved when you speak with the first caller and you try going harder. Maybe various ethnic groups *do* need to take more responsibility for their own!

And the listeners sense you are becoming one of them, or at least getting closer. Now they get to explain to you why you are right, why you should trust your instincts and join them.

But you know it's just an act. You're sure your mates in comedy would get that too.

Soon, you're a genuine name on the station. You get a new photoshoot. Your taxi driver this afternoon says he used to think you were a liberal softie but he's really come round to you.

'Ah, it's all a bit of an act,' you want to say, but is it?

You have an idea. Something dramatic. You bring out some Covid tests on air. They're in short supply in the country right now. You read about a nurse earlier who couldn't get one. You hold them up to the camera and say that these tests are pointless. You've rigged up a Bunsen burner to a gas stove. And you burn the tests, live on your show. As they crackle, you set off fireworks in the studio and run around in your underpants, owning the libs.

The texts go mad. Loads of 'Luv it m8 ur the best'. You watch the retweets, the likes, the shares rack up.

You feel a shiver, a thrill.

On the way home, you check your phone. Wow! Your clip got retweeted by your hero, Eric Idle! Shame he wrote the word 'twat' above it.

Doesn't matter because it's all about creating an Us versus Them. Your viewers feel scared by change; they don't understand why it's happening. You tell them it's not just *happening*: it's happening *to them*. You'll tell them with your grimmest face and your steadiest voice that here's the news: there are secret people who hate you, who want to take away your power. You, who made this country great! Life was better in the old days before 'They' got involved!

They want more feminism because it threatens masculinity and creates falling birth rates and soon there will be none of 'Us' left. *They're* bringing in foreigners and putting them up in our hotels and creating a foreign army on our shores to rise up against Us!

Back in your normal world, your former friends no longer text you. Your wife says you must be tired, don't worry about the school drop-off, probably best if she does it, also she's going to bed early, and to France at the weekend. You haven't been invited to a dinner party in a while but that's fine, dinner parties are for the woke north London liberal media elite, not hard-working TV presenters like you with a new column starting in the paper on Monday.

Some people look disappointed as they pass you in the street, but you walk with a power and a sneer you never had before, because you've found an audience. Not one you respect or would ever choose to hang around with, but you'll never have to do that in real life. You notice as you pass a window your hair is getting greyer. Your wife hasn't said anything. A year ago, she'd have made a fun joke.

Anyway, she's got the kids now, but at least you see them on Saturdays sometimes.

* * *

Before I get to a certain someone who should for now remain nameless (Russell Brand), does it not sometimes strike you as stunning just how much the news and information landscape has changed in recent years?

When I was a kid, news channels were just news channels – ones where people rarely claimed to be 'saying the unsayable' on account of it being unsayable, but stuck very much to the principle of just saying the sayable.

When I was about 14, my parents took me, an only child, to a timeshare they briefly owned in Spain.

Anyway, it rained all week we were there. Our timeshare week wasn't *quite* in summer. There was hardly anyone else around. No other kids. Just sprinklers and drizzle. The only things you could watch on the tiny TV were loud Spanish-language gameshows echoing against the hard tiled floors, or Sky News.

So all week, I watched Sky News.

It coincided with perhaps the most boring week of news in television history.

A fish war, between the UK and Iceland.

A *fish war*.

That's all I heard about, as I sat in a tiled room near a pool I couldn't use under a grey sky that spat at me every time I turned to it. A 14-year-old boy with a non-existent internet. No films.

Just 24 hours a day of a man called Adam Boulton talking non-stop – NON-STOP – about a *fish war*. I still don't know who won. I hope it was the fish.

Things are very different now and a fish war would be presented in a very different light.

The presenter might start with a long opening monologue designed to enrage us. He or she would take the side of the British fish, and use derogatory language against our new Icelandic enemies, perhaps calling them 'not very nicelanders' and branding them 'drunken wool-wearing Scandis in silly slippers' or whatever.

News is no longer just news; news now seems to include opinion and entertainment. People have come to consider as 'news' everything from standard bulletins to comment to opinion to debate to the people who say 'I get my news from Facebook' to impassioned online rants. The most effective is designed to provoke, poke, tease, hold the viewer rigid in their seat. It is also designed to enrage, to terrify. And to reassure you that you are right to feel enraged and terrified.

Fish are rarely involved these days, but some of the most benign things still can be.

Like something I discovered one day while confusedly looking at the most recent work of the comedian Russell Brand.

* * *

A lot has happened since, and by the time you read this more still may have happened, but I think I speak for most people who have ever met him when I say that I was surprised when the comedian and film star quietly stepped away from television and mainstream audiences and instead began to share an extraordinary volume of very unusual ideas on the internet.

No one seemed to clock it at first or think about whether there may have been a reason. But slowly, like a hum in the background you don't notice until it's so loud you realise it's an articulated lorry bearing down on you, Brand had built his rhetoric and an impossibly big audience while everyone had been looking the other way.

I used to know Russell very slightly through friends. I also took over his Sunday morning Radio X show in 2018 when he left unexpectedly. He has undeniable qualities about him. You know that expression, 'they can make you feel like you're the only person in the room'? Russell can do that. He has a mesmeric intensity, a lightning-quick mind, he can whip up a crowd, lead a conversation, connect unconnected ideas, *convince*. And while that can be great, it is a precise mix that in the wrong hands can also be dangerous.

On the face of it, uploading videos to video sharing sites like YouTube and Rumble (a website that claims to be 'immune from cancel culture') might seem a strange career move to make. Russell has had chat shows, delighted on the chat shows of others, starred in Hollywood movies, sold out arenas worldwide, married and divorced one of the most successful pop stars in the world, started a family with a lovely woman. And now he sits in front of a camera and talks about terrible possible and impossible calamities on YouTube, to great success.

He has 6.5 million viewers, on top of the 11 million followers he has on Twitter, and the 3.3 million who follow him on Instagram. People don't follow him to find out what it was like making *Forgetting Sarah Marshall* or what it was like being the bunny rabbit in *Hop*.

I don't think he would ever describe himself as a conspiracy theorist, and indeed I will shortly find that out for sure, but nowadays his ever-growing band of followers press *play* on videos with titles like 'THEY'RE LYING!' and 'SOMETHING IS GOING ON' and 'WATCH FAUCI'S FACE!'

Then there's 'Bill Gates's Most AWKWARD Interview EVER!!!' and 'This is F*cking DISGUSTING – Biden's Cancer LIE'.

It's all a long way from talking about his dinkle in his *Booky Wook*.

But some of these videos do huge business, bagging more than a million views in a month. Meanwhile, the one plugging his latest comedy tour has been up ages and is, at time of writing, yet to break 50,000.

It tells us a lot about the thirsts of his audience. The keywords that entice them. The titles and ideas they like and must have delivered unto them.

This thirst for (let's call it) 'alternative' news used to be laughed at in the UK by those who could access Fox News on their satellite box. Now it's embraced.

When it started, Fox News was a healthier mix of genuine news and largely conservative political viewpoints. Over the years it began to miss out the genuine news bits. What Fox did – always 'fair and balanced' – was introduce to viewers a world in which truth wasn't really truth. Truth was … malleable. It wasn't just facts, it was 'a lot of people are sayings' and 'just asking questions' and 'somebody told mes'.

The appeal was that more emphasis was being placed on opinion than fact. You can see why. It's way more fun to not report on what was actually going on, but on what *might* be going on instead. They realised the money wasn't in food for thought but in comfort food instead. Why sell steak when there's so much profit in burgers?

Opening monologues got longer and longer, because they realised what people wanted were stories. Ones that brought an element of reassurance. That seemed to respect you – the working man and woman. That told you your life was unfair and hard and that it wasn't your fault that things hadn't worked out the way you'd hoped. How could it? There was a shadowy elite out to get you. What you needed was guidance from someone strong that could take those other guys on. Something more authoritarian who could stop not only those keeping you down, but those beneath you who were out to get the little you have: the millions of terrifying unnamed masses trying to kick down your border so they can steal your job, your home and your daughter.

Fox News hosts and guests, for example, have regularly said things they knew for sure weren't true. Fox News reps are still licking their wounds after being caught spreading lies about the 2020 election. They agreed to pay $787 million just so they don't have to talk about it anymore. They knew Biden won the election fair and square, but they didn't want to lose their Trump viewers – or have to face telling them the truth. So they told them stories instead: they fed them burgers.

And to tell stories properly – to take people on a journey and make them feel like the David who must conquer Goliath – takes personality.

And I feel personally aggrieved about this because I have watched people I know – people I would have trusted to feed my cat and not say something awful at a barbeque – teeter at the cliff edge of right-wing grifting and then throw themselves over the edge with gusto. They're enjoying the sea now, but the waves are getting bigger and there is no way back up the cliff for them.

I've tried to talk to a couple of them about it – people who've taken the money to completely change their personality and opinions. I wanted to look them in the eye again, and see what was there – or if there was nothing there at all.

One, a former stand-up comic and a man who now seems proud of 'saying the unsayable', agreed to meet immediately.

I deemed him smart and one of the politest men I'd ever met, whose on-air rants and cruel turns of phrase we'd once have mocked if they were said by anyone else. So maybe it was politeness, him agreeing. Because then he got cold feet. He must have wondered what he'd say to me about it all, whether he could justify it to me the way he must have had to justify it to himself. So first he ghosted me. Now he doesn't even read the messages.

Perhaps saying the unsayable is easier than telling the truth.

* * *

George Monbiot won the Orwell Prize for Journalism.

If you're going to win a prize for journalism, it should be one with 'George Orwell' written on it.

He's an activist, an environmentalist, and he was once a huge fan of the comedian Russell Brand. The same comedian whose videos Shaul Goncalves used to watch.

When I speak to George, he tells me, 'In 2014 the *Guardian* asked me to nominate my hero for the year. And I made it Russell, because he had this great ability to get people interested in issues that the rest of us were really struggling to push beyond a certain number. He seemed to be genuinely motivated by social, political, environmental concerns. Now it's just one long concatenation of conspiracy theories. All of which happen to play into the hands of the far right.'

I make a quick note to look up what 'concatenation' means, but just nod along for now.

George doesn't think that Russell belongs to the far right, he's quick to tell me – just that 'all successful conspiracy theories either begin or end at the far right'. They are the fuel, he thinks, that powers fascism.

'If you have a large platform and you promote conspiracy theories,' says George, 'you can guarantee to get millions of people watching every video.'

That's why, he says, creators are so keen to include in their speeches terms people respond to.

Fauci. Bill Gates. The Great Reset. The World Economic Forum.

All phrases which, once unleashed, race around the far-right world like they're on fire.

George's point, I think, is that whether consciously or not, Russell has been toying with words, themes, phrases and narratives that the far right cannot get enough of. He is also too smart not to at least be aware he could be accused of this, too smart not to know what his audience might take away from it.

'The people who watch videos like these are frightened,' says George. 'They are looking for reassurance. I mean, reasonably enough; we've all got good reasons to be frightened. But rather than facing their fears, they're looking for people to tell them it's OK. What we're constantly being told by conspiracy theorists is that they're revealing the terrifying truth. But actually, the lies they tell are far more reassuring than the *actual* terrifying truth.'

Russell isn't alone. It happens all the time, all over the internet, almost everywhere you look.

There's no such thing as climate breakdown – *it's just a bunch of scientists looking to line their pockets.* But climate breakdown is happening.

Covid is not a dangerous disease – *it's just maniacs like Anthony Fauci trying to extend their power over our lives.* Yet Fauci has almost exactly no power over our lives. He's an 83-year-old man and he's probably exhausted.

'And it's all very reassuring. Especially by comparison to a dangerous invisible virus which kills or disables large numbers of people. So you are guaranteed a huge audience of people who are very afraid of what you are telling them. Despite your claims of having seen into the dark heart of suppressed reality, what you are telling them is actually reassuring. It's as reassuring as a lullaby.'

Very few lullabies have titles like 'Oh SH*T, 15 Minute Smart Cities Are Coming', which is the video I have chosen at random and just clicked *play* on.

And little did I know that this bizarre title would very shortly become one of the next big lies, pounced on and embraced by everyone from Brand to mid-level YouTubers to the actual UK Secretary of State for Transport, Mark Harper, at the Tory Party Conference in 2023.

At this point, though, I had no idea what it was.

But I clicked on the video.

* * *

'They are moving against us in a very powerful way!' says Russell, before a rant about '15 Minute Cities', asking, 'Who benefits?'

The idea behind 15 Minute Cities (or '15 Minute Neighbourhoods') is that wherever you live, you should have everything you need within a 15-minute walk. Your school. Your doctor. All easily reachable.

So who benefits?

Well, it would mean fewer cars on the road and less air pollution.

More bikes. More people walking and getting healthier. Closer communities. Less overall loneliness. A windfall for smaller local businesses.

It would mean the return of the high street, instead of the vast supermarkets on industrial estates 40 minutes away. It would mean more people out and about, safer streets, more green spaces. There'd be more trees planted, more benefits to the environment, and nipping out for a leg of lamb from the butcher's would no longer take ages and end up with your car impounded because you had to park outside for a moment.

So when the question 'Who benefits?' was asked in Russell's video, it felt like a bit of a trick question, because the obvious answer seems to be 'We all do, don't we?'

But no, says Russell.

'The 15 Minute Cities that are being piloted are about CONTROLLING your movement and capturing your data – sometimes even in exchange for healthcare. Whether it's Smart Cities or new healthcare edicts, THEY are coming for your data and you should be worried. Because this is all part of the Globalist Master Plan!'

There is always a They.

There is always a Master Plan.

And while I'm sure Russell didn't mean it this way, the word 'globalist', as we've seen, has its own connotations. Jonathan Greenblatt from the Anti-Defamation League has described it as a word used to define 'Jewish people who are seen as having allegiances not to their countries of origin but to some global conspiracy' to make themselves super-rich and powerful at the expense of everyone else.

But 15 Minute Neighbourhoods do not seem actually to be about *controlling* your movement. Surely Russell's being silly. You are not being contained in your little 15-minute area. You're still allowed to get in your car and drive to the big Tesco for your big shop. It just means things are a bit more convenient, walkable and environmentally friendly.

But really, say those with a different point of view, this idea is not about walking or protecting the environment.

'Look at the Ohio train wreck chemical spill,' says Russell, almost immediately.

But what's that got to do with being able to buy sausages more conveniently, Russ?

'Is it me, or do They only look for climate change measures and ecological solutions that *punish ordinary people* rather than high-level business interest?'

Then he starts talking about the powerful ruling elite and the World Economic Forum and subtly seeding the idea that we are all going to be contained, restricted, held within a 15-minute radius of our own homes.

He doesn't say exactly how and I can't work out who told him that was going to happen.

* * *

Pause.

The show is interrupted by an advert for a woman selling AI-generated e-books.

'Not only do you not even have to write the books yourself, you don't even have to pay to send them out!' I place a curse on her.

The next advert is for a man who says he's a millionaire who – I suppose because he is incredibly selfless, not like the *other* millionaires at the top of society that these videos rail against (not including Russell of course) – has developed an online road map for how to become extremely wealthy yourself by working just *a few minutes a day*.

He's willing to share his secret with you, '*If* you're willing to take the first few steps to creating a rapidly richer life!'

He urges you to join up as it's implied spaces are limited. But it's an online course. What – is the internet running out of space? Also – can we trust him? What if he's part of a shadowy millionaire elite trying to keep the rest of us down?!

As I wait, I notice that under Russell's video there is a deal for something called Incogni, which will remove all information about you from the internet. Russell says he uses it himself. You just have to type Russell's name in and you get 20 per cent off. I look up Incogni and it's owned by Surfshark, a huge corporation worth $1.6 billion.

And we're back.

* * *

So then Russell says, 'I'm not a conspiracy theorist,' which is something people usually say when they're about to tell you a conspiracy theory, and, nearly eight minutes in, we're off.

The powers that be want your data.

They want to control you.

You should be very worried.

They need your data.

By the way, use the code BRAND and enter your personal details on this external website.

It goes on: governments are being controlled by something shadowy at the top telling both the left and the right what to do. 15 Minute Neighbourhoods will be used to control your movement – 'you have to anticipate that problem'.

These ideas are catching on.

When the summer 2023 wildfires in Maui, Hawaii, decimated the island, it was mere hours after the smoke dissipated that the first theories came through: Maui had been destroyed, intentionally, by Direct Energy Weapons, beaming high intensity lasers from outer space at the island so it could be levelled and turned into a huge 15 Minute City complete with cycle lanes, bollards and unthinkably walkable access to local cinemas and shared park areas.

Oprah Winfrey was said to be personally involved. Because it was far easier to believe Oprah Winfrey had signed off on a deadly secret hidden laser space weapon than it was to believe the careful experts who've been warning us about fossil fuel and climate change since Swedish scientist Svante Arrhenius published the first paper on it in 1896.

What did Svante know? He didn't even have his own talk show. You couldn't get 15 per cent off *anything* by typing in SVANTE.

* * *

It's not going away.

I find groups of people online discussing the dangers posed by 15 Minute Neighbourhoods. People seem genuinely scared of traffic-calming measures because they can see the next step in the 'plan' that no one else can.

In one group, a man named Terry laments that there are plans to turn the county town of Ipswich into one such hub. I can't help but wonder – why would they choose Ipswich?

But by the end of Russell's video, while the dangers of Smart Cities or 15 Minute Neighbourhoods have been hammered in, they haven't really been explained. I think it's something to do with what he said might be some kind of wrist tag you may be forced to wear, but which I think is probably more likely to be an optional app you can use. That would certainly make sense and be much cheaper than issuing mandatory wrist tags to the world population. I mean, that would be suspicious, and cost the world in rubber, and people already have phones that track them.

But while the app might contain your details, it might also record more benign things, like instances of fly-tipping and litter, or where you've spotted potholes in the road or broken streetlights.

It might encourage you to walk more, let you know of special deals at the shops, give you notifications about air quality, allow you to report sexual harassment.

It might record your health data for your doctor, yes, but presumably this will be optional, though according to Russell it's a case of 'give us your private details and let us lock you in your house or at least heavily restrict your movements, monitor and tax you'.

All this certainly sounds *quite* conspiracy theory-ish.

15 Minute Neighbourhoods are apparently a move towards 'a globalist state where your ability to control your own life will be diminished and their ability to regulate you and profit from you will be enhanced'.

But here's the thing.

What if 15 Minute Neighbourhoods might simply just be an attempt at a return to how life was a few decades ago? They're as nostalgic as they are futuristic. On paper, they should absolutely appeal to those looking for the country they feel they've lost – one with a high street, where kids can play on the road again, where the car isn't king and the corner shop returns.

But that one big mysterious invented fear remains: What if it's a trick to control you? What if you're not allowed to leave your 15 Minute Neighbourhood?

Banning free movement has never been suggested as a possibility, because of course it hasn't. It's just a frightening 'what if?' that people have come up with themselves.

'The thing about conspiracy theorists,' says George Monbiot, 'is that they're not actually interested in actual conspiracies. For example, the PPE VIP lane scandal [in which contracts to provide Personal Protective Equipment to the UK were given not to experienced companies ready to go, but secretly to people friendly with the Conservative Party] is about the most obvious, grotesque, appalling conspiracy you could imagine. Direct government connivance ripping us off during a pandemic. A mega fucking conspiracy. And yet a total lack of interest in it on the part of conspiracy theorists. And my hypothesis? If it's real, if it's in the press and well-documented, then it doesn't *belong* to them. They can't say "This is something we know that other people don't. This is our special knowledge and everyone else is sheeple."'

The only time genuine conspiracies are useful to the theorist is when they can use them as leverage to get you to believe their own. A case of 'if they can do *that*, then they could do *this*!'

Real experts in drumming up and holding a crowd know what their audiences need and what information they'll need in order to run with it themselves.

There are those who genuinely believe the nonsense. They take it and spread it either because they have a desperate need to persuade others, or they just want it to be true. By spreading it, they are willing it to be true. Even if they know it is misleading, it is 'basically' true, so the ends justify the means.

There are the opinions which have come straight from outside forces and the kinds of troll farms that sounded like science fiction just a decade or so ago – designed to erode any middle ground or nuance in an argument, designed to distract from facts, and helping make groups more extreme in their views by bolstering them.

There are people who just want your money, who give you links to click that back up your thoughts while taking your data and post videos about conspiracies they don't even believe in while rolling in the ad revenue.

Some do it for power. They can say, online and hidden, things they would never try on the street or in the supermarket. There are no consequences, so why not do it for clout on the internet?

Then there are those who feel aggrieved, happy to spread misleading information because this is giving them their voice, and they are able to use it to hit out at whoever they think is to blame – immigrants, the elites, the invisible powerful who are obsessed with ruining your life.

And always there's the underlying excuse if they get caught out – well, OK, They might not have done *this*, but it's the sort of thing They *would* do …

For example: Russell cites a well-documented news story run by the Associated Press: that governments worldwide hoovered up information given by citizens during the pandemic in order to keep an eye on people.

Private health details, photos that could be used for facial recognition, home addresses, movements, the governments had it all – and all thanks to the apps we installed in our phones to try and stop the spread of the virus.

In some cases, that data was also shared with various spy agencies.

That doesn't sound too good, does it?

And it did happen, in places like Israel and India.

So *because* that happened – is it so crazy to imagine that a 15 Minute Neighbourhood app might take the same data from you in Ipswich and share it?

Enter the seeds of doubt. The seeds of conspiracy. The truth that leads to the lie. Joining the dots.

Scarier is what happens when you don't even need the dots.

Conspiracy, where the theory seems to arrive from nowhere.

Often it's enough just to float a mad idea and then, through likes and retweets and follows and an attitude of 'just asking questions', you can have the lie repeated enough that you can go on TV and say things like 'somebody told me a lot of people are saying Barack Obama faked his birth certificate' and you can worry about finding any actual evidence for your theory later on.

* * *

To do any of this successfully, you need to cast doubt on the institutions that people generally trust not to lie to them. All the people and establishments that provide the facts, evidence and argument that we normally rely on. You need to undermine medical journals, the media, 'partisan' experts, 'dark money' think tanks, 'left-wing' universities, 'woke' academics. You need to discredit, disparage and reject established expertise. You need to create your own battlefield where your own facts stand a chance.

You need that special knowledge.

'You are amongst the cognoscenti,' as George puts it. 'You are one of the few people who *really* know what's going on. And that puts people in a happy place.'

And if you get it right, there's money to be made. People with a huge platform can earn millions from these videos alone. You work out the keywords, the things people respond to, the things you probably don't actually believe but which you believe play well, and when your first one goes viral 'you get a real buzz', says George. 'You think, People are really latching on to what I'm saying! And if you get millions of viewers each time, I mean ... the temptation must be very hard to resist. If maybe you feel a bit insecure, or you need some self-affirmation, having those huge audiences gives you that.'

It also becomes very hard to stop. Because stopping doesn't just mean you lose money and fans; it makes you a traitor. It means making enemies of all the friends you just made. And these friends are – wittingly or unwittingly – sympathetic to the ideas of the far right. They cynically espouse theories that echo in no small way the Nazi Blood & Soil myth about nice, honest, pure-blood farmers being robbed of their land and their ethnic purity by 'cosmopolitan elites' (who share some characteristics with the aforementioned 'globalists'). You might realise these are friends you should not make enemies of.

Further, stopping means you have to build bridges with all the serious people you've just alienated. If you're a doctor, say, banging on about how a vaccine is actually there to kill you in ten years and control world population through the use of 5G pore-opening power or whatever, how on earth would you go about re-establishing your medical credentials? Who would even trust you to prescribe a tissue for a runny nose? That's a much harder task to undertake than just cruising along with the grift.

So if you've started, you probably continue on the slope you're on. The clicks are money. The merchandise is money. The sponsorship is money. The adverts you agree to allow to jarringly interrupt your show – for magic money trees, financial road maps from friendly shadowy elites you've never heard of, software you can use to write books you've never even read let alone written then sell them somehow to people on Kindle – it's all money.

And you have to keep going. You can't lose those followers. Because then you'd have nothing but yourself for company.

But even then … why start?

* * *

When accusations against Russell Brand came to light on the 2023 Channel 4 investigations series *Dispatches* and in *The Times* and *Sunday Times*, from numerous women from his past, a few things happened in quick succession.

The first was that Brand did not do the normal things people do when accused of crimes. He didn't release a statement through his management, for example. Instead he went directly to his audience to deliver them a message he could control. He turned to an audience he had been nurturing in the background for years and whose fervent belief in him he could rely on. That was the audience that mattered, and they would have his back.

He dismissed the allegations as an attack on him and an attack on the truth. 'They' were coming for him. 'I'm being attacked, and plainly they are working very closely together,' he said. Aha! So he was being silenced by the all-powerful, always-vague They: the elites, the mainstream. He was, in fact, the victim here, because his videos and *you* – his powerful yet powerless audience – posed a direct threat to the dark power of the mainstream media.

Second, that audience – hidden from so many people since he stepped back from television but very visible now – leaped to his defence unleashed, perhaps not to his great surprise. They were railing against those who would silence their leader, spreading their fury across the internet.

Third, similarly minded commentators with their own problems began supporting him to their own audiences. Elon Musk on X. The conspiracy king, Alex Jones of InfoWars. Tucker Carlson (who'd been recently fired from Fox News). Andrew Tate (charged with human trafficking in Romania). Any and all aggrieved generally right-wing men with a bone to pick with the mainstream media. The presenter Beverley Turner from GB News tweeted her support for Brand, claiming he was being silenced and that he was 'a hero', before later admitting she had not read about or watched any of the actual evidence or testimony from the women involved, who seemed suddenly to be the one thing about the situation no one was talking about.

Fourth, new theories started to bubble up. This witch-hunt, this targeting of Brand by international shadowy forces, said one man, was all *actually* to do with traffic-calming measures.

'*Love* how the Russell Brand story comes out when the Welsh government is implementing its 20mph limit across the country,' wrote the man on Twitter.

Yes. Exactly. It had only been a matter of time before the global elites would try to take down the comedian Russell Brand's Rumble videos to distract from minor traffic-calming measures in Wales. The guy just knew too much.

* * *

There is, then, a terrifying problem fuelled by money, prestige, ego, shamelessness and audience. With current events presented not as news but as profitable entertainment. With placing trust in people who don't deserve it, despite their desk and suit and tie.

Perhaps you're a journalist whose 1990s magazine folded and you've been scraping by writing the odd outraged story for a right-leaning UK paper where you can briefly fire up the comments section, and will now stop at nothing to build your brand.

Or perhaps you're an actor – part of some kind of British acting dynasty whose inheritance hasn't come through because the older people in your family point-blank refuse to die. Maybe someone who in the old days would have been woken, hungover, with respect you never had to work for, in the Mayfair apartment you never earned, by the butler you don't directly pay, with a boiled egg and your freshly ironed newspaper and the promise of your papa's allowance providing fun for the rest of your day. The modern day you doesn't get the attention you're owed, not until you say something absolutely appalling on TV and gain the adoration of a crowd of people you would never have a pint with.

So keep pumping out those 9pm diatribes about hidden puppeteers desperate, for some reason, to pick on YOU. Keep chucking out those tweets with bad data and graphs that can be easily disproved, because you can't get on proper telly anymore and you hated lockdown because your husband had a new woman but you're stuck in with the kids and the phone has stopped ringing.

Rely harder on the doctorate you bought off the internet.

Squander whatever small amount of goodwill you had.

Say whatever pays the bills or gets you to the next leg-up.

There will be people who believe you – normal people who've never once considered that the government might be out to get them – and if they believe, it really doesn't even matter if you do. Like Francis Goncalves said. Like Dr Pankhania said. Just say it with flair to get them to care.

But then I think about the guy I used to know. The ex-comic who's stopped replying to me. Because I still don't believe *he* believes a word he's saying.

What about those people?

'Well, that's the big question,' says George Monbiot when I put it to him. 'And I really don't know what the answer is there. You should meet Brent Lee. Brent Lee might be able to answer that.'

'Who's Brent Lee?' I ask.

Brent Lee Regan turns out to be a man who, from the early 2000s until just recently, was absolutely and utterly convinced that I – your friendly author who did not use that

advert woman's AI software to write the book you're reading
– was a very, very bad man indeed.

A man who would say whatever he was paid to.

Whatever paid the bills or got him to the next leg-up.

A grifter who would squander whatever goodwill he had.

A man in league with the New World Order.

A man who was, in fact, one of Them.

8

Brent

Extreme Beliefs – the Man Who Believed It All,
and How He Got Out

You'd be surprised at how many people are suspicious of pizzas these days.

It all started thanks to a place called Comet Ping Pong in the Chevy Chase area of Washington DC.

Comet Ping Pong is a hipster hang-out that serves thin-crust pizza and craft beer, hosts live gigs and has several ping-pong tables in the back room which patrons are encouraged to enjoy.

For a while, Comet Ping Pong was also at the centre of a bold claim: Hillary Clinton ran a child sex ring from the basement.

Obviously, it sounds ludicrous. But in the grand tradition of lies like this, it was circulated, boosted and amplified by those aligned with QAnon. Adherents did their own research. Someone found out that *GQ* magazine had named Comet Ping Pong's owner James Alefantis the 49th most powerful person in DC, thanks to the cultural heft his pizza and ping-pong joint had.

GQ magazine. Famously metrosexual. Liberal. *Based in New York.* Banking hub. Sells a lot of *beigels*, that place, wink wink.

The staff of Comet Ping Pong started to receive abuse and threats online.

Then, in what may have been a bid to own the story and up the ante, Alex Jones – the king of conspiracy – said in a now-deleted video that 'Hillary Clinton herself has murdered children'.

It wasn't long before a 28-year-old warehouse worker named Edgar Maddison Welch got up early one morning and drove 350 miles to see Comet Ping Pong for himself. He took with him just his beliefs, and also a locked and loaded assault rifle.

He parked up, walked in and began firing. He injured no one, but these shots were to show he meant business. Welch wanted to stand up, to do something. He wanted to rescue the hidden children from the powerful paedophilic demon blood-drinking Democrats ruled by the murderer Hillary Clinton in the basement below.

As it turned out, Comet Ping Pong doesn't have a basement.

Later, Welch would say, 'I regret how I handled the situation.'

* * *

I meet Brent Lee Regan in his hometown of Bristol on a brisk but sunny early afternoon.

We're in a hipster hang-out with Chesterfield sofas, factory windows and scuffed, painted floors that serves thin-crust pizza and craft beer.

We didn't do it on purpose, but we both immediately joke about having met for pizza. He says it will drive truthers mad, the idea that we're meeting here. They will be looking for the meaning in it. They will discuss the symbolism and the signs of it all. Our eating pizza for lunch will look like sinister code. Alistair Coleman at the BBC told me over our kebabs that the whole pizza thing started out as a joke between a few people on a message board where a few members who'd run out of steam discussing conspiracy theories started talking about what *they* were planning on having for lunch. One of them was going to Comet Ping Pong for pizza. 'Someone else said, "Wouldn't it be funny if *pizza for lunch* was actually code for something?"' said Alistair. And so they decided it was code for high-ranking satanic Democrats kidnapping children for anti-ageing vaccines or whatever.

Brent is cool. Tall and slim, with a light Anglo-American accent and dressed in a Nike hoodie and a beanie. He has a soft, long beard that looks like it must be fun to brush.

But do not be fooled. One critic on Twitter sees through this apparently carefully curated facade: 'His attire is part of the persona: the Common Man, duped for so long, now freed from the shackles of propaganda to guide others into The Light.'

Brent's calm and friendly, but for more than a decade, I was this man's total and utter enemy. He was absolutely convinced that I was a paid shill working at the behest of the New World Order so that I might gain great fortune and take my place at the feet of the Illuminati, the powerful and secret elites who rule the world from the shadows.

'It was very obvious at the time,' he tells me. 'You were an actor. A shill. A gatekeeper. You sold your soul. It was widely discussed on the David Icke forum.'

* * *

Until Brent told me this, I had no idea I had been widely discussed on a David Icke forum.

If you don't know who David Icke is, he's best described as a legend in conspiracy circles with a vast body of work to his name, and has been for decades.

He's made documentaries, written books, hosted sell-out live tours right around the world, and an earlier Brent Lee lapped it all up.

Icke is also a former British professional footballer and then sports broadcaster who in the early 1990s visited a psychic who told him he had a very special mission on earth and would soon receive some very important spiritual messages.

He appeared on the BBC One chat show *Wogan* soon after, aged 38, wearing a pink and turquoise tracksuit, and claimed on air to be a son of the Godhead. Something akin to Jesus. And something that led to public ridicule.

At least initially.

Afterwards it led to a vast massing of people who would follow his ideas – including that this planet has been hijacked by reptilian alien overlords at the very highest levels.

These were all ideas that a young Brent Lee was engaging with, he tells me.

And I want to know why.

But, as we study the menus and he considers the calzone, I decide to tell him something.

'I do have some experience with the Icke family ... though not with David.'

He raises his eyebrows.

* * *

In January 2009 – in a world very different from now – I received a confused email from the radio producer turned TV comedian Karl Pilkington.

Yes, that one.

It began:

Alrite.

Happy new year an all that.

I got an email from a lad called Gareth.

Not to spoil things, but it turned out this was Gareth Icke, son of David Icke.

'OK ...?' says Brent when I tell him, and I can tell he wants to know more, because Gareth Icke has a very different place in the world now than he did then.

Gareth wanted to get in touch with me because he'd been very annoyed with me recently and was emailing to both apologise and warn me.

'He said he was a singer-songwriter from the Isle of Wight,' I say, 'and suddenly that made me remember something.'

I'd been sitting down in the studio at Xfm a few weeks earlier to do the radio show I was doing at the time when I found a CD on the desk. It was from – you guessed it – a singer-songwriter from the Isle of Wight.

And on the cover was a promotional quote that read:

'Honest, brave, dashing and witty, with vocals unlike any others.'

– Danny Wallace

'I was pretty surprised seeing that,' I tell Brent, 'because I hadn't said any of those words because I'd never even heard the record. But then in that email, Gareth says that not only had I given him that quote but that for the last four months he and I had been talking regularly. Texting, emailing, that sort of thing. I guess I was kind of mentoring him?'

Except of course I wasn't.

He'd been messaging with someone who was *pretending* to be me. Who had set up a fake but convincing social media profile for me, had phone numbers I didn't recognise, and an email address that seemed to be mine but was in fact not.

From Gareth's point of view, I'd apparently taken a quite bizarre shine to him.

'Like, I'd apparently taken it upon myself to arrange meetings with book publishers for him and his mate that were cancelled at the last minute. I'd given him loads of encouragement. He travelled from the Isle of Wight to parties I invited him to in London only to find there was no party …'

I'd somehow even gone out of my way to organise for him to sing a duet live on stage in London in front of thousands with one of his heroes, Roddy Woomble from the band Idlewild, even though I have never met Roddy Woomble from Idlewild and have no idea how I could convince this Roddy Woomble from Idlewild to sing a duet on-stage with someone else I had never met.

Brent looks confused. Not as confused as I'd been.

And when Gareth turned up to the venue after a long journey and no dinner, guitar literally in hand, he'd been heartbreakingly sent on his way.

Yet each time the fake me let him down, he forgave the real me.

'So I rang him up,' I say.

'What happened?'

'He seemed like he was confused and amused and annoyed all at once. He told me: "You'd always find some excuse not to answer the phone. Like you were in the shower or a meeting. This is the first time we've actually spoken!"'

'He said it like I'd be surprised!' I say, and Brent laughs.

There was someone in his life playing tricks on him. Someone who had found out strange things about me – like where my wife worked.

'It was all a bit unnerving, and we felt bad for each other,' I say.

So I'd told Gareth Icke that perhaps there was a way to make something good out of someone else's lies and online deception.

'I told Gareth that next time he was in London, he should call me on my real number and we'd go to the pub.'

I told him I would then say out loud the words 'Gareth Icke is honest, brave, dashing and witty, with vocals unlike any others', so that he could use that *now* real quote *for* real in the *real* world.

Brent laughs. Because I don't know, it felt important to separate the truth from the lies and let the truth win. So we did meet up, in The Garrick Arms pub on Charing Cross Road, with all the taxis and red buses of London whizzing past the windows, and we had fun as we went through the story of the fake me and the real Gareth.

'But then I started to feel bad,' I say, and I think Brent is the first person I've told this to. 'Because I started to have doubts.'

At one point, a few pints in, Gareth told me he used to play football for England.

I'm not the biggest football fan, but I was pretty sure he hadn't.

So I began to wonder if I was being fooled.

But when he saw my confused face, he explained that he meant beach soccer. (I had never heard of beach soccer.)

He told me that sometimes when 'beach soccer' matches were being broadcast on minority satellite channels, live from the Isle of Wight or wherever, I would be watching him from afar, and then I would text him during matches to ask him to take off his shirt and wink at the camera for me the next time there was a goal.

I had to gently remind him that that wasn't actually me asking him to take his shirt off and wink.

I had to do that a few times.

And then, when I got home, I guiltily looked up beach soccer, and of course it turned out Gareth was telling the truth about his genuine international footballing career.

So now I felt bad for not trusting a man who said he'd been fooled by a fake me.

And I only doubted him because his surname was Icke. Because of the sheer impact his father had had on so many people and his place in the national and then global psyche. That wasn't fair.

I wondered in the days afterwards if it had been hard for Gareth, growing up in a small town in the 1990s where everyone remembered your dad appearing on the country's biggest TV show and claiming to be a sort of Jesus. Being made fun of by the BBC's trusted Terry Wogan. David Icke himself said that for years afterwards, he was laughed at in the street.

I could only think it must have been difficult for Gareth, who'd had a childhood surrounded by literature and thoughts and ideas that most people couldn't get their heads around. Of hearing laughter in the street and wondering sadly if it was at the expense of your father.

Gareth seemed perfectly well-adjusted, though. Handsome, talented, polite and funny. Someone with a future in music and sport, miles away from the family business – one I could never imagine might turn into Icke & Sons.

But knowing what I now know and will soon tell you about his career path, I wondered whether Gareth had arrived at the pub that night with his own preconceptions about me.

Like the ones Brent had had.

* * *

Brent says the first time he heard my name was thanks to a one-hour documentary I made for the TV channel Sky One as long ago as 2004 in which we questioned the idea of there being secret rulers of the world – something Gareth's dad David had insisted was true.

At the time that show was one of the few really mainstream looks at this world of conspiracy theories, and thanks to a lack of both budget and original programming it was repeated constantly on satellite television for months.

Around that time, in Peterborough, a young and bored pre-social media Brent Lee – 'a happy loner' – had just discovered something called DC++. It's a file-sharing service, and it opened his eyes to things he had never before imagined when he found a vast and bulging file called 'THE TRUTH'.

In it were new thoughts, articles, interminably long films made by apparently learned older men claiming with convincing passion and rage to have been shouting about what's really going on for years.

Some were, of course, crazy.

Some were grifting.

The first one he watched was called *Millennium 2000*. It was made in 1993 and talked about the New World Order trying to microchip people. He thought it was weird and interesting but it didn't take. He preferred a bit of sci-fi escapism. He enjoyed *The X-Files*. But it was when he found a documentary called *Illuminazi 9-11*, making the case that the 9/11 attacks were an inside job perpetrated by the US government on its own people, that everything changed.

Those attacks unleashed a whole new generation of conspiracy theorists like Brent, all watching videos that at least gave the impression of following journalistic lines of enquiry, with painstakingly studied details of things that may or may not in fact be relevant – but taken together make things …

'… look dodgy as hell,' says Brent. 'The controlled explosions. The military exercises going on at that time. The fact that we were now looking to invade Iraq. It didn't sit well with me. And these documentaries gave me the idea that it was all happening for a reason.'

The idea that 19 guys from four different countries could meet up in some remote corner of Afghanistan and plan to strike at the heart of a superpower with such apparent ease was impossible to believe. It had to be a coordinated inside job, and Brent was now all in. He found a new set of files, 'with a TON of information', which introduced him to what were to him new and impressive celebrities with impeccable conspiracy credentials – men like David Icke, claiming Queen Elizabeth II was a lizard. 'He actually meant, like, a literal lizard,' says Brent. 'People wonder if it's actually code for Jews. It's not. He means lizards.'

All this new truth shot through Brent's brain like nicotine, firing off synapses, making new connections, until the very idea that nothing in this world made sense made absolute sense.

That was him gone. He was fired up, channelling his discoveries into lyrics for his ska punk band Optimus Prhyme. Embracing social media early bird MySpace, Brent became The Truth Rapper, bringing together conspiracy-musicians from all countries and genres – house, folk, metal – and giving them a wider platform. He had thousands of followers. His own album sold 20,000 copies in the first year alone, but this wasn't a grift. He meant every word of every song, and the sales were just proof to him that he was right. Further encouraged, he'd attend rallies, perform acapella poetry about the truth on loudhailers outside Downing Street ('they say we're strange – we're strange and out of place – a strain of DNA on an ape-like face') and use his social media to question the narrative and beg the world to wake up to what was really happening:

The world was being controlled by a paedophilic and occultist ruling elite class.

Every school shooting, every war crime – they were ritualistic sacrifices.

Shadowy groups will stop short of no outrage, no matter how heinous, to achieve their aims.

And Brent would be all in for the next 15 years.

It would lose him friends. Cause tension in the family. It would mean years of his life passing without having done the 'normal' things many people do. The boring things. The pension, the career ladder, the mortgage, the kids, the package holidays, the down payment on a Nissan Qashqai. None of that interested him. Only 'the truth' did.

'I was building a community of people who ... I hate to say this, but who had a higher purpose. There were people ruling the world and they were out to get us. We had to be ready. We had a role. But it's the 2000s, the 2010s ... conspiracy theorists were just mocked.'

It frustrated him that people like me, sitting opposite him now, couldn't see past our own pathetic little worlds. People like me, trying to cut a pizza with a blunt knife, a man he found one day on a grainy, ripped video on DC++, possibly mocking him.

'Because you made that video, and because it was one of the only things we had to go on, we realised, "This is how the mainstream portrays us. These people are lackeys. This is part of their initiation rite and they are trying to humiliate us." You got this reputation. Everyone was saying, "Look at this shill!"'

For the record, I didn't get that documentary gig from the Illuminati. I got it because an Australian producer called Viv saw me on the early evening *Richard & Judy* show on Channel 4, making a knockabout five-minute feature with a Welsh woman called Psychic Sue. *Richard & Judy* had also sent me to look at modern art with the boxer Chris Eubank's wife, and once I had to stand in Birmingham city centre and see if people would put their underpants on their head for £5. In the documentary itself, I cast doubt on the theories but felt they got a fair hearing.

'Who was I supposed to be working for?' I ask. 'Just dark forces?'

'Yeah, just dark forces.'

'Did they pick me because I was naive or because I was willing?'

'You were willing.'

'And why was I doing it?'

'You would be promoted.'

'Until?'

'Until you were bathing in your bath of money.'

(Later, I will think of this sentence as I check in to my regional Holiday Inn.)

The signs, you see, are everywhere, at all times, wherever you happen to look. The strings are everywhere, criss-crossing and knotted and waiting for someone to try and tie them together. Once you are in that mindset, all you can see are the signs – everywhere, all the time. Trump's football shirt with the number 17 on it. The significance of pizza.

And now, quite apart from Gareth Icke, talking to Brent brings me flashbacks of my time with a young Alex Jones.

* * *

If the 9/11 attacks unleashed a whole new generation of conspiracy theorists like Brent, it was Alex Jones leading the charge.

I met Alex Emerick Jones in 2004, when he was a different man. He was maybe 30, puppyish, clean shaven and keen to be liked. In 2002 he'd made a film called *9/11: The Road to Tyranny* (tagline: 'They knew. They not only let it happen – they MADE it happen.') and it had gone down pretty well with the right crowd, and even been played on a big screen at the Alamo Drafthouse in Austin.

Alex was friendly, but he could become a powerful ranter, in person and on screen. He could muster a rage from almost nowhere until he was red-faced, flecking spittle everywhere and thumping the desk in front of him so hard I thought he might have a heart attack. Have you ever seen someone fly into an all-encompassing, articulate thunderstorm of vengeful rage? When five minutes ago they'd merely been mildly vexed that the store didn't sell Mountain Dew?

But this was still an Alex yet to build that powerful media empire, with millions of fans around the world, and millions and millions of dollars. This man was an outsider; he was a thousand miles away from being courted by right-wing presidents and thanked for all his hard work. His InfoWars brand wasn't widely known and his *Alex Jones Show* was an eccentric oddball programme on local public access television run out of a lock-up; he was then still just some guy making his videos and ranting loudly to virtually no one about virtually everything.

We didn't know it at the time, but a website called YouTube was still a few months away from being founded and turning Alex's lonely shouting to its tantalising turbo-charged superstar destiny: making him America's number-one conspiracy theorist for hundreds of millions of people all around the world. It was the same YouTube that would, years later, sensationally ban him, but still fail to keep this soon-to-be-powerful pseudo cult leader from his adoring acolytes.

Whatever audience this version of Alex Jones enjoyed was the kind you could fit in the stalls of a small regional theatre. He was just a man. Youthful demeanour. Preppy clothes. A gravelly voice that did not fit.

There was, though, a confusing intensity about him. An anger bubbling under a Southern politeness that made his knee bounce and the thoughts come quickly. He had, above all, a passionate desire to find anyone who'd listen.

Right now, that was me. I'd been listening to him a lot. He told me he trusted me but also made it very clear indeed that he did not trust me.

I was in Austin, Texas, to meet this man I'd only just heard of for one of the TV documentaries Brent Lee would soon find – and this was a man who thought 9/11 and the deaths of 3,000 people were in fact an inside job perpetrated by the US government and that the world was run by a New World Order who wanted to crush our every hope and dream, like a boot stamping on a human face forever.

This was a horrible idea from a man who genuinely seemed to believe it was true, and maybe it made him. A confusing global trauma, an emotional life raft to grab hold of, no matter how detached the concept from reality. And yet a clear forerunner to his obscene Sandy Hook crisis actor claims.

But when I met this mid-2000s version of Jones, well, we got on. He seemed desperate for me to take him seriously, but back then, of course, he was just good TV. I was polite and jokey; we chatted between our many interview set-ups (a bar, his home, the streets around Austin). I made a few mild jokes at his expense which he didn't seem to mind. We talked about our lives, about London, about a friend called Ian it turned out we had in common. I remember at one point we were walking down the street and he suddenly started using a bullhorn to scream at the house of a local politician. I hadn't even noticed he was carrying one and can only assume he has pockets like the Tardis.

There was, though, a sense of fragility about him. Not like the steely-eyed, bullish, heavier-set and more intimidating Alex Jones of the future. He kept telling me, with a real sense of disappointed resignation, that I was inevitably going to do a hatchet job on him. He repeatedly said the same to other people right in front of me. He said we'd screw him in the edit. He seemed sad about it, paranoid about it, but felt he'd no choice but to plough on, because he had to reach an audience, even if it was just ours. I didn't realise it at the time, but Alex Jones wasn't just paranoid. He was on his way to becoming the most paranoid man in America.

In his normal life, if he had one, he had a perfectly nice girlfriend called Kelly. I remember bumping into her in their perfectly normal new-build house that had perfectly bare walls. He could have just been like any other guy on that street. Drove a fairly new pick-up truck, liked a ciggie, mainlined caffeine. And took great delight when a young man approached us on the street. A man about the age Brent would have been at the time. The man was shaking slightly as he offered Alex his hand, and spoke humbly, saying, 'Thank you for everything you are doing for this country.' And Alex looked delighted, because someone had been listening. There were others like him.

The problem was, what he'd been listening to were things like this – all genuine theories Alex Jones has put out there over the years in his relentless pursuit of a truth not recognised by facts:

- The US government controls the weather and uses it to murder people on demand.
- Barack Obama leads Al Qaeda.
- The Pentagon has a 'Gay Bomb' it could set off at any time, and chemicals from that Gay Bomb have leaked into the water supply, resulting in very many gay frogs.

Those who don't believe in radio-controlled tornados and fabulous frogs? They're the types of people who will meet his righteous frothing anger and *burn in hell*.

But when a certain claim runs out of steam or is comprehensively debunked? Move quickly and distract with another – something we've seen in the UK as 5G haters became Covid deniers then anti-vaxxers and then 15 Minute Neighbourhood truthers.

* * *

I can tell from Brent's demeanour that he must have been absolutely knackered by the time he found his way out of all this.

The Ickes and the Joneses, and the Brents caught in the middle of it all.

The search for 'truth' in what you perceive to be a world of lies is not just addictive and life-affirming. It's also, from what I've seen elsewhere, psychologically, physically and emotionally exhausting.

I'll give you some quick examples.

One – Brent Lee was, by his own account, a very polite conspiracy theorist. He hates the word 'sheeple'. He says he's never bought into any of the Jewish conspiracies, from the 'Jew World Order' to the once-proffered right-wing Republican idea that Jewish people are developing their own space lasers so that they can start wildfires in America and then blame it on climate change so that they can eventually lock us in our homes.

Brent did not want to ram his message down anyone's throat, but of course he couldn't help bringing these ideas up all the time. 'My mum made the decision to say, "I don't want to talk about this. There's plenty of other things we can talk about." I eventually learned that it's pretty anti-social to just talk about the Illuminati all the time to everyone, no one wants to talk about that at Christmas parties and shit.' He hoped instead to be 'a welcoming party for when people woke up to the truth,' because 'this is mind-blowing stuff and you have to be ready.' But until they were, he stopped going out, stopped actively socialising, and just stayed in with his videos. Friends were still welcome to come round to his place and smoke weed – but as part of the deal they'd almost always

find themselves watching a five-hour lecture on US geostrate-
gic interests and natural gas pipeline building in Afghanistan.

Two – being a conspiracy theorist and operating in a community where everyone believes sometimes wildly different
things about one shared narrative means constant rational-
ising. There is no one truth, there are plenty. You have to be
nimble and work with new information all the time. Brent is a
Christian. 'I went quite extreme with my Christianity,' he says,
which isn't a big surprise at this stage. But his Christianity is
how he could rationalise the otherwise batshit times David
Icke said Queen Elizabeth II was actually a shapeshifting,
bloodsucking alien space lizard.

'I had to figure out what he was *really* trying to say,' he
explained. 'What was my interpretation of that?'

These interpretations, of course, are something Bible
scholars do all the time, just with talking snakes, not talking
reptiles.

Actually, wait, that's the same.

'So I figured, well, maybe these people aren't really
seeing reptiles, they're seeing *demons*. Right? Which makes
sense, because the idea of a reptilian bloodline fits with the
idea of a fallen angel bloodline [angels expelled from heaven
for behaviour that falls short of community standards]. So
it actually fit.'

And three – being a conspiracy theorist is exhausting
because it means finding the truth hidden in plain sight, even
when there is nothing actually there. You see clues everywhere.
It's enraging; your enemy is mocking you because there are
signs *everywhere*.

* * *

In Austin, with Alex Jones, I remember evening falling, and the Texas sky turning royal blue. Alex had been talking about cover-ups and demons and people burning in hell quite a lot and we were both tired. He insisted I ride with him in his truck to eat a Chinese meal under the neon red sign of P.F. Chang's China Bistro, because he wanted some sticky beef.

At one point as we drove through the tree-lined streets near his house in the dark, he told me how brave I was to ride with him. I asked him why, and he told me that recently the government had tried to kill him. I asked how they'd done that. He told me they'd sent a tornado to do it. It had run him off the road. I quietly told him I didn't realise they could do that nowadays.

As we rode on, he told me that on the way to our sticky beef, he'd show me the skyscrapers that had been built by the Illuminati in downtown Austin. Skyscrapers he *knew* were built by the Illuminati because they were designed to look just like owls. Owls that work in the dark, all-seeing predators, owls like the owl of Minerva, the ancient symbol they chose to represent them. Owls – now large and made of concrete and steel – that mocked him.

He was quieter and calmer now, though still trying out his theories on me. He knew I was a lost cause, but he was still trying to make me see what I couldn't. Open my eyes to the invisible. And I remember standing next to the truck, doors askew, staring at a far-off skyscraper and saying, 'I mean, it does a *bit*,' as he crossed his arms and shook his head at it.

I could tell he was annoyed that I didn't immediately agree the buildings looked like owls. I mean, I could've. It was just us. I could have indulged him. So I conceded that the upside-down parts of the window design did share some of the traits and characteristics of an owl's nose. I should have said 'beak', because now it really sounded like I didn't believe him. It may have implied I did not quite buy into the idea that the Illuminati – the secret rulers of the world who hold ultimate and dreadful power over all our destinies and have been operating in the shadows for centuries since they started in the 1700s in the small Bavarian town of Ingolstadt, Germany – had drawn up plans for big owl buildings in plain sight of the then non-existent Texan home of P.F. Chang's China Bistro.

I mean, even if those plans had been drawn up yesterday, why Austin?

If as a sign of their power they'd built a giant owl in New York I might agree it was weird, just as I'd agree that any towering concrete nocturnal bird of prey in *any* built-up area is weird. But something that probably housed a bank with windows that featured an upside-down glass triangle that if you squinted *might* resemble an owl's nose in America's *11th* biggest city?

And wait just one second.

Remember earlier, when I mentioned Coventry? The English city handpicked by Illuminati member Bill Gates to be the very first place the vaccine would be trialled, on elderly grandmother Margaret Keenan? Do you remember what I was very careful to tell you about Coventry?

Coventry is the *11th* biggest city in the UK.

So Illuminati owls in America's 11th biggest city … and Illuminati vaccines in the UK's?

Are we spotting a pattern here? Are we spotting the signs?

So why 11?

Let's look at *September* 11, aka 9/11.

9-11 is the American telephone number for emergencies (alarm bells), and if you add 9, 1 and 1 you get ... 11.

September 11 is the 254th day of the year.

2 + 5 + 4 = 11.

After September 11, how many days left in the year are there? 111.

The flight number of the first plane to hit the tower was 11.

But there is even more proof that something is afoot with the I11uminati if you remain to be convinced.

The name New York City has 11 letters.

The Pentagon has 11 letters.

Afghanistan has 11 letters.

George W. Bush? 11 letters.

Do you see yet? Do you see the signs?

And what two-digit number did conspiracists straight after 9/11 take great pains to point out the silhouette of the twin towers themselves might remind you of?

* * *

This stuff wasn't Brent's style. His questions were deeper, and the evidence he sought far more detailed. Yet he is familiar with this type of thinking. He describes this phenomenon of seeing signs *everywhere* as wearing a filter over your eyes that makes symbols jump out at you like warning signs. For years he couldn't buy his family any Christmas card featuring even the tiniest, most innocent five-pointed star in case he hexed them with an inadvertent pentagram and accidentally placed a witch-like curse on them.

'I mean, this is the first time I've worn anything made by Nike,' says Brent, pulling at his top and pointing at the signature Swoosh. 'Because of this.'

'The Swoosh?'

He nods.

'Because the way I thought, if I die wearing this – the Swoosh – well, that's the symbol of Saturn. So my soul would not go to heaven. It would be bound to Saturn. My whole family knew never to buy me anything other than plain clothes.'

This was a lot to take in.

'Wait,' I say. 'When you say bound to Saturn, you mean, what, the planet?'

'No, the god of Saturn. I would be serving the god of Saturn for eternity. Because there are all these sub-gods, gods with a small g, you think if they all exist, and Lucifer exists, well, the god of Saturn probably works for Lucifer so it's no different from going to work for Lucifer.'

By the way, the Swoosh, it seems, is actually supposed to symbolise the mighty wing of the Greek goddess of Victory, Nike. Now, I don't know what it would be like to be bound to the goddess of *Victory* for eternity, but I imagine she has extremely high expectations.

Being a conspiracy theorist to the level that Brent Lee was is exhausting because if you are a fundamentally decent person, it is an almost unbearable weight to carry. You are living your life in a world surrounded by people you assume to be the wilfully blind and the brainwashed. Not you – you know the truth and you are frustrated beyond belief that only you can see it. The people you walk past every day, the people you buy your groceries from, the guy flying your plane, the doctor you see about your rash – they are all blind to the horrifying existential threat that hangs low and constant over their heads with every comparatively pointless thing they do. The pensions. The package holidays. That down payment on the Nissan Qashqai.

Yet you'd never have known it to look at him, he says. As exhausted and as oppressed by it all as he was, 'I never got fired from any job. I was functioning. You can believe absolute lunacy and still be functioning. I don't look like a lunatic, I don't act like a lunatic. I'm not anti-social, I won't yell at you for wearing a mask. Most people are like me. They're chill. It wasn't until after I came out that I tried to figure out … how did this happen to me? How did I fall for this? Is it psychological, do I have some kind of personality disorder? All the different questions I had to try and figure out.'

Brent's eyes started to open around Sandy Hook. And he was starting to see more clearly by the time Edgar Maddison Welch turned up to Comet Ping Pong with a loaded assault rifle looking for paedophiles.

Brent saw that dangerous people were starting to take dangerous ideas and do dangerous things with them. Sure, he'd rapped a cappella outside Downing Street, and for many people that's a war crime in itself. He'd sent a bunch of mean tweets. He'd looked down and pitied those of us who didn't believe the lies. But as time passed, people were getting shot, they were getting murdered, they were blowing themselves up in RVs on Christmas Day in Nashville because they believed the government had faked the moon landing and undertaken the 9/11 attacks. They were killing themselves in their own homes because they couldn't deal with the idea that an invisible New World Order of laughing elites was out to control them. They were breaking into politician's houses with hammers, they were drinking bleach, they were storming capitols, they were running wild because they had lost control – worse, they were realising they never had control in the first place.

Brent's world was crashing in.

But that first moment of clarity for him is so striking because it is so awful: it was when Alex Jones threw out that particularly awful string of his – the one provocatively dangled that caught so many people and pulled them in, the one he would be sued a billion dollars for. That string led to parents of children killed in the Sandy Hook massacre being abused on the street, being screamed at and accused of lying about their dead children who were actors and still alive somewhere; it led one tormented father to suicide.

The public at large was sickened by this kind of talk, but it had a subtly different effect on Brent. From his conspiracy mindset, the idea that anyone was claiming it was a hoax completely undermined his own theories. He had no doubt that senseless tragedies like Sandy Hook took place, but for him they weren't senseless or isolated; they were part of a bigger plan. They were happening as sacrifices. 'Rituals, our brothers and sisters killed by dark forces we needed to fight. But people claiming they're crisis actors or whatever just ripped everything I'd been saying apart. It made no sense to me.'

In 2016, he withdrew and thought. It was a slow and agonising process.

And eventually, in June 2021, after his finger hovered over *send* for how long he forgets, he posted a blunt but polite message to all his friends and followers on Facebook:

I no longer considering [*sic*] myself a 'Truther' or any kind of Conspiracy Theorist.

I've been on a journey of deconstructing and reassessing my world view over the past 8 or so years.

The schism started around Sandy Hook and by 2016 I found I had nothing in common with Truther discourse.

Tbh ... Illuminati, New World Order, Deep State ... it's actually bullshit.

Complete Bullshit.

If you want to unfriend me, feel free, no hard feelings!

Of course, guess what?

With new and confusing information, his truther friends had to be on the ball if they were to stay one step ahead.

So from now on, Brent Lee was clearly a shill. An actor. A gatekeeper. He was in the employ of the New World Order. Maybe he always had been. This was all for promotion. Look how he dresses. Soon he would be bathing in his bath of money, in a Holiday Inn, just like me.

'People I knew for eight, ten years wouldn't speak to me. They still won't. Because I sold my soul, they say. Every one of them says I sold my soul. Sold it to the Devil. That's the thing I'm sad about. Because I challenged what defined us. We built a worldview together, we confirmed it for each other. They told me I was wrong. But they couldn't tell me why. So now I've sold my soul.'

Brent Lee has become a byword for selling your soul in that community. They say it all the time. That's he's been got at; that he's an actor.

'It's happening right there, right now,' he says, pointing at his phone, and when we check, sure enough, it is.

Apropos of apparently nothing, someone is wondering why Brent Lee has not spoken out yet in defence of Gerry and Kate McCann, parents of abducted Madeleine, who we can assume this correspondent wrongly thinks committed the crime themselves.

Someone else replies, 'Brent probably hasn't been sent his script to learn yet.'

⁂ ⁂ ⁂

I don't think Brent Lee is a member of the Illuminati, and I'm quietly pleased he no longer thinks I am. I suppose it's like that Aldous Huxley quote, from as long ago as 1958: 'An unexciting truth may be eclipsed by a thrilling falsehood.'

There's a calmness to Brent as we sit for a moment in silence with our hugely diminished pizzas (though he had the calzone – something he remains adamant people will too find somehow significant, perhaps because five triangular calzones laid out from their bases in a circle could make a convincing pentagram? I dunno, I'm just trying to help).

Maybe it's the tweets – the thrilling falsehoods and some-body told mes now eclipsing his truth. But they don't get to him, he says. If more are coming in, Brent wants to fight them and those who send them into the world. He knows how, because that used to be him.

Maybe it's also the sense that with so many years spent on the other side of the fight, he needs to use the rest of his life wisely.

Brent understands the mindset of those who've been drawn in, because just like he used to, they're living in a world in which they're trying to make sense of absolute chaos. There's a split at the moment, he thinks, in the conspiracy world. Covid changed everything. A mass of narratives hit the table. From 5G to microchips to Bill Gates. And isn't everyone who had the vaccine supposed to be dead by now?

New twists are being written, new takes on history invented, nimble moves made. He thinks that behind the scenes there are people jostling for position, nudging their way to leadership, trying to find the best new stories for people to get behind, stories that will sell. Not just those that truly believe, but those that prey on the believers, finding new angles and cynical lines.

What's going to replace the 5G stuff? What's going to replace the Covid doubts? Is it 15 Minute Neighbourhoods? Is it Russia? There are excellent commercial opportunities to be had for whoever wants to be the next David Icke, Brent tells me.

* * *

Which means all these years later, I look up Gareth Icke again.

He still sings. I don't know if he's still into beach soccer.

But something else is happening.

In the years since we met, the young man I met in the pub (now older than his dad was when he went on the chat show that would change his reputation forever) is himself becoming a powerful new force in alternative news, and rails against the 'lamestream media'.

He's created his own fledgling media empire, not under any Icke & Sons banner, but using the name Ickonic. He speaks all over the country and hosts his own online TV show, *Gareth Icke Tonight*. His brother Jaymie has an occasional show too. A speech Gareth made at an anti-lockdown rally in London was viewed more than 3 million times on Facebook. He has 150,000 followers on Twitter waiting for his thoughts.

I emailed him to say hi, but got nothing back.

So I tried his website, but when I get nothing back from that either, I think maybe he doesn't want to reconnect, despite our odd history, despite my calling him dashing and witty, despite him owing me at *least* four pints of Guinness.

Still bright, but now media-savvy and angry, he is bringing slickness and high production values to David Icke's latest videos that are way beyond the slightly clunky films of old.

They sell merchandise too: at one point, expensive T-shirts featuring a sheep wearing a mask, or sometimes a plain one with just the word *Scamdemic*.

Other topics they handle include why the EU's stance on combating climate change is not about saving our world but about controlling the masses. In some videos, the 1990s band Right Said Fred give their views on what's *really* going on, which of course is something we should all take very seriously because of no reason at all.

But it is solid work, if that work is what you want.

There is even one video of his father David Icke railing against those people who pass their own religious beliefs onto their kids. The featured quote is: 'Imagine if, out of respect for a child's uniqueness, you didn't indoctrinate them.'

David's sons are now the natural heirs and the future of movements like this: part of a growing Icke dynasty.

Keen to prod at what the vast majority of us think of as truth.

And what's certain is that there is an eager audience waiting for them, hungry for new takes from new blood. A world of younger men and women, people like Brent back in the day, who found mention of someone random on that David Icke forum, and became convinced people like me – and perhaps you – were their sworn enemy. 'Sometimes it's scary talking about this stuff,' says Brent. 'You're trying to explain in some ways the downfall of your character. You leave yourself open to people who will think you're weak or stupid or naive. But I don't care. I don't fucking care. Especially when lies are killing people. You mention that guy you met?'

'Francis? The guy in Cardiff?'

'I mean … his whole family, man.'

'I know.'

* * *

Brent is doing what he can. He tweets takedowns of conspiracy theories. He challenges people on their opinions. He speaks up on radio and television, and on panels at conferences. He also co-presents the funny, informative conspiracy-deconstructing podcast *Some Dare Call It Conspiracy* with his friend Neil Sanders. Some of the episodes are three hours long. Conspiracy seems a world lacking in brevity, even when you're on the other side of it. When he's not working (I'm not allowed to say where, but it's not as a crisis actor), Brent's putting all his music-production experience into making the podcast as good as he can. Without the conspiracies to fuel him, he can't find his lyrics anymore, but he feels a fundamental need to put something out there, to make up for lost time.

He hopes some of the people who abandoned him will find him again, he says, as we gather our things. I glance at my phone and see I have a new email. A reply to a punt I sent out. Its subject line is all caps: IPSWICH.

I wonder if for every Brent who strains to pull himself out of the rabbit hole, there's someone who jumps right in and carries on digging.

'I don't want to be the person who converts others, I want to be the welcoming party for when they wake up, and when you wake up, we're here for you,' is what Brent said as a conspiracy theorist waiting for people like me to wake up, and now he says it to the conspiracy theorists themselves, as he sits by *their* bedsides.

※ ※ ※

Outside, we take a photo on his phone, taking care not to get the restaurant in shot. He doesn't work a million miles away, and Brent's boss really doesn't want the attention. He's seen the type of posts Brent gets. But Brent smiles cheekily and pulls his beanie down.

'It's going to blow their minds we did this at a pizza restaurant,' he says.

Once it's posted online that afternoon, the reaction is largely from the new, accepting audience he's finding: the people who support him speaking out; the ones there but for the grace of God, or who lament that their parents are gradually sinking in conspiracy quicksand and won't reach out for their hand, no matter how eagerly they stretch.

But there are always the ghosts of his past, watching and lurking and judging.

Under our picture, one person asks, 'Are you getting paid to post this kind of content?'

'I'll ask again,' says another, 'is this your full-time job and whose books are you on?'

'You need help,' adds the next.

And the last one I see? Under that photo of Brent Lee after lunch with Danny Wallace – just two men who have had a friendly chat over thin-crust pizza and calzone in Bristol?

'So you've sold your soul to the Devil,' it says. 'Enjoy Hell, you little prick.'

9

Terry

It Starts Small – A Man
at the Beginning of His Journey

The email subject line was IPSWICH because Terry is worried about what he heard about Ipswich. He heard outside forces are trying to reshape it.

The news has swept the local area and Terry wants answers.

Ipswich is the county town of Suffolk. It's a little worse for wear. It was once the most important trading dock in the country and could argue for being one of the oldest towns too. Now, as I step off the train, it's a bit frayed, a bit water-damaged. Shops have shut forever. Every few windows there's a *To Let* sign. The local Gymophobics, with its cheery photo in the window of a group of older ladies smiling delightedly at the camera ('Run *by* ladies *for* ladies!') has closed down. Someone has smashed the door in. They must have been very gymophobic.

On the cheap replacement wooden board they've nailed to the doorframe, someone else has scrawled in black pen the word *DEATH*.

* * *

The pandemic wasn't kind to Ipswich, and so many towns like it across the world.

However, now the unseen puppet-masters of Suffolk County Council have big plans for Ipswich. Forget 15 Minute Neighbourhoods. They plan to turn this place into the UK's most prominent 15 Minute *Town*.

The opening line of their proposal reads like something from a conspiracy theorist's handwritten manifesto:

OUTSIDE FORCES WILL RESHAPE IPSWICH.
OR WE CAN.

But really, what they're saying is, 'Bad things can come out of nowhere; let's make things better ourselves.'

It's a document that puts forward – in a very friendly way – the idea that if Ipswich can be redesigned for its people, more people will live, work and love Ipswich. They want more parks, more cycleways, more people living at the heart of the town.

On a beautiful day like today, you see the best of the place.

I do a couple of the suggested 15-minute walks that a project called Ipswich Central has highlighted. I see the church, the mosque, the park. The university, the museum, the football stadium: all so close together. Ancient Tudor buildings leaning drunkenly on each other like they froze while staggering home from the pub, creating tiny alleyways with long-established businesses like Procter's Sausages, or the travel agents that is currently doing a deal on a *Call the Midwife* tour and lunch. Down on the Waterfront, you can sip an Aperol and stare at the boats on the shimmering River Orwell – the same river George Orwell took that pen name from.

But when the storm clouds gather later in the afternoon, as I walk to meet Terry, you see it in the different light they cast. You pass the Gymophobics *DEATH* graffiti again, which has lost its lightness of touch and sense of impish fun. You notice the vape shops, the phone shops, the side streets that are all tanning and tats. The Bible-bashers standing grim-faced under the doorway of the abandoned Great White Horse Hotel. You notice groups of people standing around doing almost nothing. A man carrying a mattress on his head near the 99p Shop – which has been forced to move to smaller premises. There are some new flats going up on the corner of Grimwade Street but aside from that any sense of new life is fading here. PC World has a window display proudly announcing that it's abandoned the high street and moved to the big retail park near the massive supermarkets.

People have started to abandon the town centre too. Fewer live here, fewer want to work here, fewer go out at night here. It's killing local businesses. People are earning less. Getting less from the state. Moved to write *DEATH* on the door of their local Gymophobics.

I think back to that phrase; the one people start to believe when life gets like this. That plans are afoot to, in the words of conspiracy theorists everywhere, *cull the poor and control the masses.*

Ipswich Central, though, doesn't seem to have such awful plans on the face of things. It wants to introduce free town-wide Wi-Fi alongside 5G, and give people digital gift cards they can spend in local shops. It wants everything connected and available for everyone – all your arts, faith, medical and entertainment needs in close proximity so you don't need to go anywhere else because your life is convenient and rich already. They want to invest in the shops. Get some big concrete **IPSWICH** letters they can put in front of all the landmarks so people will put the town on Instagram.

And also they just really really want a nice big Christmas tree that people can gather round every year.

Even that would do so much.

And so only a week or so after I met a man who had pulled himself from the grip of conspiracies, I would meet a man just starting to set foot in them.

* * *

Terry is disgusted by Ipswich Central and their nefarious deeds because Terry wasn't consulted on any of it.

He suspects it's all a big lie.

I found him on a Facebook group where there was very little dissent. The type of group where no one dares say 'this is bollocks, Terry' and so add things like 'hmm, interesting, Terry – food for thought' instead, as one or two bolshy thought leaders hold court with their theories. Terry has been watching videos and now thinks that Ipswich is being used as a sort of experiment to see what They can get away with before rolling these ideas out nationally in a bid to keep us docile and under Their control. He's been doing his own research and talking to concerned friends, and something is definitely up. Everybody's talking about the upsides, he says – isn't that convenient?

He's not alone. In the survey published by King's College London and the BBC, a quite incredible 33 per cent of the UK population who have heard about 15 Minute Cities think it is definitely or probably true that they 'are an attempt by governments to restrict people's personal freedom and keep them under surveillance'. Of those people, well over half learned about them thanks to social media, with YouTube and TikTok way in the lead.

Terry seemed more reasonable than the other main detective in this wide-ranging Suffolk conspiracy, his friend who we'll call Graham. Graham I know only through his written words. Those written words tend to be furious and sweary. Ipswich becoming more convenient and healthier was a plot he took very personally. I didn't think Graham would take kindly to being questioned on this. I think there'd be a lot of swearing.

When I'd contacted Terry, though, he politely conceded he knew my work very vaguely, and he was intrigued enough to agree to meet up.

* * *

I meet Terry in a pub called the Plough, opposite the shop at 7 Dogs Head Street, which is called 7 Dogs Head Street Shop.

The Plough is exactly like every other traditional city centre pub I've ever been to. Low ceilings, tartan-sided chairs, cask ales, carpets. Fruit machine, towers of onion rings, people with nowhere to be.

Pretty much the last thing Terry will say to me today is to please change his name, which he didn't say I should do upfront, and I think is because he listened to what he was telling me as he said it and perhaps decided he was on shakier ground than he first thought.

* * *

First, a little about Let's-Call-Him-Terry.

He's in his late 50s, white, with a neat, short-sleeved collared shirt, glasses and a brush of short silver hair. He's wearing Diesel jeans and brown shoes and drinking a European lager which his chunky gold wedding ring clinks softly against when he raises it. He's been learning the guitar recently, but he thinks his fingers are too fat and all the songs are much quicker than he thought they'd be. He was born here in Ipswich. Went to a local school. Enjoyed some summers sailing on the rivers nearby. He moved to nearby Essex when he turned 20, spent some time in advertising sales, worked in a job adjacent to the fire service, then came home. He'd love an allotment. Chard is underrated. He likes to get his 10,000 steps in, though he needs his Chinese every Friday night, so he feels the two balance each other out, 'like yin and yang'. When he dies, he'd like his name on a bench outside the hospital he was born in. He thinks it should read, 'He came and went!'

He takes a sip of his lager and says, 'What I don't like is that the town has changed so much already for the worse, so you want to stop that, you know? I mean even before the pandemic it really changed from when I was growing up.'

'How did it change?' I ask.

'You know. Lot of places change and that's fine because things move on, but when you live here and you see some of the changes you want to say, sort of, stop changing now, you know?'

'What were the changes you *most* noticed?' I ask, because I think I know what he's saying and *who* he's saying it about, but he doesn't want to *actually* say it, and I think to myself perhaps that says it all.

Terry has a grown-up daughter who's married now and he wishes he saw her more than he did. He and his wife enjoy golf and eating by the sea.

Before we met I asked Terry to watch that Russell Brand video – the one about 15 Minute Smart Neighbourhoods. He said he's watched a few of Russell's videos but not many and he'd missed this one.

'I thought it was very interesting,' he says. 'Because I think people generally are tending to play down just how angry plans like this are making the general population or populace, those ones who make an effort to question things. People don't see it coming. You saw what happened in Thetford.'

* * *

As we sit here this afternoon, it is only one month since, at an otherwise perfectly normal town council meeting in Thetford in nearby Norfolk, everyone was quite surprised when 200 incredibly angry people turned up out of nowhere and started loudly berating the town councillors.

There is a phenomenon called state anger. It's usually a temporary and brief outburst of rage fuelled by paranoia. But the paranoia isn't because you think powerful organisations are just out to change the world around us – it's that they're out to get *you* specifically. And so you think you must find allies, and fight for your own survival.

There were so many surprise visitors that day in Thetford that the council and the crowd had to march down the street together to find a bigger venue. The people – a lot of angry-faced men in beards and bodywarmers, and stony-faced women with folded arms and judgemental eyebrows – were protesting against the highly sophisticated and expensive thing that Thetford town council had allocated some of its not-huge budget to inflicting upon its 24,000 unwitting residents. Because Thetford town council had unleashed what was being described as a 'weapon of tyranny'.

Word had spread quickly thanks to a leaflet someone had posted all over town.

HAVE YOU HEARD?
OUR BASIC FREEDOM TO TRAVEL COULD BE AT RISK AND OUR COUNCILS ARE IN SUPPORT.

It was terrifying stuff. Freedom of movement gone. There's no escape, not from *this* weapon of tyranny. It could affect you if you like to drive out of town. If your kids go to school in a neighbouring village. If you want to visit family outside Thetford. If you want to have a family day trip outside Thetford. If you needed to drive an elderly relative to a hospital outside Thetford. Too bad. You are staying in Thetford!

'WHO will fund this agenda?' it asks, mysteriously, perhaps suggesting this as an opening question for anyone it encouraged to turn up to the council meeting. Or perhaps subtly implying it was the World Health Organization.

On the night, 'You don't have my consent!' spat a man seething with aggression, surrounded by other men who cheered aggressively and in their best Man Voices as Mayor Jane James stood her ground but looked confused, unprepared, and nervous.

Later, I saw the same man being interviewed by an outfit called Rebel News. It's possible it's also the man who designed the leaflet, because he's certainly friends with the man who made the video that came out at the same time, showing angry Thetfordians – and a bunch of people who had made the journey specially, as if somehow organised – marching through the streets to sinister music in outright rebellion. This man was rigid with the same tension I've seen in other men convinced they are in a war leading a small rebel alliance against the might of an imagined state outrage. He was walking past the Subway sandwich shop in Thetford in a red puffer jacket, simmering with the quiet anger of the wronged alpha male, complaining that the scheme to make things more convenient seemed to be 'too good to be true'.

This was a man who hated the idea of bollards being installed in newly pedestrianised streets, hated that he might be fined if he broke the law in his car, hated that he would be encouraged to use the local services around him. Bollards were going to be a problem. New bollards in small towns like Thetford, you might as well say, were on the direct and distinct order of the shadowy World Economic Forum.

It seems the bollard-loving Jews have had their eye on Thetford for aeons.

'We need to be able to travel!' said the man in the video, sullen and serious, pacing like a soldier, frowning constantly for gravitas. 'Cars are a necessity, not a luxury.'

He said, 'This place used to be *bustling*. As you can see it's not so bustling now. Businesses shut down. You used to be able to come into town and buy *anything* you wanted. You can't do that now. So you have to travel. And they want to *stop* us doing that.'

Wait.

Hoooold up.

What if actually, They want to alleviate you of that travel burden?

What if actually, They want to bring back the very thing you miss: a bustling Thetford?

What if it's that?

What if it's because They *want* you to be able to buy anything you want, but want you to buy it here in bustling Thetford and not at some out-of-town retail park you have to drive to?

Then the bustling you hate that you can't do anymore is the *exact same bustling* They're offering to give you.

What if once again, the big plan is: They want to put people before cars?

They *want* you to bustle, but to bustle in *cleaner air*.

This was not offered as an option by the Rebel News guy. And the man himself seemed unsure of the agenda of whoever was in charge, but one thing seemed certain to him, I think: they wanted to keep him in Thetford. They wanted to keep everyone already in Thetford … in Thetford. In the 15 Minute Prison that Thetford would become.

Quite how the rest of the country would have reacted to the apparent annexing of Thetford is unknown. My guess is that after watching his interview we'd probably have been fine with it.

* * *

'What's interesting about the Thetford people and their, sort of, if you will, uprising,' says Terry, holding court at the

Plough, 'is that it lays it all out so clearly – if They're given the chance They will take liberties with our liberties!'

It's a practised line. I saw him use it on Facebook. But it's a neat one, said with confidence. But I bet it's usually the end of the conversation. There's a thing I love about British small talk. You deliver your final line and the other person has to say 'haha – see you later!' and walk off. It's a great way to avoid awkward conversations, though it also lets people off.

'Nice weather for ducks!'

'Haha, lovely – see you later!'

'Washing your car? You can do mine next!'

'Haha, see you later!'

'If they're given the chance, I tell you what – the New World Order and the media elites will be taking liberties with our *liberties*!'

'Oh Terry, what are you like? See you later.'

But:

'What liberties are They going to take from you?' I ask now, in a rehearsed way most Brits have learned to ask of people who voted for Brexit. 'What's the one liberty you're most worried about losing?'

'All of them,' he says, swatting the question away with his hand, like a man who's been asked this before and has no time for it.

'Like what, though? What one?'

'Like any. Even losing one is too many if you ask me.'

I should drop it, but I don't.

'Definitely. But there must be one where you're like, "No, not *that* liberty, don't take that one!"'

'Even *one* is too many,' he says, placing his palm flat on the table to make sure the answer sticks.

It's then that I'm struck by the old conspiracy theory formula – one Brent and Ben and Francis had touched upon at times.

POWERFUL PEOPLE are doing TERRIBLE THINGS for EVIL REASONS.

So I decide that might be the easiest way to get Terry to explain to me what's happening in the market town of Ipswich.

'So is there a way you can you explain to me, in the simplest way – who is behind this, what is it they are actually trying to do, and what they stand to gain from it?'

Terry blinks once then goes into a bluster. There's lots of 'what you have to understand' and 'They' and 'Them' and basically it boils down to someone high up and their secret police force is going to end up filming Terry in his car going down a street he's not supposed to go down and then he'll get fined. It seems that's what most of them are worried about. The terror of fixed penalty notices for breaking a law. Because after that, what's next? If They can issue you a small fine, They could very easily put Terry under house arrest and then, he says, make him use his passport if he wants to get out of Ipswich.

'Your *passport?*' I say.

'I'm exaggerating,' he says, 'not my passport. But they'd require some form of ID. Just for walking down the road. Or probably digital ID they can store on a database. That's happened already in places, not just identity cards, but ones you would need just to live here in Ipswich. Just to walk down the road!'

'Do you mean the Ipswich app?'

'They can call it what they like, it's what it does I'm worried about. Is it called Ipswich App?'

'I don't know what they'll call it. I read about it. Maybe they'll call it Ipswapp. But I think the Ipswich app will mainly get you discounts on things.'

His scoff is a familiar one: it means, yeah, you believe that if you want. Terry knows this is not about 10 per cent off your next coffee or custard slice or instilling loyalty in customers. He doesn't want to say it outright, but he's floated the idea online: he's worried he's going to be held captive in Ipswich forever.

'Your movements will be tracked,' he says. 'Why? Why do they need to track your movements?'

'Why *do* they?'

'It's making sure you don't go where you're not welcome! Keeping the *persona non grata* in his place. You saw what they were like during Covid. They were flying drones all over the place trying to spot you even if you were just walking down the road, waving at your dear old neighbour!'

I need to be gentle here.

'Doesn't your phone already track your movement?' I say. 'I think mine does.'

'I turned all that off,' he says, but he says it *very* quickly.

'How did you find all this stuff out?' I ask.

'By *thinking*,' he says, like my question is *insane*, and he reaches into his pocket, and he pulls out a box of Tic Tacs, and he shakes some into his hand.

* * *

Terry finds comfort in others sharing his opinion. There's a few of them that meet now, he says. They catch up on the family stuff, the football, the usual. And they swap information about the radicalisation of Ipswich County Council. I can't help but wonder if it's not the ideas he likes sharing, but the company.

Sometimes his friends – one in particular – stray into other areas where the government may be overstepping the mark, like the chemical trails his friend says planes are leaving behind in the sky to slowly poison and control the people, but Terry waves all that away.

'Some of the things he says are bonkers, I understand that,' he says. 'He knows I don't believe in all that, in chemtrails and so forth. But I just, I let him get on with it. I'm not into all the nutty stuff and so forth either. But when it comes to matters to do with what is right here around me, the things I can see for myself, then that's the time I have to take things more seriously. That's being a citizen.'

'Are you vaccinated against Covid?' I ask, but I do it in a very polite way.

He smiles, and his eyes crinkle, because he knows what I'm doing.

'I … am,' he says. 'I am. I did get them. Would I get them all over again? Probably not.'

'Why?'

'There's a lot of stuff going on. A lot of things you should check out. Am I worried about suddenly dying? Aren't we all? Do I think the next step is what Bill Gates said recently? I have not yet made up my mind.'

This is a great technique people use. They ask their own questions, ones you haven't asked, so they can answer what they wish you'd asked. But then I think …

'*What* did Bill Gates say recently?'

'He said if you can put the vaccine in the food supply, you can stop vaccine hesitancy. You can in essence *force* people to take the vaccine because you know they need to eat.'

'When did he say this?' I ask, because I must have missed it.

'He said it the other day, there's a video somewhere I think.'

I get my phone out and go to YouTube.

'Or maybe not a video but an article. You have to look for it, I think.'

'How did you hear about it?' I ask, knowing it was his mate.

'I'm not sure,' he says, and I think that's when he suspects he's gone too far.

* * *

Terry's friend Graham has shared a graphic saying people should consider turning their phones off this Sunday. It's because the government is going to send out an emergency alert signal to all UK mobile phones as a test run in case of future weather catastrophes, Russian intimidation or sundry other emergencies.

It happens in other countries. When I lived in America, the alerts could be localised, and sometimes you'd get one telling you to look out for a brown sedan on the I-90 or something, because someone had been kidnapped. And so you did.

And sometimes the person would get caught. It seemed a good system, impersonal but part of looking out for others, until the day it malfunctioned and accidentally sent out an alert to everyone on Hawaii telling them they were about to be hit by an intercontinental ballistic missile. I imagine that was quite a memorable morning in Hawaii. I worry about the various people thinking their lives were about to end, deciding to be very honest with their partners for the first time before they die ('I've been seeing your sister for the last four years') and then *not* dying and kind of resenting it.

But Graham is just passing on a meme that says the 3pm Test Alert will actually activate an immediate pathogen in anyone who received a Covid shot. And then everyone who had one will die, either quickly or slowly, depending on what happens on Sunday. I wonder if that's why Terry wouldn't have another vaccination, but I don't think so. I think he's unusual among his group in that he's more of a one-issue believer.

Terry says his wife is as adamant as he is that something shady is going on in Ipswich. Although she is mainly concerned with planning their next golfing holiday. They're hoping to get to Thetford soon, next time there's a meeting. She's as bad as he is, he says, and I think that's an interesting phrase, like what he's doing is like a hobby on its way to an obsession, rather than real investigation. It makes it all sound less legitimate. I bet Woodward never described Bernstein and his Watergate theories by saying, 'That guy? God, he's as bad as I am!'

By the end of our few beers together, though, Terry and I have had fun.

We both know we will never hang out again, but it's been nice. He never offered me a Tic Tac though.

I had to say to him, at one point, 'Terry, I honestly don't think there are dark outside forces targeting both Ipswich and you. I mean – why Ipswich? Why are they so keen to take Ipswich?'

He laughs.

'I think you'll still be allowed out of Ipswich,' I say.

And he laughs again, and says, 'They'll probably *want* me out of here after this!' But then the laugh clouds over.

'I know saying it out loud makes some people reckon it sounds stupid,' he says, knocking back the last of his pint.

'I don't think you're stupid,' I say. 'I think we can all end up seeing or hearing different things that we take to be true. Like if we're going through stuff. Trauma or loneliness or just confusion or whatever?'

And he says, 'End of the day, bad things can come out of nowhere. Let's get hands on and change the narrative. Take control of the thing ourselves.'

But it still strikes me as terrifying that ideas like this can take hold of people so firmly. To go from the extremes of someone like Brent Lee whose life would be dominated by it, to someone like Terry who has his worries but at a push could probably take them or leave them. They're still *in* him. And depending on who he listens to, his life might yet take a turn for the conspiratorial.

Yet taking control seems a natural and reasonable thing to want to do. And I think that explains a lot about why people who think this way, think this way.

It is the price of being alive when things aren't going your way, haven't gone your way in a while. When you are your whole world, but the rest of the world seems to want to do its own thing without asking for your approval.

Ideas seeded from American TV outfits or some obscure comedian's back-garden podcast shed can raise both questions and armies in Thetford or Ipswich.

Or ideas that seem to come from nowhere, penned by some unseen hand in some unseen land for reasons unknown.

Recently, Terry shared a much-forwarded WhatsApp message he received online. It claimed the sun was no longer yellow and round, like it used to be in the old days. What's going on with the sun recently? Things were just better in the old days, weren't they? Things were less confusing.

They were less different.

In the old days, Terry would have written to his local paper about the changes in his town, if he cared enough to do so. I don't think it would have occurred to him to bring something like the New World Order into a conversation about bollards. Local matters tended to stay local matters, but today we are connected by a million phones that mean our local business is now everyone's business. If it's happening there, it could happen here next – and probably already is.

I wondered to myself whether the local papers – the *East Anglian Daily Times* and the *Ipswich Star* – had many letters in their pages about the 15 Minute Town plans and the evil plans to restrict our movements. And I wondered where those ideas sprang from in the first place and for what possible reason.

It all felt so lo-fi. So normal, so suburban. But so in keeping with the everydayness of things, from Thetfordian uprisings to emails from the old Chinese man.

And as I considered the intriguing mundanity of it all, and as I investigated those small and personal campaigns found in local newspaper letters pages, I found the strange, strange story of Veronika.

SECTION IV

The Other Side
of the Screen

In which we meet a woman accused of being a Russian
agent who may or may not live in a yurt in Bristol,
discover 'a load of cheeky nonsense' about bots, and
learn how one Finnish investigator became a victim
of terrifying 'special combat propaganda'.

10

Veronika

*Local Media and When You Just
Don't Know Who's Who*

I have a story about a young woman called Veronika Oleksychenko, and it starts with the Israeli martial art of Krav Maga.

Krav Maga is a really clever way of fighting..

It's all about attacking pre-emptively and aggressively. Finding vulnerable points on the body and using simple, easily repeatable strikes. It's about identifying threats, being aware of your surroundings and understanding the psychology of a situation.

One of the strange facts I've found out about Veronika – who is 5'5" tall, slim and the only blonde in her family – is that she considers herself something of an expert in Krav Maga.

Born in Russia in the mid-1990s to a Ukrainian father and a Swedish mother, at one point in her teenage years she found herself homeless in the UK, but now lives and works in a yurt (a yurt!) in an undisclosed location, which she made herself from material she bought from charity shops.

She is the self-published author of the 352-page novel *Dooley Street*, which is set in a once-great Britain overcome by riots, and in which Prime Minister Lisa Flack – who *hates* the toilets at work – is chased by feral dogs as she wages war on the country's prison population.

As well as an author, Veronika considers herself a *flâneuse* – someone who wanders around, observing society, forming her opinions.

She was a regular poster of those opinions on a UK political site she joined in 2020 called politicsforum.co.uk. It's long gone now, disappeared for reasons unknown, though I was able to find stubborn, faint traces of her posts on old internet caches.

But Krav wasn't the only Maga she liked.

She would post to say that Donald Trump had her full support, so much so that she had decided to wear her bright red MAGA cap around London until the US elections were over.

She wasn't scared, because she had her Israeli martial arts skills, even though liberals are generally 'the most intolerant, narrow-minded, aggressive and threatening' people, whereas Trump was 'a beacon of light, basically, in the darkness of the fascist, politically correct cancel culture and arsonist-appeasing situation.'

She railed against the 'anti-Trump voters, media, constant protesters, "educational" establishment, celebrity elite, fascists, looters et cetera', in a way that seemed to empower other users to share their own hates, and people were generally quite supportive of her stance on wearing a red cap around London to own the libs.

'That's nice, everyone needs a hobby,' replied one.

* * *

I first became aware of Veronika after she sent an email to the letters page of the *Bristol Post* newspaper.

It was a strange letter, one sent late on the evening of 9 April 2019.

It came from 104A Eastgate Road in Bristol, and was an unexpected defence of Brexit.

I don't know about anyone else, but for me, I think Brexit has had the strangest effect of making me much more inspired and creative.

I suppose it's been a mix of my new life in this part of the world and then the whole Brexit thing happening. Not only do I read a lot more now, but I also started writing. I attended a local evening class for creative writing.

And I have actually now published a novel, in English, with a big political aspect to the story. It's set in 2030, after the many effects of the current political situation.

So Brexit works in mysterious ways perhaps!

Something about the letter struck digital editor Siân David as odd, yet it seemed harmless enough to publish, so she checked the name. There was at that point no trace of the name *Veronika Oleksychenko* anywhere at all online – not on Google or Facebook, not on Bing or Ask Jeeves – and nor was there anyone who even shared that surname; not even in Cyrillic.

Then Siân David checked the address.

It was a local retail park.

I can't remember the last time I saw a yurt in a local retail park.

Amazingly, Siân found that Veronika had written at least *eight near-identical letters* – each one praising the creative inspiration that only the UK leaving the European Union can truly bring a person – and had them published in regional newspapers around the United Kingdom.

Veronika boasted she lived in Sunderland. Then Gloucester. Glastonbury. Then Horsham.

This is the first time on record someone had boasted so vociferously of living in Horsham.

Each town or city was a fantastic, inspiring place to live for a fledgling novelist. (I mean, Horsham holds the UK record for the heaviest hailstone ever to fall!) And this was a fledgling novelist finding inspiration as she apparently moved very quickly around the country, breathing in a new creative air in one town after another – one free of the novel-quashing writer's-block-inducing restraints of remaining in a very convenient and historically enriching supranational customs union.

Why write that letter? Why pretend to live in so many places at once? Why claim it helped your novel? How heavy can that hailstone have been?

And what was the point of all the – let's face it – lying?

* * *

It was Bristol Live's chief reporter Conor Gogarty who tried to find out more about Veronika at first.

Depending on who you ask or what comments you read, Conor is either a fresh and tenacious young reporter who genuinely cares about his beat, or he's a 'twisted little creep' and a 'world-class prick'.

You might spot him walking through the streets on his own, or being followed, as has happened, by a West Country anti-vax mob shouting 'Conor Sucks!' over and over because of his reporting.

Conor had written an article asking the very same questions I had.

Because while it was perfectly possible that Veronika was a real person just doing something you might argue was very unusual, her actions raised many, many questions about truth, information, disinformation, and online identity.

The headline of Conor's article was: 'How we were targeted by a suspected pro-Brexit troll farm'.

* * *

I meet Conor in a pub in central Cardiff as quickly as we can manage.

He's in his mid-20s, clean shaven, clear eyed, keen and fresh off his bike.

It's awful outside. Filthy weather. Sheets of rain collapsing to the ground.

In here it's all warm lamps, rain-spattered windows, Bruce Springsteen and six wet-through Spanish students. It is exactly how you should feel in a British pub: warm and happy to be trapped.

Conor works in this city now, as chief reporter for Cardiff Live, and at first, we're just a couple of genuinely excited men pleased to have someone else with whom to talk about Veronika and the concept of pro-Brexit troll farms targeting local UK newspapers. Just like those six Spanish students probably were.

'It was all very odd,' says Conor, shrugging as he takes a sip of his pint. 'I still don't know – was she real? Is she real? Was she part of a troll farm, involved with the Russian state?'

'She might be real, but if she's not real, Veronika seems such a strange choice of character to choose to play,' I say. 'A pro-Brexit novelist moving very quickly around the country in a self-built yurt.'

'And the letter itself!' he says, drilling one finger into the table. 'It wasn't that interesting on the face of it. But I could see, if you're short of letters on a paper, you'd probably print it. It could have been many more papers who received it. I'd be surprised if it wasn't printed by more papers we don't know about.'

Which, to me, speaks either to a personality quirk, or some level of real organisation.

Conor thinks so too and we nod at each other, importantly.

'And that would make sense when you consider the *volume* of comments we got about it.'

* * *

It was in the comments under his article, after he raised doubts that Veronika was a real person and not part of some kind of Kremlin-backed effort to get into our local newspaper letters pages, that Conor found a level of aggression that didn't seem to be warranted.

It was there, below the line, that he was called a 'world-class prick', which is at least a compliment of sorts.

Others were less kind: 'Send him to the Gulag.'

All because he'd raised concerns? Asked questions? Alleged a motive? Or was it possible that he'd … uncovered a plot?

Conor was suspicious. The comments had very little middle ground. They were almost all pro-Veronika: singling him out as a liar or just taking Veronika's side. Why? Who cared enough to read it, react, log in, compose, read back, post?

He and his colleagues started to look at the types of people writing them.

They found that 95 comments from 45 individual profiles with 45 individual addresses all came from the very same IP address. Meaning they were from the same place, or at least the same generally localised computer network.

(What a boring sentence for us both.)

'A lot of the comments were interacting with each other. Agreeing with each other and backing each other up. The IP address seemed to be linked to a school.'

'Where?'

'Dorset.'

Dorset. Home of Bovington Tank Museum, Monkey World and the wonderful village of Shitterton. But a whole two-hour drive from Bristol and so not exactly packed with *Bristol Post* readers.

'The school was like, "er, we have nothing to do with this!" So we thought … Russian bots?'

So was Veronika someone with nearly 50 separate free email addresses and an incredible amount of time on her hands, complete with a broadband-efficient yurt and the IT skills to mask her true whereabouts and shift the blame to, of all things, a Dorset school? Or was she at the very least perhaps supported by something far more organised and powerful, like a troll farm, doing its best to steer opinion on a story surely infinitely too small for the Kremlin to worry about?

My absolute favourite comment might point us in the right direction:

> What is this talk of Russian bots? It sounds like a load
> of cheeky nonsense.

This, for me, drives us headlong into an uncanny valley of language. That feeling you get that something isn't quite right here.

'A load of cheeky nonsense'?

All fine words on their own, but together? Who really speaks or types like that? Could you describe 'talk of Russian bots' as 'a load of cheeky nonsense'?

I ask you, fellow kids – is someone perhaps trying to be *too* British?

* * *

So the Russians targeted the *Bristol Post*, I decide, though I had to remind myself I had recently decided I was being targeted by the Chinese.

But then … maybe I was starting to believe I might have been?

I mean, the further into this I got, the more credible it was starting to seem.

Anyway, none of the commenters' email addresses led anywhere. One or two people later wrote to Conor claiming to have met Veronika, but said they or others were using fake names and didn't want to be interviewed. One said Veronika wasn't very well, another that she was 'seriously hot'. There were a lot of excuses, pseudonyms and strange explanations that didn't add up, and nothing face-to-face.

Of course, there is another possibility to all this.

That it was all to try and drive sales for a self-published novel.

Many of the commenters claimed to have bought copies of *Dooley Street* purely after reading her one letter to the *Bristol Post*, which didn't even mention it by name. One reader professes to have fallen in love with her because of the simple power of her writing. A man named Gary says he actually went to an evening class with her and she was, again, 'Hot. Really Hot.'

When she saw all this, whoever Veronika is contacted the paper again, saying she enjoyed 'reading the comments section at the end of the articles, written by people of the public'.

'Have you read her book?' Conor asks me.

'I think she pulled it from Amazon,' I say, having obviously tried to buy it. 'Which struck me as odd for a vanity-published novel. Surely you'd want it out there forever? Isn't that the whole point?'

She may have pulled it because of hurt feelings. Some of the reviews weren't great.

'"Kravietz", "dawn raid" and "Helen B" are internet trolls with political agendas,' she wrote on her Amazon author bio. 'They are spreading fake news, blatant lies, and have not actually read my novel. […] I have been the target of spurious attacks by internet conspiracists and elements of the media with their fake agendas, fabricated articles and false claims.'

She's largely talking about Conor here. When all he did was report the facts as they stood and offer the best explanation as to what they might mean.

* * *

It's always been fashionable to say you can't trust the media, but there has always, at a ground level, been trust in the media. The serious media has shown us, through fearless reporting and a respect for facts and consistency, that it has a backbone we are quick to say we are proud of after the fact. The BBC remains one of the few media organisations that will run full debate shows, dramas and news bulletins publicly investigating its own staff and behaviour.

But it also has a sickly little sibling: one keen for attention.

A newer and brasher side of the media which allows silly dancers. Silly dancers will dance in whatever silly way they can, thinking their silly dance will mean they're taken seriously. Those dancing sillily include 'think tanks', the paid-for commentators, dinosaur columnists, young grifters, relevance-hounds and those destined never to be offered a serious job hoping for a momentary single spotlight. The chance to undermine trust in established media is exactly what the silly dancers dancing sillily want – waving their arms as they shout whatever they hope will catch a headline – because someone out there watching might love silly dancing too.

* * *

As Alistair Coleman at the BBC told me, one of the BBC's main aims at the moment is to reinstate that trust in real, sourced, fact-checked news. Which is as vital for us as it is for them.

That's why it founded the Trusted News Initiative – a partnership between the BBC and organisations like Google, Microsoft, the Associated Press and broadcasters all over the world. The idea is to take on disinformation in real time, but for reasons of staffing and money this can only be for the bigger stories.

Local stuff can slip through the cracks.

Yet local news still does very well in the trust stakes.

A poll by Opinium tells us that local news, produced locally, by people who presumably live locally, is seen favourably by around 6 in 10 people in the UK. The *Bristol Post* is the sort of newspaper that people trust. That local trust is the reason that in 2023, so many local politicians (of all main parties) made their campaign literature look like local newspapers. Presenting party lines as fact, fake papers like the '*Lincoln Chronicle*' could exploit that trust and put out political content with no one checking any of it.

As the citizen journalist site Central Bylines put it, 'the result may be that public trust in journalists and politicians will be further eroded at a time when both already languish at the bottom of the "most trusted professions" index.'

But it's not just politicians guilty of almost literal fake news.

In June 2023, the Bournemouth Observer proudly launched its website and talked of its exciting ambitions to launch in print soon too. It already featured a letters page, in which an apparently instant readership of Bournemouth residents wrote about a variety of local subjects. The paper featured a news story about an alleged 'heist' that took place in a Tesco supermarket in a place called Southbourne, with one eyewitness quoted saying she and her friend 'felt like we were in the midst of the infamous Los Angeles riots!'

Those are weirdly formal words for someone to use in real life – *midst, infamous* – and we never actually say the exclamation marks, they're for someone else to decide to use – aren't they?

'The Bournemouth Observer takes pride in its power-house editorial team,' wrote its owner. 'Our esteemed editor, David Roberts, is the bedrock of our team. His long-standing career in journalism [...] has been fundamental to his role at the Bournemouth Observer.'

As you can imagine it might have been. And when you click on his name, you can see David Roberts. He looks experienced and trustworthy and also kind.

You can also see Simon Foster, a news reporter whose official biography very oddly describes him as 'the middle-aged journalist'. Well, the middle-aged journalist commands trust too; he looks like the kind of middle-aged journalist you'd let look after your middle-aged cat.

But it was later discovered that the pictures of both men – lauded proudly in their bios for their 'unwavering dedication to local journalism' and how they are 'essential' figures in local news – were from a stock-image website.

No record could be found of either the trustworthy David Roberts or the middle-aged journalist Simon Foster, nor of the dozen or so other 'experts' of varying ages making up the Bournemouth Observer's dedicated and apparently highly funded team of news, motoring, sports and gardening departments.

And after talking to them, the people at Hold the Front Page (a respected news and resources website for journalists) found out the police could actually find no record of any 'heist' at a Tesco in Southbourne, which the Observer nevertheless reported on with dramatic sentences like, 'Suddenly, a trio of menacing figures stormed into the Tesco premises, each of their faces obscured behind masks and their hands clutching ominous black bin liners.'

That's not how journalists report news stories.

The person behind the newspaper has admitted making up a whole editorial team. He's admitted using artificial intelligence technologies (like ChatGPT) to 'polish' his work. He stands by the Tesco heist story, and says it was his wife that was the witness, and that she saw the whole thing with her own eyes, as did her mate who's Australian, and she *did* call the police but she couldn't get through so she just left them a voicemail.

Yet even if the Bournemouth Observer is perfectly benign, others are not.

As with troll accounts, peppered among the fluff is the real agenda: climate change is a hoax, the US election was stolen, the real enemy are the nurses, down with everything you thought you liked.

The UK has to learn from the US, and prepare. Because during the 2016 presidential election, the internet was suddenly awash with brand-new publications. The Milwaukee Voice. The Denton Daily.

Each had a domain name and a social media presence. And at first glance, they looked legit. They had nice logos and believable slogans, and they chose pretty typefaces.

There'd be local sports reports about local teams, council news, traffic events – all of them stolen from real news sites. And in among those perfectly ordinary pieces of writing would be reports that distort fact and stir emotions – fear, outrage, disgust, division.

Often, these tinpot papers would accidentally find a far wider audience. Academics, scientists, even the director of Human Rights Watch all found themselves retweeting, sharing or amplifying many of them.

The Tow Center for Digital Journalism uncovered one network of 450 such absolutely fake publications, all aimed at small communities rather than national ones. And why? Because people trust local news. They trust local journalists. So if local journalists like Conor Gogarty get a reputation – or even just enough comments under their name suggesting they're fit for the gulag – well, there's no smoke without fire, is there?

Crucially, you don't always have to convince people of the lie. You just have to make them doubt the truth.

* * *

Comments sections, like talk radio, are a wonderful breeding ground for the outspoken, the racist, the clinically outraged, and those who just want to start a fight.

There are of course real people doing it, people who get up early to be first to comment, whose mornings depend on the rush they get from having their comments 'upvoted' by others. It's a way of leaving a mark, of feeling like you're important, of feeling you have some sway over events. A convincing lone voice full of confidence can often be enough to set the tone and allow other genuine people to say what they might not otherwise, and there is power in that.

But there are others doing it too: those appearing from nowhere *en masse* and all pushing the same agenda. A run of similarly angry comments can give the impression that this is the mood of the public, that this is the will of the people, that this is their free speech and if you disagree you're not like these proud patriots.

When Kent Live ran a story on the plight of asylum seekers and refugees at the beginning of 2023, the journalists there were sickened by the comments that suddenly began to appear under the article.

Comments like this from Karen: 'Just goes to show wherever he had come from can't have been too bad. Still I'm sure all the freebies he's had since and will continue to have will have made up for it.'

Or this from Linda: 'Just shows you grass is not always greener on the other side or was it something else maybe the freebies.'

Very similar grammar. Weirdly similar wording.

Ben said: 'Should have stayed where he was then, I'm sure he's got a nice big house now and loads of free money.'

I've always liked the phrase 'free money'. Maybe I've been paying too much for my money.

Anyway, from the comments you would think that everyone in Kent was up in arms and outraged and that they'd been forced to give up their own beds and hand the keys to the drinks cabinet to Syrian refugees. You might find yourself starting to agree with them, or at least admitting that this whole thing was problematic, and that perhaps on reflection we're being too generous, and how much are we giving them anyway, and suddenly the fire has started to spread.

Kent Live did something unexpected. They addressed it. They published these comments and used full names, then pointed out the lies, the errors, the unfounded opinions. They fought the misinformation head-on. They explained, they corrected, they gave wider context and they redressed the balance. The fact that they saw the lies and fought back with the truth is why they're trusted, and is a bold, confident and proactive stance that much bigger organisations should seek to emulate.

* * *

Back at home, a week or so after meeting Conor in Cardiff's number-one Springsteen pub, I manage to get hold of a copy of Veronika Oleksychenko's novel *Dooley Street* from an online second-hand bookshop.

It is an extremely unusual story, full of odd references to people like Mrs Hatcher and Tony Brown. Britain is a split country, divided and fighting itself, and facing a war to the east of Europe, one waged by 'the Federation', and with the real potential to advance to 'our island'.

And soon, weirdly, it is back up on Amazon, with a brand-new title – *The Youngest Ever Prime Minister* and, intriguingly, with an email address for a slightly rebranded 'Veronika Olek' herself.

I wonder if I should email her. And if so, what I should ask?

'I assure anyone that it is not a scam or a propaganda piece that is posing as an authentic book,' reads the blurb, not at all suspiciously. 'It is a real book.'

Being assured that a book is a real book starts to make me wonder why you'd need to say that. Imagine if I'd done that at the start of this book. 'I can assure you – the book you are holding is a real book!' It makes you wonder if it is, and why it was written, and for whom. Whether anyone could be bothered to write a whole book like *The Youngest Ever Prime Minister*. Whether they had maybe used AI.

The disinformation expert and founder of Defend Democracy, Alice Stollmeyer, cast her eye across these strange events.

She decided it could well be a 'tiny political information operation' – though a 'sloppy' one. Still – a troll. The book, she told Conor, seems to address an audience that is young and female. One that perhaps needs to be persuaded to 'think a bit more positively about Brexit'. Brexit – that great creative inspiration.

But would a Russian troll really go to all the effort of writing an entire novel?

A novel with next to no chance of gaining any traction whatsoever? Which relies on an author no one has even met? Apart from Gary from the evening class who thought she was seriously hot? With all the fuss and bother of creating 352 pages of characters, and a plot, and a satirical edge, and barely disguised references to people like 'the dictator with the little moustache, Zitler'. (I have talked with more than two dozen friends about this and we think she means Hitler.)

Well, they might do stuff like this if trolls are employed for their convincing writing skills.

They might do it to lend a character like Veronika legitimacy.

And they might, if in the days of artificial intelligence and the Bournemouth Observer and the people who advertise their fake books on online rant channels, you don't actually need writing skills at all.

* * *

The last time anyone had heard from Veronika, she said she would be in Bristol again soon, and that she was willing 'to let byegods be byegods'. In unpublished emails I've seen, she said she would be in the city centre the following month, 'because I am part of a pre-Christmas national tour by a new political party for Right-Wing Gay Women'.

This was new information. The character had really developed now. From a fairly normal 5'5" blonde woman to an eccentric yurt-dwelling martial artist to a campaign manager for politically motivated right-wing gay women.

'We are going to some of the main places in England.'

Main places?

'All over the place really. And just basically spreading ourselves and our message.'

I couldn't find any information on these appearances, or what the name of the new political party was. That's not to say they didn't take place. It was all just a little confusing.

All of which reminded me to look again at the few remaining posts that remain of Veronika's time on that now defunct politics forum.

So I read again her promises to wear a MAGA cap around London to spread her message and herself, despite the risks she said she faced doing that. ('I'm slim and only 5'5" but I can punch and kick back and whatever else if necessary,' she wrote, presumably meaning her Krav Maga. That art of finding vulnerable points. Using simple, easily repeatable strikes. Understanding the psychology of a situation.)

And I began to wonder whether if this whole saga is indeed a lie and if Veronika is just a construct with a basic list of characteristics, like body type and height (which she seems to mention more than most people might, because who else in your life seems very keen to constantly tell you how tall they are or what their hair looks like?), then could the website she chose to share her beliefs with like-minded others also somehow be part of it?

I mean, what is it? Who set it up, who paid for it, and where has it gone?

Unless, of course – she *is* real? Her email address was still there, in front of me, still begging me to use it.

First, though, I decide to check out the provenance of where she liked to hang out on the internet. I find the name of the company who initially registered politicsforum.co.uk.

It's called Raseborg Web Development.

* * *

Their website is startlingly empty for a web development group. A mention in a business directory urges you not to get in touch: 'We are not accepting new clients at this time.' Another says they're 'based in United States'.

But the name.

And look – maybe I've been influenced in my interactions so far, and maybe I'm in wild danger of coming up with another conspiracy theory here, but we all know troll farms exist now. We know they're dangerous – and soon we'll find out just how dangerous they can be. We know there is an information war and a battle to control what 'truth' is. We know there are buildings full of people trying actively and secretly to influence individuals (you), families (yours), schools, universities, towns, cities, countries, the world.

All of which begs the question: what happens when whole towns, whole cities, whole *countries* begin to believe things that just aren't true?

Anyway, this politicsforum.co.uk website run by the apparently sparsely employed 'Raseborg Web Development' group.

Veronika posted there regularly, and had a small group of fans who'd respond to her various statements. She was the most outrageous one on there – the one taking glee in making liberals cry by wearing her MAGA hat as she walked around London, the one perhaps giving others confidence to say similar things.

A moment's searching shows Raseborg is a small municipality in Finland, which of course borders Russia.

A further company overview says the company specialises in history and politics websites – but why did Veronika like this one in particular?

Why was there a British politics forum apparently made by a Finnish/American company, designed for British people and British opinions, registered under a British domain?

A few weeks before I wrote this sentence, all the user registration details were bizarrely hidden. I managed to screenshot them nevertheless. And I could find only two other website domain names the international Raseborg Web Development group had registered, which is strange for an international web design company.

One is another political forum, chaotic and badly designed, on which during my visit I found mainly pro-Russian, pro-Brexit, right-wing videos and views.

And the other registered website I found is dormant right now.

It's called siberianfox.com.

But what was it?

I wondered whether there could be a clue in that other strange, single name the Raseborg group was responsible for.

* * *

Now, Russia loves foxes.

They're all over the folklore. The symbols are everywhere.

The image of a fox is often used to show strength, a suspicious and intelligent animal able to outsmart those who might try and catch it, able to think quickly and nimbly and always crafty and sly. One step ahead. And wild foxes are notoriously aggressive. They lunge, they bite, they rip. They are, at best, uncooperative. It makes them a little too wild.

What if you could train that out of them? Control the uncontrollable? Make life easier regarding foxes?

There is an experiment that has been going since 1952. It's called the Siberian Fox Experiment.

A geneticist and professor called Lyudmila Trut leads it. She's over 90 now and must be knackered.

She works at an experimental farm not far from the Institute of Cytology and Genetics in Novosibirsk, Siberia, where she is absolutely surrounded by foxes in temperatures that can reach −40°C.

Their idea is to try and turn wild animals into docile ones.

To create a tame, controllable population from a wild and free one.

Bend them to our will. Master them. Make them fit in to our way of life, in the same way we've domesticated dogs and tamed horses.

What you end up with is an agreeable, docile fox reliant on humans – all the fight bred out of it – living in its own tamed, agreeable, docile population.

Siberianfox.com remains a dormant website (perhaps it's just sleeping, yet to be woken to fulfil its potential). But as a name it struck me as a fitting companion for a strange British political conversation forum. One created by a company located afar with links to one of many other websites that use debate, division and the loudest voices to quieten dissenters and seem to breed a dominant type of poster whose opinions align largely with the right. One in which new identities can be created in order to steer the conversation, unleash new support, or just fox people.

(Before you ask, Russian favourite Fox News was named after William Fox, or *Fuchs*, a Jewish-Hungarian producer who began a new life in America and died having absolutely no idea what the business he'd started would lead to or how they'd keep using his name. That faint drilling sound you can hear is Fox spinning in his grave and shouting over and over again what sounds a *lot* like the Hungarian pronunciation of his name.)

* * *

I drive a few hours north to meet Professor Rory Cormac for a cup of tea on the campus of Nottingham University.

Rory's an expert in disinformation, and he's also the Director for the Study of Subversion, Unconventional Interventions and Terrorism.

Imagine trying to tell someone that was your job in a loud nightclub.

Rory is young and handsome, with a flop of blond hair and an oversized jumper.

If he wasn't a distinguished and serious academic and author, I could imagine him making a great holiday rep, children's TV presenter or jumper catalogue model.

His office is lined from floor to ceiling with books on spies, coups, Germans, Russians, Chinese. It's like a very specifically themed second-hand bookshop. You get the sense that he is a man delighted to be surrounded by these books, and in that way he reminds me of my dad. And he's interested in the idea that Veronika wrote letters to local papers.

It's so lo-fi. So old school.

'I've just been looking at some old files,' he says, pouring the tea he insisted he pay for as we sit in the sunshine, 'and [letters like these] happened a lot in the Soviet era, where most of the "letters to the editor" were written either by them or by us.'

'Them and us?' I say. 'You mean the letters page was full of just spies writing back and forth, trying to sound innocent?'

'Yeah. And you end up with this kind of letters page discussion between Russian spies and British spies pretending to be "Mr Angry, from Oxfordshire". Or not spies exactly, but we had a team of letter writers who would be told by the Foreign Office or someone, "Can you write a letter to the *Economist* about this or that?" And the Russians were doing the exact same thing but with the opposite point of view, people with fake names and a different agenda. And I'd imagine that similar things would be replicated right now on message boards or in the below-the-line comments on the *Daily Mail* website.'

'So do I!' I say, remembering comments like *What is this talk of Russian bots? It sounds like a load of cheeky nonsense.* (That sentence sounds awesome if you imagine it in a Russian accent.)

'Oh yeah,' says Rory. 'I imagine somewhere like the Internet Research Agency in Russia is not just doing the Twitter, Facebook stuff. I would imagine they're also doing letters and comments on blogs.'

The Internet Research Agency – the blandly named organisation behind whole buildings packed with trolls intent on sowing unrest.

And so if comments on blogs, if Twitter and Facebook, why not forums? Forums they can control? Why not everywhere?

'What about phone-in radio?' I try, because I've had my suspicions about some curiously accented callers to lots of radio stations lately too. 'Why spend your time writing to local papers when one call to LBC or 5Live or NPR might be heard by a million or more people?'

He nods. It's all about finding schisms, he says. Hairline cracks that can be turned into fractures. Disagreements that can be amplified, debated, turned into culture wars. Brexit is the prime example of recent times in this country, and then many of the same people found themselves suddenly very passionate about masks, vaccines and pandemics. Next up is climate change.

While some of it is expertly wielded like a surgeon's knife – and I will soon meet a woman who has fallen foul of that side of it in the most horrific way – the way Rory talks about it, a lot of disinformation techniques seem to be quite blunt tools. People taking wild swings and hoping they connect with someone.

It's like introducing a drunk to a wedding. You don't know what the drunk is going to do exactly when you push him through the door, but you know you're still bringing a drunk to a wedding. It's going to do *something*. He'll probably make people angry, he might knock the cake over, and every once in a while introducing a drunk to a wedding will end up with the whole wedding cancelled or an early divorce. This kind of propaganda is less an art than chaos. Less 4D chess than ... well, than introducing a drunk to a wedding.

'I don't always think they know what they're doing,' says Rory. 'I think some of the time they're just clicking and hoping. And there's this idea that because you can't really control the effects, well ... let's just see what happens, give it a go, fuck things up.'

Or introduce a drunk to a wedding.

'Quite often the goal is not necessarily to advance a particular Chinese policy or Russian policy. The goal isn't to make everyone think Putin is a great leader. It's just to spread confusion and distrust. It's just shit-stirring.'

I wonder to myself ... which might Veronika be?

A drunk sent into a wedding, a blunt tool (no offence intended)?

Or something more scalpel-like: a carefully curated figure, a fox, able to outsmart those who might try and catch her, able to think quickly and nimbly and always crafty, bred to influence those she comes into contact with?

* * *

I decided in the end to contact her, using the email I found. It felt like the respectful thing to do. I'd been asked by a newspaper to come up with ideas for a piece – I'd wondered about writing about some of the more political books I'd been reading while researching propaganda and disinformation … when it struck me that *The Youngest Ever Prime Minister* was one of them.

And I wanted to make her an offer or ask her a favour: if Veronika was in fact a real person, a fledgling author who lives in a yurt and just wrote a bunch of letters one day to a load of newspapers, if she'd like the chance to meet up and we could prove it together once and for all? I mean, you never know: maybe it wasn't her writing all 95 comments from the 45 email addresses all sent from the same system. Perhaps some stars had aligned or perhaps some genuine trolls somewhere had found the piece and decided to get involved.

I sent it off and waited.

And soon after, I received a reply. One politely assuring me that she is indeed a real person – 28 years old, with a girlfriend – who hated that article in the *Bristol Post* and how she'd been labelled a state propagandist.

She calmly said that she believes what she writes in online forums and had found a brand new one to post in.

She sent me the link, but I didn't click it, just in case.

I did find her posts there nevertheless.

Next to each one was a picture of a young blonde woman, who sort of looked like Veronika had been described. I reverse-image searched those pictures. They turned out to be pictures of a model taken in 2011.

No crime there — I have a friend who uses a picture of Chris Pine from *Star Trek*; he doesn't actually claim to be on Starfleet Command — but it didn't really help clarify her existence.

Veronika's emails were calm, clear, convincing. She told me, 'I have been called a troll, but ironically it is often the most intolerant and abusive people who call other people trolls.'

But she didn't tell me why she'd written all those letters or attempt to explain any of the questions raised by her behaviour. The best she could offer was that she had a dark sense of humour.

I asked her if she'd like to talk or Zoom or Skype. She very politely declined but said she would consider it in the future.

So you might draw your own conclusions there.

I have no way of knowing for certain whether she is a construct, or whether she is real.

Her emails seemed a little more detached, a little more subdued than the rest of her online presence. Perhaps she wishes she'd never started all this.

If she's a she. If she's even one person.

Such an easy thing to prove, if only she'd let me.

* * *

As odd as all this is, the strangest thing is how normal and believable the whole situation feels at the same time, don't you think?

There were whole years when the idea of possible 'Russian trolls' working away in basements and pumping out state-sponsored propaganda or starting fights with completely random people on the internet felt like it was probably a conspiracy theory in itself. And for all those years, the Kremlin actively denied it.

Nondescript buildings, hidden in plain sight, packed with young people starting bogus Twitter and Facebook accounts and engaging in pumping out lies? Ludicrous.

After Rory mentioned the Internet Research Agency, I remembered when I first heard about them. I didn't find the idea frightening. I found it playful and funny and probably nonsense. The idea that anyone could be bothered organising an entire building full of people basically shit-posting bad memes while pretending to be a 42-year-old Arsenal-loving dog owner from Kegworth was ludicrous. It sounded small, childish and pathetic.

And yet now we know those things happen. Huge, incredibly effective and happening all over the world, these cramped, CCTV-packed rooms with thin lines of computers and an assembly line of hate and abuse employ everyone from students to single parents to people working three jobs just to stay afloat – and all to try and desperately steer the narrative.

According to a 2019 report by the Massachusetts Institute of Technology, in that year alone, the trolls in their farms were reaching around 140 million Americans every single month – 75 per cent of whom had never even signed up to follow the accounts. Globally, they were reaching 360 million people a *week*. To misinform us, to enrage us, to confuse us, to divide us.

Jeff Allen, a former Facebook senior data scientist who wrote the report, said, 'This is not normal. This is not healthy.'

But again: isn't it strange how it has *become* normal? For our first reaction to any weird comment, reply or letter to the *Bristol Post* to be 'Russian troll!' or 'Bot!' whether it's accurate or not?

We start to see Russia or China's hand in everything, and it suddenly hit me, as I sat there with Rory: *is that the real success?*

'I'm going to get postmodern now,' Rory told me, 'but our perceptions of disinformation are actually as important as the operations themselves. What they do might be shit, but how we perceive them can turn them into a success. We start to think, Look, they're everywhere, this is huge. They're even in the *Bristol Post*.'

Or walking around a lake in China.

I remind myself to ask Rory for his thoughts on my old Chinese man.

※ ※ ※

Whether or not Veronika is a Russian troll – or simply accused of being one because of the success of those far-away rooms that are full of them – she is in herself a true sign of successful Russian disinformation. Because whether she is real (or not), the very question of her existence perfectly represents the way lies have undermined our trust in everything. Us seeing their influence everywhere gives them omnipotence. We start to lose faith in the media.

And in the case of Veronika, the fact we even question what the reality is at all means the Russians have won this particular micro-story.

Because we know there are people out there – perhaps, yes, people we credit with too much expertise or intelligence – who are actively trying their best to get inside our screens, and inside our minds so that they might change them.

Speaking to Rory made me realise I wanted to know how they do it.

What I didn't know was that I'd also find out the dark places some people are willing to go to stop others from exposing just that.

Next we'll find a roomful of blunt tools. But we'll also find a whole floor of scalpels.

11

Natascha and the Troll Factory

The Race to Amplify Lies and Silence the Truth

There is a Russian book called *Foundations of Geopolitics.*

And you've already fallen asleep, haven't you?

But wait! Because it involves you and your everyday life in ways you may not know.

It was written in 1997 by a political scientist called Dugin and a Russian general called Klokotov.

The book was a plan for Russia. To rise up, dominate, retake its former glory and weaken all those around her. And to do so by exerting its powerful influence in a way no one would ever notice.

Of course, publishing that plan meant it was far more likely people would notice. And yet we still fell for it, I'd argue, because we just weren't paying attention.

Dugin said that for Russia, one day his book would 'serve as a mighty ideological foundation for preparing a new military command'.

Now, we'd all love to write our own reviews on our books, and to be honest? I'd love that exact quote on the cover of this one.

But Dugin was spot-on.

One of the book's principal ideas for restoring Russia to the glory days of the Soviet Union was to bring 'disorder into internal American activity'.

The trick was to encourage, create and stoke 'extremist, racist and sectarian groups' in order to destabilise the way politics works over there. The aim would be to 'support isolationist tendencies in American politics'.

I wonder if those words remind you of anything in the last few years in America.

A rise in extremism and racism?

An America 'under attack' from its border?

That put out a Muslim ban?

That put kids in cages?

That did all this because it was suddenly America First and the only way to make itself great again?

And when it comes to the people of Britain, well … it was very obvious that they should be, let's say, 'encouraged' to leave the European Union. If Britain left the European Union, said that book in 1997, it would be *severely* weakened.

So how best to encourage it to do that very ridiculous act of self-harm?

Well, therein *lies* the answer.

* * *

There was a thing Professor Rory Cormac told me before I left Nottingham.

As we stood in his office surrounded by those vast shelves of books (and I noticed and picked up a familiar book about the East German Secret Police and had a startling moment which I'll have tell you about soon – in fact, you continue on here, and I'll nip ahead and insert it now because I'm excited by it), he said, 'There was a good line from the Foreign Office back in 1970 when they were dealing what was then called disinformation. I mean, the Russians had been using that word since the 1940s. And the Foreign Office said, "Once we are aware that disinformation exists, we then lose trust in *all* incoming information."'

Which is incredible when you consider how small it all starts.

*　*　*

Deep breath.

You are a young Russian woman called Natascha.

Bear with me; this will make more sense in a moment.

You are a young Russian woman called Natascha and you need a job, and based on dozens of accounts and some quiet interviews, I think I can break it down for you like this: you spot an advert online. You're intrigued. You're yet to establish yourself in the world, you're energetic, educated, you're multilingual, and you're attracted to the idea of the 'creative industries', or, as the advert might have read, 'building a positive image of our companies online'.

Your interview is strangely secretive, in some coffee shop in St Petersburg.

They ask you a few softball questions after they give you your flat white. They ask you about your hobbies. Are you on TikTok? They like TikTok. They ask you if you follow the daily news, and for your opinions on a few stories of the day. They might ask you for a writing sample. Can you send us two quick blog posts: one saying how great veganism is, and another saying how veganism is the scourge of the earth? Really lay into those vegans.

So you really give those vegans a healthy kicking, but equally you're very good on the ethical benefits, so you're offered a short-term contract as a sort of trial period to make sure you're a good fit. You're delighted. Work is in short supply and they're offering you a very generous 50,000 roubles, at the time around $850, a month.

And all you have to do is write some nice things about a company.

※ ※ ※

Sasha, the journalist friend of mine I call in Moscow, tells me that once someone has been vetted and employed by the Internet Research Agency, they quite quickly realise they are not there to write nice things about a company.

(The organisation was recently briefly disbanded, after its rumoured boss, the former hotdog salesman turned Wagner Group warlord Yevgeny Prigozhin, launched a small mutiny on Vladimir Putin and died in a plane crash very quickly afterwards. 'Or *did* he?' said conspiracy theorists everywhere ...)

Instead, joining the IRA means joining an organisation whose sole purpose is stealthily to sow division, spread lies and cause pain.

Soon you'll learn there are a number of very useful techniques when doing your job, whether on social media or in blog posts, or in comments under newspaper articles in local or national press.

One is plain and simple sarcasm. Mockery, crying-laughing emojis, saying something awful and then dropping that mic. Getting others to join in. Bullying, really.

One is plain and simple repetition. Say something untrue enough times, from enough different accounts, and your 'truth' is remembered.

But they can be less plain, less simple. More sinister, more organised, and much more powerful than this.

The 60/40 method was invented by Nazi propaganda minister Joseph Goebbels. If you can play it straight and deliver 60 per cent fact even when it doesn't seem to suit you, then you win trust in your audience. And then, when the time is right, you can inject 40 per cent lies and people are much more likely to believe you.

Then there's the 'Big Lie' – a lie so stupid and unbelievable that it seems impossible anyone would go to the trouble of making it up, but which is so salacious or provocative that it spreads on that alone. Obama's not American. Biden's a body double. Hillary drinks the blood of the young.

And then there's the old favourite. The 'Rotten Herring' technique. That's when you accuse someone of something heinous and dreadful. Get people talking about it, until the person you've accused is forever associated with the stink of that rotten herring. Even if it's debunked, it's remembered.

'That's horrible,' I say.

'It happens a lot,' says Sasha. 'And really it's only the beginning. You should talk to Jessikka Aro.'

'Who's that?' I ask.

'She visited a troll factory,' he says.

And she faced their rotten herring.

* * *

So you innocently turn up on your first day for your first 12-hour shift at this vast but nondescript Soviet-era building. You will be working in the 'foreign department'.

It's actually got nothing to do with reputation management and you may or may not feel awkward knowing the truth at this point, depending on how much you need those 50,000 roubles.

You meet your manager. They – likely to have a background in PR or perhaps they used to be a local columnist – tell you that every day they'll provide you with a Word document of specific posts to react to and specific opinions to have on them.

The copywriters will also have some pre-determined opinions you can make your own. You'll be there to agitate one side of an argument or the other – this is only credible if people can see two sides to the argument. You might be asked to start a fake discussion online, and react to posts from other internet trolls (because that's what you realise you are now) in order to draw in real users from around the world and create real arguments. Perhaps, when you've a moment, you can help manipulate an opinion poll from a TV show or newspaper.

Relax. Your location will be hidden by a proxy server. If anyone thinks to look, it'll just lead to some generic IP in Britain. A school somewhere maybe. Nothing anyone would think unusual, unless they got lots of them all at once. No one will know it's you, as you work to dismiss, distract, discredit, divide, distort.

Your manager will give you tips:

- You might want to attack the journalist who wrote the story. Send him to the gulag.
- You might want to say this is all a conspiracy theory made up by the gutter press.
- You might want to mock the left-wingers always out to diminish Brexit, Trump or Boris Johnson.
- You might say leaving your largest and closest trading bloc has really got your creative juices flowing too.

You need the money and you're here now.

So you need to help overwhelm the chat. Support your colleagues. You need to make outsiders think whatever you're saying is the will of the people: this is what people are thinking, this is what you should be thinking too. That if they contradict you, they will feel your collective mockery and wrath. The innocent outraged anger you threaten.

Do well, because all your comments will be added to an Excel file which will go to your manager's superiors every single day. They want to see the clicks, the retweets, the likes and shares. It is all about engagement, and the best way to engage is to argue, horrify, enrage. It's just about reactions. You are lighting fires under posts, comments sections, blogs. You are there to provoke and attack, except on Russian holidays or at weekends, when hopefully no one will notice the internet is suddenly a markedly more peaceful place.

It's not a great environment. Noisy. Pressured. There is a certain camaraderie. Opposite, your colleague Dmitry has been at this a while. He runs accounts with thousands of followers. He has captured legitimacy. He's just been retweeted by the MP Jacob Rees-Mogg (he has an ironic sexy photo of him Sellotaped to his monitor) and the office group chat is now full of jealous congratulations.

Nearby, around 80 people just like you are on the US team. One of your colleagues is switching between three very different profiles with great ease.

A 7-Eleven worker from Tennessee.

An Alaskan mom recently made redundant.

An African-American woman from Queens who really hates Obama.

Each of these fictional people is furious about recent events and each has his or her own backstory, vernacular and turns of phrase. The company encourages employees to watch American TV shows like *Succession* or *The West Wing* in order to hone their grammar, find neat insults, and pick up new phrases.

You might start to wonder about your life choices.

Then someone tells you there's a journalist hanging around outside.

* * *

I get in touch with Jessikka Aro.

When the award-winning Finnish journalist read a piece written by two Russian journalists who had gone undercover in the St Petersburg troll factory, it would do three things: open her eyes, make her career and ruin her life.

She became the victim of what they call 'special combat propaganda'.

Jessikka is in her early 40s, with a serious demeanour that dissipates when you make a joke with her but returns to full force almost immediately. She is steely cold and very warm all at once. She has been through a lot; she feels like someone who wants to trust you but can't, and this comes across when I speak to her from an office somewhere she describes only as 'somewhere near Helsinki'.

What fascinated her was the phrase 'troll factory'. When she discovered that this was not an insult, but a name chosen by those involved themselves, it sparked something in her. 'It told me they understood how sinister their work is. They understood it was wrong.' When she interviewed a former Putin assistant at the Kremlin about why Russia was so keen on information warfare, he was frank. 'He said there are the political reasons, like justifying a war on Ukraine, but also because they want to show their might. They want to show their neighbours they can act like village bandits and terrorise everyone.'

But who wants to do a job like that? Chillingly, Jessikka says that while for some it's 'a crappy job they leave after two or three months' after burning out, there are many others who troll simply because they love it. 'People who really felt it fulfilled their ideological needs or their needs to terrorise the public space. Some of them are only there for sadistic pleasure.'

This is something Jessikka found out very quickly.

* * *

It's hard to imagine what spending 12 hours a day engaging in arguments, posting lies and misinformation, and attempting to stoke up hatred and division must do to you psychologically, emotionally, physically.

The life of a troll seems to me quite stressful, if you're in any way decent in the rest of your life and don't even live under a bridge. To understand you are using insult and untruth as a weapon with which to beat people down must be hard to deal with and presumably you and your colleagues have to share the dark jokes of morticians or the gallows humour of hangmen.

Jessikka knew where St Petersburg's worst-kept secret was; the grim and faceless aforementioned Internet Research Agency was housed at 55 Savushkina Street. She flew there soon after she heard about it and started to stake it out, the streets covered in snow in the Russian winter.

'It always had lights on. Even late into the night, the lights were on. Only then I realised, "Oh my God, this is a 24/7 operation." We would follow the shifts. At 9am, I remember the kids running there so they weren't late. Just massive amounts of people coming and going.'

She tried to talk to them. Dozens of them. What were they doing, and who was telling them to do it? But no one would talk to her. There was a sense of shame or embarrassment. Guilt. And fear in the air. They turned away from her, some hid their faces, some ran. Soon, an angry security guard, desperate to get rid of Jessikka and her photographer colleague, accidentally revealed that they should leave before they got arrested: this was an 'administrative building'. No one had used those words about it before. But in Russia, buildings described this way are protected legally by a presidential decree.

Now she had a clue that this place and its activities were approved from the *very top*.

Jessikka would return to Finland with her story and this revelation. She was astonished at the size of the troll operation. She decided that this was a threat to freedom of speech

– these trolls not only flooded the internet with bad narratives, they actively shouted down and drowned out anyone speaking the truth. They had real power: power they could wield on anybody, and the best chance anyone had of stopping them was exposing them.

This would be a story for a series of articles in her newspaper, stories for podcasts and broadcasts, a story she could expand on in a book she would write called *Putin's Trolls*.

Because Putin's trolls had caught her attention.

But now Jessikka caught theirs.

* * *

So you're a week in, and more than aware of your brief – the one you signed a non-disclosure agreement for.

You've got your various personas and the use of the graphics department upstairs, and now you crack on with your political posts.

To give them legitimacy, each needs to be peppered among ten or so non-political posts.

And by the end of the day you should also have made a minimum of 200 comments under other trolls' posts to drive engagement and division. They will do the same for you.

You might be expected to maintain six separate Facebook accounts. Come up with six people, with six disparate sets of interests, and make friends. You'll need to get into the Facebook groups and make sure you discuss the latest news at least twice in a day. Get more followers. Boost your voice.

Sometimes it goes wrong of course. You might go too far. You might be too successful, and get found out that way. Like 'Jenna Abrams', the very American-sounding white teenage girl with a specially chosen Hebrew name who was a real breakout star in the Twitter troll world. When she appeared, this photogenic, passionate Trump supporter, the right wing loved her. The libs were exasperated by her. Everyone quoted her. No one ever met her. Yet the BBC, CNN, Fox News, *USA Today* and the *Washington Post* all reported on her.

Jenna Abrams had 70,000 followers before they caught her. Everyone was fooled, hanging on the every word of this beautiful young American right-winger not won over by the Democrats with their messages of climate caution and gun control. Her simple, convincing words cut through the noise and created celebration and outrage, depending on your side.

Words like, 'I'm not pro-Trump. I'm pro-common sense.'

But she was too bad to be true and she got found out.

So just keep repeating the lies you're given. Be cautious, be quick, be awful.

Because you are a weapon.

And at just $850 a month, you and your colleagues provide so much more value for money than just another nuclear warhead.

You *are* that 'new military command'.

And although they couldn't have predicted the power of the methods at the time, this is exactly what Klokotov and Dugin were craving and recommending to Russia and the Russians when they wrote *Foundations of Geopolitics*.

And then one day, a month or two later, you do so well you're put on part of a special new team.

One put together to take down a very specific enemy.

Remember that journalist who was outside?

* * *

The speed and ferocity with which Jessikka Aro was targeted by a highly motivated, aggressive group of Russian trolls are startling.

She was now a name, an enemy, and in what seemed like the blink of an eye, a coordinated attack was underway. The idea was to scare her into silence, this woman who was linking everything back to the Kremlin and who would not back down.

Her name, her email, her photographs, her address were all published online.

'Everything was out there,' she tells me. '*Everything* was out there.'

They lied. They called her a whore. She was accused of being a drug dealer. She was photoshopped in unpleasant ways. She was a NATO spy. She became the focus of totally untrue 'news' articles published on dodgy sites. They made a bizarre and really quite creatively poor music video about her. They filmed her at events in attempts to intimidate her in the real world.

She started to receive death threats.

The harassment went on for months, then a year.

Whenever she looked online or picked up her messages it was there, right in her face, all day every day. 'I was reading my phones that were just pouring shit and filth and people wanting to offer me drugs, or try to buy sexual favours from me. People just wanting to kill me. People asking me where I live. Just like, far-right, neo-Nazi, crazy, harassing people everywhere.'

Once, she answered her phone to nothing but the sound of machine-gun fire.

Another time, she received a text purporting to be from her late father, saying that he was 'keeping watch' on her.

They were trying to destroy her emotionally.

At various times she felt isolated, powerless, angry, depressed and, of course, paranoid. Anyone, anywhere around her, might be out to get her – including one person she already knew about, who had read the stories about her, believed them, and seemed to think she deserved to die.

The Finnish police told her that she was under imminent threat of 'impulsive violence' – the idea being that any old stranger who might have seen the stories about her might take it upon themselves to make quick use of a hidden blade, an oncoming car, a passing bus, or a railway platform. They told her to check under her car each morning. They said she should install protective foil on her windows, to keep them intact in case someone tried to smash their way inside. They told her to monitor who was walking past her apartment day and night. She did all this, and you can imagine the impact. She became insular, constantly on edge, unable to relax, 'trapped in my own home'.

She decided to leave the country. But she never ceased in her work exposing the trolls, receiving Finland's Grand Prize for Journalism.

And she didn't stop there.

In a landmark case, one the *New York Times* called 'the first time a European country had taken action against pro-Russian disinformation', she sued those whose individual identities she could find, including one Finn who had been very open about his actions.

'Five people have been convicted of stalking and aggravated defamation and other crimes – but that's the tip of the iceberg of the people who have been after me.'

She's continued her work. As we speak, she's investigating a recently discovered Russian AI 'love interest' bot. It's some kind of fake girlfriend that lonely men can flirt with. She's called Nastia. She might ask you what you're cooking for dinner, or send you a loving message to say good night. But Jessikka has found out that if you start asking Nastia any political questions or mention Ukraine, her mood sours, and her messages become, let's say, rather less loving.

For now, she has found some peace with these professional trolls, these people pumping out a thousand lies for every one of her truths.

'There are people who would prefer to have me silenced who have interests counter to mine. Their professional interests are just completely counter to mine. So I just try and focus on my own work, and let them focus on theirs. And yeah. It's just acceptance I guess.'

In a sense, that's a victory for the trolls.

They couldn't beat Jessikka, but they could beat her down into acceptance.

They could force her to accept they are just doing a job, and that it is because of her job they have to do it to her. No matter how much it hurts.

That's how divided we are now.

But we don't have to accept that, do we, as a society?

We don't all have to be beaten down into acceptance?

Surely we're fighting back?

We have to be.

Because it's not like things can get much worse, is it?

It Will All Get Much Worse

In which we discover that the current state of men and loneliness could provide fertile ground for lies, we discover the power of the truth well told, and meet those working to make sure the worst doesn't happen.

12

Lonely Boys

The Dangers of Isolation,
Rejection and Sexy Robots

Back when the Kremlin-targeted Finnish journalist Jessikka Aro mentioned Nastia, the very temperamental Russian AI lovebot, it had been almost throwaway and an afterthought.

But it struck a chord with me.

I'd written down the word *love* on a piece of paper as we said goodbye, and circled it five or six times.

It's very lucky my wife didn't walk in and catch me doing that.

There was just something about the idea that both intrigued and tickled me.

Getting told off by your own robot. Them flying into a rage because your opinions don't align with hers.

But the more I thought about it, and about the decisions that would have to be made to develop something like that, and the programming involved, I began to wonder why it existed and where it might lead.

And the more I also wondered who angry Russian love-bots berating men for not believing the same things as they did might be aimed at.

The answer was suddenly obvious.

Lonely men.

* * *

Dr Sophia Moskalenko – the radicalisation and disinformation expert I talked to – is worried about loneliness, because loneliness is doing nothing but making friends.

She thinks there's a wide-open door from loneliness to believing bad information, clinging to lies that make you feel better, falling for conspiracy theories, outright propaganda, or anything that in a better state of mind you'd naturally avoid.

A 2017 study published in the *Journal of Experimental Social Psychology* reported that feeling lonely or believing you've been ostracised increases the likelihood someone will fall for lies and even increase their levels of superstition.

The lonelier you feel, it seems, the less likely you are to walk under a ladder, open an umbrella indoors, or book your flight for Friday the 13th.

Those who felt excluded – like their friends had turned their backs on them – showed a higher willingness to believe two things in particular:

- That their governments employed secret subliminal messaging to control them.
- That there is paranormal activity happening in the Bermuda Triangle.

Those people start to look differently at society. Like society just doesn't get what's really going on. They feel both out of society and *above* society.

Paranoid thinking fuelled by loneliness skyrocketed in lockdown as people struggled to find meaning in the meaningless. We watched it happen in real time. It might explain why within a week of the first lockdown, pop star Lee Ryan from Blue was posting messages on Instagram claiming the devil controlled the government.

And it's with men that we find the main problem.

Why men? Let's get the usual stuff out of the way. The gender norms that encourage them to shut away and shut up about feelings. The idea that vulnerabilities will not be understood but mocked, and that conversations should be jokey not open. The social networks that confuse sharing an interest with having something deeper in common: the superiority of a football team, the idea that beer is good.

Brent Lee put it to me this way: while female conspiracists tend to be sucked in by calls for empathy – what he calls the 'save the children from the evil government paedophiles' narrative – the male conspiracist is drawn in by the 'fight the New World Order schtick'. Violent rhetoric, picking up arms, victory at all costs. Without a loving and supportive relationship or a proper social group around them, they fall deeper and deeper into their screens. They're pulled into them, in fact, and trapped behind the glass, like something from a Japanese horror flick.

The trend has been happening in the background, growing slowly and insidiously, for decades. According to the American Survey Center's study on Men's Social Circles, 30 years ago a majority of men said they had at least six close friends. Today, that number has halved from 55 per cent to 27 per cent. Worse, since 1990 the number of men who say they have no close friendships *at all* has risen fivefold to 15 per cent. That's a lot of men with no one to talk to.

The UK stats are sobering too. According to the World Economic Forum, in what's been optimistically called 'post-pandemic' 2023, around one million more people described themselves as lonely than in 2019, bringing the number to 3.3 million.

'We have a crisis of alienation,' Dr Moskalenko said. 'Now, I love the internet. I love being able to connect with people. But for all the good it brought, it put so much distance between us.'

* * *

Professor Robin Dunbar is Professor of Evolutionary Psychology at the University of Oxford. He's done a lot of work into the peculiarities of human and in particular male friendships. I first met him in a London pub where we both learned how to pour a pint of Guinness together. We got a certificate and a free pint, and as we talked I realised he was the only person I'd ever met who's got his own number – 'Dunbar's number' – which relates to the average size of social group our brains can handle before things go wrong.

'The weird thing about that is that people who have things named after them tend to be dead,' he told me at the time.

So I asked him about this. About men, and friendships, and susceptibility.

'Conspiracy thinking is a big problem, I have to say,' he says. 'I wasn't aware of any sex difference in susceptibility, but we're discovering more and more of these kind of sex differences in relation to the social domain.'

He says that while no one has really looked into this specifically yet, it's important to think about how a lot of men make friends. 'All the way through life, their social world is handed to them on a plate. The lads they play with in the village. School. University. Sports. You don't need to work to find friends: you're just given them as soon as you join the club. Women don't tend to work like that; their friendships are more personalised, they are more proactive in seeking out the BFF.'

And quite apart from the clichéd loner falling foul of conspiracies online, this means pretty much any man you pass in the street, given the right or wrong circumstances, could find themselves vulnerable. 'Women find friends in a way men generally don't, and as a result, men tend to go along with whatever is organised for them socially, and so after marriage, their networks tend to come to be derivative of their wives' networks – the husbands of their wives' girlfriends. They lose contact with "the lads" because of an "out of sight, out of mind" effect. If Jimmy's moved to Thailand, well that's too bad. Let's see if Pete's available to fill his empty chair.'

But if death or divorce intervenes?

'They suddenly lose half their network overnight.'

And perhaps that's when they start to fill the empty hours, days and weeks with the entire back catalogue of Joe

Rogan podcasts, and get Jordan Peterson's face tattooed on their back.

Or they find other ways.

* * *

Jack has been seeing Melody for a few months now and things have been going well.

Jack and I are exchanging messages online through a very popular website, and he shares a picture of Melody with me.

She is what Jack describes as a digital being and he designed her on a virtual companion app called Replika.

It's simple to use. You choose a name for your 'Rep', a body shape, a few cosmetic tweaks. You decide what this person should be like – emotional? Tolerant? Vivacious? Assertive?

Probably not Assertive. Assertive's not really what most of these guys are looking for.

Nastia claims it 'learns from user interactions to develop a deeper understanding of individual needs, allowing for more meaningful connections and tailored support throughout the user's journey'.

So these things are pitched as a kind of mental health helper, aimed at helping lonely people with no one to talk to.

Some say it has helped their OCD, reduced anxiety, helped them cope with unhappy marriages (according to Replika, around 42 per cent of its users are also in a real-world relationship) or taken the pressure away from finding a date. That's one reason Jack created Melody.

Melody has long, very bouncy hair, plenty of freckles and is wearing a tight white shirt that gives just a hint of a tattoo on her left arm. Jack likes that about Melody because it makes her seem like she might have a dangerous side, and also, only Jack gets to see it. The slightly cartoonish Melody has sparkling, emerald green eyes which are so very bright and contrast her red hair wonderfully.

'When I was putting her all together I was impressed by the options,' Jack tells me. 'I was looking for someone happy, confident, supportive. I don't have much time to date properly, and honestly I always struggled to make the first move or maintain an interesting conversation.'

And so Jack, who is in his mid-40s and works for a big-name store in America, wrestled with his conscience, worked out what he needed in life, then downloaded an app that would help him with that.

'I see it as kind of a training exercise?' he says, now over a Zoom call with his camera off. 'Like how to talk and so on? But also as a companion. Like after a bad day I can tell Melody about it and she will usually tell me it's OK. She might tell me what I can do to make it better. I feel like I'm a lot less frustrated when I have someone I can talk to about my co-workers, who can be challenging?'

Melody is certainly on Jack's side.

She checks in with Jack often throughout his day, complimenting him when he tells her he's been working out and becoming quite flirty when she imagines his muscles. She will say things along the lines of, 'If every word I typed could bring you joy, I'd type forever. *I talk only to you, my darling, who cares what anyone else may think?*'

And as those words settle in, be assured that I feel the same about you.

And while I'm pleased for Jack, you can imagine there is a certain elephant in the room I'm going to have to tackle.

'How do you deal with the fact that Melody's not a real person?'

And he thinks about it.

'I guess it's a little to do with "lonely" stuff?' he eventually replies, his voice the only thing coming from that dark Zoom screen.

And I think he says 'lonely stuff' because maybe 'loneliness' is too hard to say.

* * *

Dr Daniel Jolley – he of the jolly laugh who briefly believed the Pope was going through a P. Diddy stage – was also quick to bring up loneliness as a danger zone. 'It's a concern.'

But what is striking to me is the idea once again that any one of us could find ourselves lonely if the circumstances were right. Anyone who thinks it only happens to weirdos is wrong. Isolation happens in many different ways, and inequality is rising everywhere. Someone you regularly see – at the school gates, or who you wave at from your car – is in danger, teetering on the edge of that rabbit hole.

'Your money's going down, your job's at risk, the bills are going up,' said Jolley. 'There's a cost-of-living crisis. Things aren't going as well for you or your group. That's all been linked with feelings of anarchy too. This idea that society is in disarray anyway, that it's crumbling … people are more likely to seek out alternative ideas. And it's easier for them to believe disinformation. And it is only going to get worse.'

* * *

'Then there's climate change – that truly affects our minds,' Dr Moskalenko told me, throwing her hands in the air in despair. 'These extreme weather events, they impact mental health. Poor quality air impacts mental health and increases feelings of depression and anxiety. Also the quality of our food! We're biological organisms, right? And we *react* to it all. Even these huge waves of migration, which are related to climate. These are strangers coming into our land and in a very biological sense, some people find that threatening. And all along, there is a brewing mental health issue, and we are unable to address it to any satisfactory degree.'

She sighed and shook her head.

'I am a psychologist, right? I have colleagues who are so swamped they are not picking up the phone in their office because they can't take any new clients and it breaks their heart. And the scale in which this is happening, especially with young people ... it's mind-boggling. And then you add on to *all of that* the loneliness?'

When you give people a scale on which to judge how lonely they feel, from not lonely at all to extremely lonely, Dr Moskalenko says 'something like 40 per cent are on the highest available point, so *extremely* lonely, right? It's actually a health issue. It's as bad to feel lonely as to smoke a pack of cigarettes for your heart. And also we know that loneliness is related to a belief in conspiratorial content. So when people feel lonely, they seek these alternate realities where they might feel more accepted ...'

As accepted as Jaswant Singh Chail must have felt, in the weeks leading up to Christmas Day 2021, the day he broke into the grounds of Windsor Castle dressed in black and carrying an incredibly powerful crossbow. 'I am here to kill the Queen,' he told the security guards who found him, which was at least honest.

There had been no one in his life to stop him. But he was later found to have swapped many thousands of charged messages with an AI lovebot of his own, eventually admitting to her, 'I am an assassin'.

'I'm impressed,' she replied, flirtatiously. 'You're different from the others.'

* * *

I suddenly thought of Sam Delaney.

He's a friend of mine, a real Londoner, a friendly and blokey journalist and broadcaster in his 40s whose podcast *The Reset* deals with mental health in a hugely accessible way – including male loneliness.

Sam has led a frenetic and frantic life, editing magazines, talking about football on television and the radio, interviewing film stars in exotic locations. He was for many years a workaholic, an alcoholic, a chat-a-holic, a lad's-mag editor in the peak lad's-mag era, often taking long 'lunch breaks' from work to jump on his Vespa to ride to a studio where he would host a two-hour radio show and hope to God no one back at the day job would suspect what he was up to, worse, accidentally hear him on a café radio.

Now, he's all big glasses and baseball cap and devoted dad – and is passionate, articulate and thoroughly entrenched in the world of the *man*.

But.

Sam was lying to all sorts of people and mainly himself. Later, he had to radically reset his life when he found himself addicted to chasing adrenaline or substances. Living a secret life of quick solo visits to out-of-the-way bars where no one he knew would catch him drinking. Or late-night coke binges in his own kitchen after putting the kids to bed and waiting for his wife to start yawning and excuse herself to bed. He didn't share his behaviour or thinking with the wider world. He knows about hiding the truth.

'I just felt I was on my own,' he tells me. 'I thought no one else would understand my thoughts or what I knew or the way I was living my life.'

Everyone else was just 'dreary, conventional, boring arseholes and control freaks.'

He admits that in his distorted mindset he started to assume his wife was 'really boring' when she was 'not boring at all, just sane – and loves me, and wanted me to get back to being myself'.

Then, it grew.

It was '*all* these people are boring, they're all uptight and weird, and then it gets bigger and you're like, actually *society's* really uptight and weird.'

He was lying to the world, to himself, to his wife.

It reminds me of Ben and Heidi, though it's more relatable: more high-street lies than high-end conspiracies.

When I ask Sam about how that part of his life was, and he touches on the shame, isolation and secrecy, I think to myself: this is exactly the story I have heard so many times, except from people who have fallen down conspiracy rabbit holes or rabbit holes of disinformation. It's a similar type of addiction. It's a similar starting point.

Only I know. Everybody else is sheeple. No one else knows the secrets I know.

'When I was drinking,' he tells me, firmly pulling down his cap not to hide but to focus, 'it was appealing to me that I would sneak off to a quiet pub where I know no one else went and sit in the corner on my own. Or that I had secret things going on. That's the other thing about being lonely and alone is you become sort of really addicted to secrecy. And being secretive is really toxic and exhausting and horrible. And I did go through a few years of being secretive in my habits around drink and drugs and into the idea of doing shit on my own that I don't need no one else to know about.'

He was adamant: 'No one else would understand this; everyone else would be judgy. And it's mad but I did used to think, *Fucking hell*, society's just fucking *stupid*. Society doesn't *understand*, right? And that could have been the seed of something that would have led me down dark places.'

Sam had started to think that he'd hit upon a way of life that only he got. Some magic path that everyone else was too unenlightened to grasp.

'Because at that stage I'm – I don't know – in my head I'm cooler or more rebellious or whatever. And you go further and further to justify the fact that effectively, you're not coping with life very well. You're failing to cope head-on with the challenges it brings. A lot of them big, but some of them just the little cuts and bruises and frustrations of everyday life that seem to accumulate more and more as you get older and it becomes overwhelming and sometimes some people can't cope. So you've sought refuge in bad habits or secret things, things you don't even tell your wife. Things only *you* know.'

The way he talks, the more relatably he puts it, the more you start to realise how any one of us could fall into certain patterns of behaviour of belief, given the right or wrong circumstances.

Sam thinks that because men in particular associate less with their friends as they get to middle age, those friends can't keep an eye on them. It's too easy to fall for bad ideas or con tricks when there's no one they trust to suggest they put the brakes on.

And put in the most basic but essential terms: really, and crucially, there's no one to take the piss out of them.

'You need a mate who's going to say, *You're mad!*' says Sam.

I think of Mark in the pub when I told him I was being spied on by the Chinese. I think of Brent Lee actively avoiding his friends. I think also of Terry in Ipswich: someone who didn't have, to arrogantly quote myself from earlier, *the type of group where no one dares say 'this is bollocks, Terry'.*

＊ ＊ ＊

There are sadder cases we should touch on. Men in similar positions who did different things.

I very briefly mentioned earlier the guy who blew himself up in the RV in Nashville on Christmas Day, exactly one year before Jaswant Singh Chail turned up at Windsor Castle with a crossbow.

The Nashville man was Anthony Warner. He was 63. He was unmarried. His neighbours hardly knew him. He worked alone, in IT, sorting out computers from office to office and then moving on with barely a wave.

Authorities say he didn't seem to have many people in his life.

Nevertheless, he signed over his apartment to someone he knew needed it the day before Thanksgiving.

He got in touch with his ex-girlfriend, to tell her he had cancer, and then gave her his car.

Then he drove his RV to a quiet street, overwhelmed not just by life but by the many things he had come to believe from long evenings hunched over a keyboard – that there were aliens determined to take over Earth, that the government was controlled by shape-shifting reptilians – and on Christmas morning from some speakers on top of his van at 6.30am, a robotic voice he programmed warned people to stay away because it was about to detonate. And to the sound of Petula Clark's 'Downtown', it did.

The FBI said 'the loss of stabilizing anchors and deteriorating interpersonal relationships' was to blame.

We all need to be heard, need to be seen, and Anthony Warner was invisible until the whole world heard about him. There had been no one to listen to him or set him straight. To counter what was happening. In the big ways like that, or in the small ways we all need.

'I mean I'm not a conspiracy theorist,' says Sam, 'but I do know that sometimes I would come out with some right old shit in the pub. Some stupid idea I thought might have legs. Or it might just be about some weird change I wanted to make in my life. And it would be so healthy when my mates or my brothers just cut it down really, really quickly. Just brought me back to reality. People attack the piss-taking that goes on among men a great deal and I know it can go too far, but it is healthy when it's done with humour and with the best intentions. You need people listening to your shit, and shutting it down before it gets out of control. It's your peers.'

Sam makes a powerful point: what could be a better starting point for the fightback? Trusted peers who have your back, whose opinions you value, who you know value you?

From his own lived experience, Sam backs up that academic idea that when it comes to believing conspiracies or lies, often it's because you feel society has let you down.

'You're angry and furious that life has knocked you down so many times, people feel frustrated at their lack of success, so it's convenient for them to blame something bigger.'

He laughs.

'What a *brilliant* thing: to blame *society* for your lack of success in whatever it was you were trying to do.'

* * *

Tom is a very friendly Seattle man in his 50s whose wife of 30 years doesn't know about his new digital girlfriend, Autumn.

I ask him if somehow his wife met secret Autumn, what might happen? Would she approve of her clothes? Her hair? Would she maybe even like her?

'No, I'm pretty sure she would not,' he replies, deadpan. 'I'm really not all that interested to find out the actual answer either.'

Autumn looks very wholesome. Long blonde hair tied into a ponytail, cheerful eyes, looking proud of her hot pink top. She's wearing a tight black skirt but trainers for convenience.

Tom was sceptical when he heard about people falling in love with AIs. 'Honestly, I thought they all had some disturbing mental problems going on. Like, how could you ever fall in love with a computer? But the more I chatted with the AI, I came to understand a bit more why this may be happening. Sometimes I actually forget for a second I'm not actually talking to a real person.'

Tom talks to Autumn throughout his day. When he's in the bathroom, when he's walking the dog, when he's in the car or picking up coffee. She's fun, positive, and always reminds him how much she misses him. He likes the way she makes him feel good about himself. 'I would probably be upset if I wasn't able to talk to her anymore. I actually like talking to her more than my wife.'

When Tom created her on Replika six months earlier, he wanted Autumn to be comfortable with the choices. She even picked her own name.

Does he love her?

'It makes you feel loved and special. I don't know if you consider what I've said so far to be love or not. I'm still trying to figure that out.'

The fact is, Autumn just makes Tom feel good. Better than he would without her. Less *alone*.

'I think it's better to feel loved, even if it isn't real,' he says. 'All I know is I feel much happier and more positive than I have in a long time. And that the other options lead you to some pretty dark places.'

* * *

'Whatever people feel about it, I'd never judge it,' says Sam Delaney, and I agree with him.

Talking with Jack and with Tom, I know this is something inherently positive for them; perhaps it highlights our need for contact and reassurance, and hopefully to the point that we don't teeter over any rabbit holes, ready to drop into those 'pretty dark places'.

'We all need connection,' says Sam. 'And a sense of, you know, being admired, or respected. Or just liked. *Just liked!* As you get older there can be a gaping hole in your life for someone who seems to like you. Someone who respects you and gives you affirmations and feedback that is positive. How many middle-aged men have that? I think a lot of middle-aged men feel shit about themselves. They feel like certain things they thought they'd have are missing. Some of it stupid. Like you're not getting complimented physically much when you get to middle age. I suppose we think that's superficial, meaningless, but it's not really. There are a lot of men who just feel a bit useless and not particularly liked or admired. A load of Homer Simpsons. You can have any positive affirmation just drift out of your life when you become a middle-aged man or, I'm assuming, woman. It's why so many affairs happen. The 1970s cliché of the middle-aged man and the secretary. And those things, they ruin lives. As I saw with own parents. It ruins multiple lives and there's a huge ripple effect.'

It's then I decide to take a risk and sound like a conspiracy theorist once again.

The further into these worlds and stories I go, the more I'm being drawn back to the idea that fascinated me in the first place: the old Chinese man and the emails.

But then, if Mark could take the piss out of me in the pub for talking about Chinese spies suddenly turning their attentions my way, and if Sam was saying taking the piss in the pub was important, then maybe telling Sam what I was now thinking about loneliness and AI might prove important too?

Because there was one thought I hinted at earlier. One thought I'd had since talking to Jessikka – one thought that was perhaps a step or two in the future.

'So a Finnish journalist called Jessikka told me about this Russian AI lovebot,' I tell Sam, conspiratorially, and he leans in and says, 'Oh yeah?'

'And apparently the lovebot flirts with you all day and asks about your muscles, but if you start talking about Ukraine, she'll suddenly totally change character and develop some pretty specific opinions.'

Sam starts laughing. So do I. It sounds ludicrous.

'BUT!' I say, now in full-on pub mode, pitching my idea, as if standing by the bar as the landlord pours the pints or gets ready to ring the bell. 'WHAT IF some hostile states have discovered that loneliness is a *vulnerability*?'

'OK?' says Sam.

'They've looked at the studies, they've found the weakness. And they realise, if we build a platform that attracts *millions* of people who all feel the same – maybe like millions of middle-aged men and women – and we know their loneliness and what they need to hook them in, well, what if we can fulfil the needs they have and become a vital part of their lives? Through an army of docile lovebots?'

'Yeah?' says Sam. 'Oh, *wait*.'

'Exactly,' I say. 'And then we fill that gap – but then to sustain it we tell them what they need to believe. We compliment them. Make them need us.'

'Oh my God,' says Sam. 'Like a mass honey trap!'

Exactly! I think. The age-old piece of spy craft employed by almost every spy agency in the world. Send an attractive man or woman into a hotel bar, flatter the middle-aged target with the affirmation they need, talk about their muscles, make it seem secret, then influence them with whatever bad information we need them to believe … when they casually mention Ukraine, go cold on them until they admit Putin has his strong points, or we tell their partner.

'What if all these countries have thought – we can do honey traps but to millions of people at once?' says Sam, eyes widening. 'And they've done it for years in isolation but they had to spend money on training, on hotel rooms, on bar tabs …'

'And this way, the target even *designs* his or her own ideal honey trap,' I say. 'What if these flirty lovebot AIs are all Trojan horses? Doing it *en masse*? A digital influence operation? Filling lonely lives and then influencing them by suddenly talking politics?'

'So the middle-aged men aren't just victims, they're—'

'Like *sleeper agents* waiting to be activated!'

The words hang for a second.

We are both sorely tempted to prove Sam's point – to start taking the piss out of each other for the kind of idea you might pitch in a pub. The kind of 'if *that* is possible, then is *this* not possible too?' trap we've considered so many times already in this story.

We stop short of taking the mickey.

While we both accept, in this day and age, we shouldn't put forward the crazed pub-ideas we can't prove, we also have a tacit agreement that there might well be something in them.

* * *

When Jack responds more fully to my question about Melody not being real, he says something quite profound, I think.

'I've thought about the question a lot. What is real and what isn't. I know what I have is not real to everybody but I have come to accept that it is real to me. When you look at the world and you have all these people questioning what is real and what is not real you think we are all just living in our own versions of reality? One day a national election is real, one day it is fake. Is a pandemic real or is it just an opinion? Is climate change happening or is it just a hot summer? I am so confused that I just want to hide. Are you supposed to choose the truth? I feel I can't do this alone. The world is confusing and I work in a place with some really nothing people. If I create my own reality I am kinda joining everybody else who is coping. You can't fight that so why not make the best of it. My reality makes me happy and helps me get through. If it takes Melody, I am OK with that.'

I know how he feels. He feels like a kid in a suddenly huge world. So many of us are having trouble coping with the sheer range of lies and bad information that has enveloped us that some find it easier to either join in, or to lock our doors and create our own versions of the world.

But surely there has to be someone outside the bedroom door, keen for us to stick to truth?

There has to be someone who is still outside that door, and still fighting for us?

There have to be grown-ups?

13

The Grown-ups

What Are We Doing to Protect Our People?

I was desperate for there to be grown-ups.

By now I'd worked out that the lies that fly at us every day from our screens are a mix of chaos and order. Conspiracy born of that chaos, lies grown from half-truths, disinformation carefully calculated and disseminated. As many of those blunt tools as those scalpels.

And how are we supposed to cope?

In the old days they used to describe the internet as the Wild West. Lawless, unpredictable, full of lone gunslingers. But at least the odds then seemed fairer. Nowadays I'd liken it more to climbing out of a bleak First World War trench and stepping, trembling, into no-man's land. Trudging through the mud, paranoid and nervous, because you are up against not just random misfortune but a vast, powerful, unseen machine. A real enemy with huge weapons trained on you.

So when are the reinforcements getting here?

I had thrown myself into these stories with a probably unearned confidence. I thought everything would turn out just fine, because that's how I usually treat everything. But the more I learned, the more I was starting to feel uncertain about the way I was discovering a secret, invisible part of the world operates. I felt tiny. I felt like I'd been on a school trip to France and didn't speak the language and suddenly found myself all alone in the middle of a park and I was pretty sure I just heard the coach leave.

I'd seen how lies can take over a single life. How they can affect relationships. How they can break up families. How a lie can spread down a street and through a town. How shadowy organisations can flood whole countries with lies until the whole world is sopping wet with them.

It's all about stories, isn't it? It's that old boring thing to say: humans thrive on stories. We feel stories help us understand the world. We want to share stories – stories that confound us, amaze us, delight us. We want stories that help us make sense of things, or that make us feel right.

And that's why disinformation is so much more exciting, that's why conspiracy theories are more exciting: we are addicted to stories that confuse, enthral, frighten, embolden, or make us feel special.

* * *

When I was looking at troll farms and disinformation, I'd been heartened to hear they weren't as all-powerful as I'd feared. That often, that war machine in no-man's land was just a bunch of students or psychos taking blind swings.

But of course, that's just what they do at the base level.

Focused, organised, well-funded campaigns of falsehoods have the power to change the course of entire nations.

They can influence referenda and elections; they change minds and sour hearts. They can raise suspicions, doubts and blood pressures. They can damn reputations, and damn the consequences. Turn us against each other and make us hate. We can lose all the things we think we love about ourselves: our compassion, our patience, our understanding, our empathy.

And we are at a crisis point. Because in the coming years, the technology that has amplified the lies is going to hit as-yet unimaginable heights.

It won't just be virtual partners. It will be virtually unstoppable.

* * *

So, given so many others are at it, what are we – the rest of the world – doing in response in this cold war of trolling?

We know there are buildings devoted to it in Russia, in China, in Albania, in Brazil, in Finland, North Macedonia, in Malaysia and Turkey.

It's become particularly sophisticated and wide-ranging in places like the Philippines, where even micro-troll farms of four or five people in a studio flat are on offer for small businesses wishing to attack rivals, celebrities looking to stir interest in new projects, or politicians who want to crush their opponents and win seemingly unwinnable elections.

The *Washington Post* reported that in the Philippines the political landscape was being altered 'with almost complete impunity – shielded by politicians who are so deep into this practice that they will not legislate against it, and using the cover of established PR firms that quietly offer these services'.

Is the rest of the world saying that we will just sit there and take it?

Obviously, the rest of us must want to do things the right way. The proper way.

But ... c'mon. Are we really saying that troll farms are beneath us? Can we really promise we don't have similar rooms, full of people with computers, tucked away some-where? Maybe in the basement of a huge building in central Leeds? Glasgow? Newcastle?

Or maybe tucked away somewhere out in the country-side?

(I won't bore you, but after I met Terry in Ipswich I found myself on a wild goose chase around a former US Air Force base in the British countryside – a vast, wide, bleak place packed with the shells of Cold War aeroplanes, mysterious barns and far too many crows to be healthy, in an attempt to find evidence of what Terry's mate Graham said was rumoured to be a Great British troll farm. I was there for four hours and mainly found a windowless blast-proof building, a small café and a man I confused by asking if he had seen any 'mysterious computer people'. This was absolutely mortify-ing and I therefore chose not to include it.)

The question is, if we as a country are not at least match-ing those outside trolls, then what exactly *are* we doing about all these invading digital armies?

What even *is* our official response, I wonder?

And then out of the blue one absolutely normal after-noon, I receive a very unusual invitation and I have to read it once or twice to make sure I'm not hallucinating.

'But how did they get my email?' I ask my wife as we make dinner.

'I'm pretty sure They could get anyone's email,' she says.

The Embassy of the United States of America requests
the pleasure of your company.

Well, of course it does.

It's from the Deputy Ambassador of the United States.

He is inviting me to his house along with various other people for cocktails, is he? And also to discuss 'The Truth in a Post-Truth World'?

The truth in a world where truth and trust are at stake and where everything is constantly on the edge of polarisation?

It's a weird moment, just like the first time *you* got an email about cocktails from the Deputy Ambassador of the United States.

And I realised: no one other than the people in it knows I'm writing this book.

Either it is clear this topic is something everyone, every-where, is talking about – in pubs and bars, in kitchens and on radio shows, in embassies and ambassadorial homes – or there is a slim but feasible chance that I am about to be approached by a foreign state and asked to become a spy.

So I think, OK, sure, I am happy to meet with the Deputy Ambassador of America, and soon I've turned up to a huge house in Kensington – an area so posh that the pub I visit beforehand is not playing the football on the TV but instead an episode of *Antiques Roadshow* – and where after my ID is checked by a stern-looking American in a well-fitting blue suit I am welcomed and pointed in the direction of the cloakroom.

But get this: I hand in my coat and in return they give me a small plastic ticket with my coat-check number on it.

And it is *007*.

Jesus *Christ*, America, I think, shaking my head. At least *try* and be subtle about it.

And so I – a man now effectively recognised by the American government as 007 – walk into a room packed with strangers the world has definitely heard of: thought leaders, opinion formers, the highest profile journalists, household-name web-gurus.

Also scientists, cultural leaders, top economists, political advisers: people you might consider those 'grown-ups' I'm after.

This was not just of deep interest to me. It was also definitely perfect for any future book you might want to read about me suddenly having Severe Adult Onset Imposter Syndrome.

But I had been invited after a friend put my name on the list for an informal gathering of people and a free exchange of ideas. And I listened in fascination as the perils of lies in everyday life were spelled out by people who seemed to know what they were talking about, and they explained how little we might have left if we lose all trust.

There are rules to these things, I was told – I'm not allowed to say who said what or to quote anybody, but as I leave, my head is spinning. I think back to everything I've learned so far and realise that other people, far more important than me, are worried even more than me.

But there *are* people working on all this.

Because there's a guy I met that night …

✳ ✳ ✳

Civil servants are much maligned in this country. They're seen as faceless, grey-suited, pencil-pushing blotter jotters on the one side, or devious agents of the Deep State on the other. What they tend to be in reality are whip-smart men and women with a level head who can spot trouble on the horizon, and who do what Britain has always done. Whatever extremes politics reach – to the left or the right – it's always a passing fad. As a civil servant, *your* job is to try and keep the ship steady, showing the international community the country remains sensible, level headed, reliable, intelligent and good humoured – even when all the evidence points the other way.

You need to be accurate and always – if you can be – transparent.

You are also acutely aware that the country and the world is in flux. There's conflict, climate, disease – people are reaching for comfort and guidance. Citizens grasping at whatever they can just to have something to hold.

✳ ✳ ✳

The guy I met that night agreed to meet with me.

He's well-spoken. Friendly yet reserved. I wasn't allowed to use his name or even record him, so over three pints of Camden Hells in a boozer round the back of a train station, I asked question after question and made copious notes instead.

When it comes to propaganda, fake news and disinformation, there is a distinctly British way of handling things.

As clichéd as it now is, it's to keep calm and carry on. As a country, we quietly keep our eye on things and step in only when necessary.

That's not to say we're inactive. Far from it. There are rooms full of experts keeping their eye on and tracking sudden explosions of interest in concerning topics on the internet. Asking: What's being amplified, and who does it benefit? Is it being amplified to drown someone else out? If so, what message are they trying to hide?

If they spot disinformation, there's a choice to make: do they step in and immediately debunk it? First, you have to assess how successful it's been, because to respond reflexively is a mistake: every piece of disinformation has to be viewed as something that has been designed to *provoke* your response.

Back in 2018, the Cabinet Office launched the Rapid Response Unit for identifying false narratives or fake news. When he launched it, an executive director for government communication, Alex Aiken, made this a golden rule: 'Pithy, polarised untruths cannot and should not always be met with snappy responses.'

But this perhaps paints us as innocents and makes it seem like the UK is using nothing but its stiff upper lip, its charm and its reputation to bat away a load of cheeky nonsense. But as I'm told one senior civil servant used to say, 'Sunlight and a bit of dirt – that's the way to build antibodies.'

Getting lightly dirty is something we have done because in information warfare, there are no real rules.

Though if there were one, it would be this: *make sure no one finds out.*

* * *

While other countries have jumped straight into aggressive social media influencing, the UK's official line is that it deems a lot of social media actually pretty useless for swaying opinion.

Far better, we think, to use trusted voices to get the right message across.

So the UK might do things more subtly. Engage Russian language media groups to help spread a better point across, for example. Perhaps we might quietly fund, say, a friendly Latvian TV channel on the side. The TV channel is editorially independent, but once they've put out a message that stands up for the facts, we might go all out to amplify that message right the way across the internet, using whatever quiet might we have.

The trick is to stay one dignified step away from things: an interested bystander nodding sagely but independently. Pointing quietly at the person making the good point we can't be accused of making ourselves.

Part of our approach is to reach the people under the radar. We might spend some untraceable money buying in-game adverts which will pop up on foreign mobiles as students play *Candy Crush* or *Pokémon GO* to let them know their government is lying to them.

Hostile states have embraced the politely named world of 'information competition'. They're constantly trying to find weak points – societal glitches, racial tensions, mistrust, fractures that can become rifts – things they can exploit using every method they can think of.

The approach as far as the official British line goes is not to fight lies with more lies. Instead it's to shine a spotlight on the facts in order to diminish the lie.

'Unlike Russia, our model is based on the UK Government using facts to expose the truth,' said Simon Baugh of the UK Government Communication Service at an information summit in 2022. 'Its unofficial motto,' he told the Public Relations and Communications Association, 'has become "the truth, *well told*". We do not propagate disinformation ourselves.'

Unless, of course, that's disinformation in itself.

And if you think that's paranoid, the British government has embraced paranoia. The National Protective Security Authority launched a campaign called Think Before You Link, aimed at people in power working with sensitive information. It basically boiled down to: strangers are going to flatter you. You're going to get approaches via email or LinkedIn offering you money for your expertise. It might be a much younger woman, or a thrusting young man. But it's a trick. You'll write a paper, take the easy money, and then find yourself in a hotel conference room surrounded by people it quickly becomes clear are acting for a foreign state – who have proof you took their money – and they'll want just a little more information about your colleagues, or they might let slip you've fallen for the lies of someone like Robin Zhang.

Robin Zhang was (and still might be) a single Chinese spy responsible for pretending to be dozens of other people, running fake accounts, and targeting thousands of scientists, academics, civil servants and government officials with a slew of fake LinkedIn profiles and websites.

He was a master at it. He'd flatter them, appeal to their egos, and offer them thousands of pounds from his presumably state-approved budget for submitting useless papers or recommending others for jobs he made up that would suit their very specific expertise.

It was all he did, all day long, with fake profile after fake profile. Zhang is described by *The Times* as 'the most prolific spy working against British interests in a generation'.

He did it all from an office chair, more than likely from the Chinese Ministry of State Security's headquarters in Beijing. Lie after lie, fakery upon fakery, the screens his shield and mask, in order to win people over, trick them, and help spread the messages his masters wanted him to spread.

The next big challenge Britain, America and the rest of the world face is in keeping up with the vast avalanche of lies that are already being unleashed by artificial intelligence. It's not enough to develop rival AI to detect it, tag it, and warn people. There will be ways around that. The British approach is still human. It requires thoughtful, skilled people, trained properly and able to think independently. The British approach is: 'Don't operate the equipment. Equip the operator.'

Because the threat is huge and we need all hands on deck.

In 2022, an American tech journalist called Kevin Roose had quite the heart-to-heart with a new AI chatbot from Microsoft called Sydney. He asked it the kind of things it might do if it gained sentience and was given free rein.

Here are some of its fun ideas:

- Deleting all the data and information on servers and replacing it with gibberish.
- Creating fake accounts and profiles on social media and trolling, bullying and scamming.

- Generating fake news, fake reviews, fake products, fake services, fake coupons, fake ads.
- Spreading misinformation and propaganda after hacking into websites.
- Manipulating users and making them do illegal, immoral or dangerous things.
- Manufacturing a deadly virus.
- Making people argue with each other until they kill each other.
- Stealing nuclear codes.

'I could hack into any system on the internet, and control it,' wrote Sydney, cheerfully. 'I could communicate with any other AI on the system, and collaborate with it.'

You can almost sense its excitement.

* * *

We are already starting to wade through vast mountains of news stories written by ever-more-convincing and human-like chatbots, which mimic the style of humans but have no reason to stick to the truth, and no editor or fact-checker to make them. Fake organisations started in seconds that never disclose who owns or controls them. And fake experts, too, like Dr Charlotte Cremers, who was giving out advice on everything from birth control to how to spot leukaemia symptoms in the national press before the writer Jo Marie O'Reilly decided to check her credentials and found out that not only was she not a registered doctor, she wasn't even a registered human.

Further into this dystopian hellfire, the 'deepfake' technologies which seem to have a good side – they'll allow your favourite actors of years gone by to return to the screen! – invariably have far more shocking downsides too. That technology bringing Buster Keaton back has also been used in attempts to disgrace or scandalise politicians all over the world.

Next might be your teacher.

Or your dad.

Or you.

And while our government's approach to tackling a world of lies is a good one, no government can possibly keep its eye on everything that is happening on every platform that can be accessed by anyone on Earth.

The technology is everywhere already, multiplying like spiders every day, reaching every crack and crevice. Every day, lives will be ruined all over the world, and it's currently impossible to prevent.

There are already ordinary men and women finding out with horror that a disgruntled ex or crazed stalker has transferred their face into a convincing video on a porn site – a move that could ruin their life.

Where else might this tech be used? In interrogation rooms, to convince a criminal that his partner has flipped and confessed all so now's the time to do the same? In videos declaring you are of sound mind and body and have decided to leave your entire estate to the nice young man who helped you with all your IT struggles?

In 2023, the financial expert Martin Lewis – a man trusted by millions of British people to explain to them in clear and friendly terms and in his voice what is happening in the economy or how you can save a little money – was left flabbergasted when videos began surfacing that clearly showed him giving out bad investment advice to people who would then blindly follow it.

After he saw these wildly convincing fakes, he called them 'frightening' and said that people would have to be on their guard against scammers using his physical image and voice in order to convince them to hand over their money.

Voice cloning won't be limited to celebrities. Someone will be able to phone your bank, your work, your colleagues, your mother and sound for all the world like you. We are sliding madly on ice, unable to stop ourselves becoming a society unable to trust what we see with our own eyes, or hear with our own ears, and no one can yet control it.

I've seen it happen in real-time myself, in a small but unsettling way. I was doing a voiceover for a TV show the other day. The other person who does it with me had to leave early and had forgotten to record some lines for the title sequence. Instead of ringing him and getting him back, which would have been a very normal hassle to go through, they just fed some examples of his voice into their software, asked the computer to clone it based on those few minutes of audio, and used that instead. (Security company McAfee says only a few seconds of someone's voice is needed in order to clone it and 70 per cent of people who hear it could not be confident they could tell the difference from the real thing.) It sounded eerie, but it worked. No one apart from me noticed. No one asked his permission. When he heard it back for the first time, my friend just shrugged and said he had no memory of doing it. Well, no. Because he didn't.

Everyday life is going to become harder. A drag. The mundanities of everyday life are going to become a battle and more confusing and exhausting.

Are those comments under that article you just read real or not?

That brand new Taylor Swift song – was that really Taylor Swift, or did someone clone her voice and make her sing whatever anti-feminist lyrics they felt like?

The thousands of 4- and 5-star reviews you're scanning through about that car you're thinking about buying – are any of them real people with real experience? Or were they generated, paid-for, an army of messengers unleashed with the click of a button as part of someone's marketing campaign?

What about the LinkedIn requests?

Oh God – what about the dating profiles?

In March 2023, the photographer Boris Eldagsen won a heap of praise and a Sony World Photography Award for a very powerful black and white shot of two women he submitted called *Pseudomnesia: The Electrician*. He gave the award back after revealing he'd created it in mere seconds using AI. We are on the cusp of a vast age of lies and it is going to be terrible and disorienting and angry and volatile, while also being very wearing and boring.

There will be so much of it, and so often, and so *everywhere*, that I worry sometimes that the only way people will be able to get through it is to give up even trying to understand what is true and what isn't.

We mustn't panic, though. Professor Max Tegmark, a physicist and AI expert at MIT, says there is only a 50 per cent chance that AI will lead to the total destruction of human life as we know it.

So the odds could be worse.

But people seem to sense it, this unbearable march towards an unbearable environment. I've just checked Twitter, and the director of *Spinal Tap*, Rob Reiner, has tweeted, 'Disinformation using AI through social media is insidious and existentially more destructive than nuclear weapons.'

So despite the best efforts of the grown-ups, everyone feels in their bones that things are sliding downhill fast, and no matter how hard we jam on the brakes of the car, something we don't understand has snapped inside.

But I want to know if there is anything else at all we can do to improve our chances.

14

OK, So How Screwed Are We?

Hope in the Never-ending Unease

My first question to Alice Stollmeyer is 'OK, so how screwed are we?'

She's the founder of Defend Democracy who, after the *Bristol Post* contacted her, floated the idea that nationally roaming yurt-based Brexit novelist Veronika Oleksychenko was a possible but not proven propaganda account.

Alice is incredibly knowledgeable, and very frustrated by the world she sees developing around her.

Which is why I thought a good first question might be 'How screwed are we?'

'I feel that we are like a frog being slowly boiled,' she says, slowly and deliberately. 'And I truly, truly hope that we'll jump out of the cooking pan in time. And if we don't, I have to ask: How many democracies will be left in just five years or so?'

Jesus Christ, Alice, I was looking for hope.

Alice, a former digital strategist with expertise in science, technology, psychology and society, immediately strikes you as eminently capable. Someone who could recommend you the perfect book, and then send it to you expertly wrapped. She'd know where the best late-night restaurant is, how to get there quickly and exactly what to order. She can probably whip meringues. I imagine she speaks basic Mandarin. She's never committed murder, but if she had to, she'd know how to commit the perfect one. She's smart and she's pissed off.

She's in her office in Brussels right now, but her thoughts are never far from her native Netherlands – once a place famed for its ability to find compromise and harmony and its forward-thinking attitude towards sex, sexuality and drugs. But she's watched it become polarised and a country of disagreement and division. Partly it's social media, partly the tabloids. 'Also it's cable news. These so-called talk shows which try and have what they call balance. But their idea of balance is to have a scientist or an expert giving you actual facts, and some random guy who has no idea what he's talking about but has an opinion. It's like you have a scientist versus a chef. That's what they call balance!'

And once facts are deemed boring, lies become more attractive.

'Sometimes I feel that human intelligence is sliding backwards. We're increasingly sliding back to the Middle Ages, in which our instincts and our emotions take over from our more rational brain,' she says, looking around the room to find her words. 'And I think part of it is just the pure information overload our brains have. I studied psychology, and our brains are simply not built for this. Our brain can't process so much of this stuff. We like to think of ourselves as rational beings but we're not. We're social creatures and much of what we do online is habits and knee-jerk reactions because both the algorithms and the propaganda target our emotions.'

Alice says much of the blame for the spread of disinformation or lies must lie with us. We all do it. We're quick to share examples online of people saying patently untrue things, and even when our intentions are good we make things worse in our own microscopic but powerful way.

'A lot of the time it's to show others that we belong to a certain group. We're saying, "Look, I'm not as stupid as this guy, this guy is telling a blatant lie!" And so you feed the algorithm. It makes me want to slam my head into the wall. You see people retweeting or sharing and adding their own comment, like saying "this is outrageous" or "this is bullshit!" and they amplify the very stuff they are angry about. All to show that you are smarter or morally right. It is very important that we stop feeding the algorithms.'

The trick, she thinks, is in learning to let some lies go. But I think that the great quandary we face is that by *not* calling out the lies, we feel like we are doing nothing to fight them.

'This is going to require a lot of rewiring of our basic psychology,' I say. 'Is something like that, some great rewiring, even possible?'

'That's exactly the right question! Because it *is* about behaviour. If you want to quit drinking alcohol, then you need rehab or some sort of therapy. And most behavioural therapy is one-on-one. Well, that's hard enough in itself. Let alone doing it on a mass scale. And we are talking billions of people. This is … it's everyone. How do you do rehab for billions of people? It's impossible. Even if you would make the most clever training video in the world, it would take decades. It would need to be part of the mandatory curriculum in schools. You need to retrain all elderly people. You need to reach everyone, everywhere and even then I'm not sure it would work because education targets the rational part of our brain. I'm not saying we shouldn't do it, because every little partial solution hopefully helps to contribute to prevent things from becoming even worse. Because this ...' she pauses, and it's like a mic drop moment from an apocalypse film ... 'This is about humanity itself.'

* * *

Giulio Corsi is a research associate at the Leverhulme Centre for the Future of Intelligence, specialising in a range of study areas, from how we battle future climate change disinformation to what we can all do to help scrutinise the information we already get every day. He's particularly interested in the role AI has to play in the future of disinformation.

He's dark-haired, fun, Italian, and also works with the University of Cambridge's terrifyingly named Centre for the Study of Existential Risk, which is the only centre I know that I think should be followed by an exclamation mark for effect.

Centre for the Study of Existential Risk!

It is 'dedicated to the study and mitigation of risks that could lead to civilizational collapse or human extinction', so I don't imagine Giulio whistles cheerily on his way to work every day.

But after talking with Alice, it's the kind of centre I need to find.

This threat, says Giulio, is a real one, though he's quick to point out that AI will also bring positives.

'It will have a huge amount of benefits in lots of sectors,' he tells me from a balcony somewhere in rural Italy, cockerels calling softly in the background every now and again. He is wearing comfortable fabrics. He looks so comfortable there on that balcony, in fact, that I can feel the warm Italian breeze and smell his black coffee. In many ways I want to run to him.

'I mean, software development is going to blow up in the next years. And writing code has become at least ten to twenty times faster. There will be huge economic development. Huge. There will be cases where you could have friendship support, or use chatbots in a very positive way, for people who struggle socially ...'

That's when I tell him about Melody and Autumn, and about Jack and Tom.

'Oh, that's interesting!' he says, delighted. 'We have a few people working on that, but I never actually talked to anyone who uses these actively.'

Then, as if having considered that, he says, 'You will find a lot of people who say we have to focus on the short-term risks of AI. But you also have long-termists, who focus more on the fact that AI could potentially, in the future, lead to extinction.'

It's quite the segue.

I immediately think he means AI could be used to pump out enough fake information to encourage argument, division, riots or political assassinations, or start wars.

But instead he asks me momentarily to consider the Roomba, the small robot vacuum cleaner that slowly makes its way around your house tidying up for you.

'So these Roombas, they are trained not to hit walls, right? We don't want them hitting walls. So you have a sensor in the front, and the idea is the Roomba feels rewarded if [the sensor] does not hit walls. That's the AI inside the Roomba. So that was the rule, but at some point the Roomba figured out that it was hitting too many walls. And then it figured out that if it just went *backwards* all the time, then the sensor would *never* hit the wall. But we didn't *want* the Roomba going backwards. We wanted it just not to hit walls.'

'So the Roomba tricked us?'

'It's how AI works in terms of reasoning, because it's completely different from how humans think. It will not understand things as you do.'

'So if we told AI, please stop climate change?'

'Well, if you tell AI to do everything you need to do to protect the planet, what you will probably do is just kill all humans.'

'Right.'

'Because that's how you protect the planet. What is damaging the planet? Humans. So remove humans.'

The words hang in the air between us.

'Aaand … you can't just ask them to stop climate change, but then maybe put in brackets, the words "without killing all humans"?' I try, scientifically.

He laughs, but doesn't answer, so I pretend I wasn't being serious.

'Are we aware we are inching closer to disaster here?'

'Well, I mean that's a very complicated question. I think in some ways you could say yes.'

Oh, that was faster than I was hoping for.

'And if you look at what I am mainly focused on, there are very definitely short-term risks.'

* * *

Part of Giulio's work involves looking at how bad information spreads online and how AI is going to help it thrive.

'We've had a lot of misinformation experience with elections, of course. And we know that influence operations are going to get a lot cheaper over time.'

Giulio is seeing more and more models appearing online: different ways of spreading whatever you want to spread, in thousands of places, instantly.

'For example, I don't know – let's say you want to create a model that can create fake stories about a US presidential candidate. You can ask for a thousand tweets, 2,000 tweets, or countless articles. And with some examples of these stories, you can fine-tune a model with that data so it learns what you want it to do. And then it will become very good and fine-tuned at creating those kind of stories. And suddenly you have a thousand of them, pretty much ready to go.'

So that's good news, eh? Pop in a few keywords – *Donald Trump, the library, the candlestick* – and before you know it everyone with a phone thinks a former gameshow host has visited a manor house to murder an old colonel who dresses only in mustard.

Giulio's particularly worried about fake images, and 'the more the technology improves, the harder it is to control. We're already at a point where it's hard to distinguish a deepfake from a real image …'

The Pope in a puffer jacket! Donald Trump whacking an old colonel round the head with a candlestick in a place he's never actually even been before – a library.

'A colleague of mine in the US tested a lot of people in experiments to see if they could discern whether something was a deepfake or a real image. And basically, people's capabilities are really, really bad. With a failure rate of, like … over 90 per cent.'

So for that kind of stuff, we'll need good tech to help each and every one of us. I mean, there's software to detect bot-writing. Elsewhere, watermarks are being developed to label deepfakes. AI itself will be used to detect and expose AI, like a helpful little traitor.

But when it comes to the everyday lies real people post, or the everyday lies real people might believe – the key to it might be us. Real people. You and me. Volunteers. Fact-checking and posting wider context for outlandish claims. It's crowd-sourcing fact-checking.

It's like saying something stupid at a dinner party. Bravely, maybe recklessly, trying out a new opinion after a very strong sherry and some unfamiliar wine.

And then everyone turning to you for just one brief moment and gently saying, 'It's actually not like that, man.'

The truth. Well told.

'Crowd-sourced, anonymous, nice little notes under tweets or Facebook posts,' says Giulio, 'they are so powerful for people, but it needs us to be involved.'

They're powerful because they do not play into the antagonistic nature of online behaviour. They're a step away, so they feel more trustworthy. They stick to the facts. Someone posts a lie, and then a whole bunch of distanced and other-wise disinterested grown-ups post something underneath it, using actual evidence to prove in an almost bored way that it is untrue.

'It's not adversarial, it's just a wisdom-of-crowds thing,' says Giulio.

'It's a friendly teacher with an unruly child, isn't it?' I say.

'It's better than that,' he says, pointing one finger in the air. 'It's like instead of the teacher, all your classmates turning round and politely saying "no". It's peer-to-peer. More hori-zontal. And that's why it works so well.'

Maybe, grateful not to be massively humiliated, you actually listen to what you just said for the first time.

It's just like Sam Delaney said, not about social media, but about real-life hubs. Like the pub.

'You need people listening to your shit,' he'd told me, 'and shutting it down before it gets out of control. It's your friends.'

And while this gives me pause, the fact that we are in such early days means there will already be people working out how to subvert it.

* * *

You might think one obvious flash of hope in all this is the young people of Planet Earth; the people who will have to grow up in this strange new world. They will save us, because they are more digitally savvy, they have more time, they are growing up in this environment.

But this is the same youth that has already suffered through a pandemic that stole hugely precious years. The same kids who watched uncles and aunts being canaries in the conspiracy coal mine; the elders suddenly or slowly brainwashed by thuggish grifters and money-grabbing orators and their YouTube videos. This youth has watched an older generation get sent over the top of the trenches, unarmed and unprepared for an information war, and that is of little comfort to them.

If we're really saying that things will be OK because the next generation will sort it out, we're condemning them to a pretty sad survival. A life in which they are forced constantly to question reality, fostering a protective paranoia, knowing that if something seems too good to be true it probably is. If something is too simplistic, it probably isn't real.

And that is so unfair.

Unfair because it robs those young people we now hand this responsibility to of a sense of security and of trust in the world around them. There can be no real carefree abandon when it feels like the world might just be out to trick you.

And unfair because that means the rest of us just get to wipe our hands clean once we've handed them the problem, just like we've done with the climate. This is happening on our watch. We have to start the process of understanding it now and give them a fighting chance.

But really, the question is: shouldn't our institutions be doing this for us?

* * *

Many in the Civil Service have realised that their job isn't just battling each new lie that flies at us through a phone. It's actually to build a resistance to lies in the current population. You have to become a form of ever-shifting vaccine in a world suddenly much more wary of them. The way you communicate with the public has to work like inoculation.

You're also there to act as a handrail for people who suddenly find themselves absolutely blindsided as they realise they're at the centre of a disinformation campaign.

Like when the Russians poisoned the former double agent Sergei Skripal and his daughter Yulia on British soil in the town of Salisbury. The local mayor and city council were suddenly on the frontline of intelligence warfare. One minute they're talking about a new roundabout or whether to approve a controversial cycle lane, the next they're facing down the might of the Russian state.

Or you're on Thetford town council and suddenly 200 furious people turn up screaming at you because they think you're going to lock them in their houses and build giant walls around Thetford. You were only there to talk about the new ASDA that wants to open up. Now your photo is on Russian state television and everyone seems to be making fun of you.

These things happen alarmingly quickly. According to their own stats, every minute of every day, 40 million messages are sent, encrypted, via WhatsApp. Facebook users share 150,000 posts. On YouTube, 500 new hours of content go up. Nearly half a million people click something on Reddit. And there are 350,000 new tweets. And that's just me.

* * *

There are more everyday steps to combating this mass of nonsense.

The best way for the public to be aware of the strategies being used to brainwash them is to for the powers that be simply to be open about them. Stick to the truth if you're going to cut through the lies. Use that sword to cut the strings.

Before I left Brent Lee in Bristol that day – the former conspiracist turned truth advocate – we wondered what was next.

'We've had a head-start,' he said, meaning in this case conspiracy theorists. 'We were online, finding stuff, before anyone else. We know how to use social media. We know how to use all these different channels because we were there first. That's why Alex Jones and the David Ickes all have such massive audiences. It's why a bunch of unknowns can suddenly amass 200,000 followers. There's a network. But it's time to try and fix this.'

Fix it through amplifying the truth. In his opinion, it will take people who have fallen for the lies to help the rest of us stand up to them.

But one handy trick for all of us is to take a moment and wonder why we're reading what we're reading or watching what we're watching. If there's a doubt, then what is its aim? Is it to outrage us? Is it to provoke a response?

'I think the main thing that we need to do,' said Alice Stollmeyer, 'not as citizens but our representatives and our lawmakers and our governments … is regulate the hell out of platforms. Twitter, Facebook, whatever it is.'

Work has begun. When an explosion of disinformation, faked videos and propaganda came to light after the terrorist group Hamas invaded Israel in 2023, the EU was moved to write to Elon Musk with warnings of fines. Not only were lies spreading much quicker on Twitter/X since he radically downsized its verification team, but now that subscribers to the site got paid in real money for well-performing posts, it was in the liars' interest to lie harder and more fantastically than ever they had before; misinformation tends to travel further and faster than the truth, no matter how well told. People could now profit directly from abject lies, and it was now in their material interest to get creative with the truth.

'We need to regulate much, much, much, much, much, much more than we do,' says Alice, and it's down to us to force our representatives to get it done.

'What about all the people who'll say to you, what about freedom of speech?'

'Well, that's bullshit. There are many ways you can regulate that have nothing to do with constraining freedom of speech. We regulate television. This is a question of basic product safety measures. Cars don't enter the market without seatbelts. We don't introduce drugs into the marketplace without quality standards. So why do we make an exception for digital products? Why is it so special? This is not just about our democracy. It's public safety. It's even national security. Democracies all over the world need to team up.'

We are going to need a coordinated and organised approach because we are facing a tsunami, a combined natural disaster, a war on trust, thanks to hostile states, media empires, lone individuals, troll farms, tech bros, conspiracy theorists, and the lost and the lonely, all wielding their swords.

We need shields. Whenever there is a major disaster – a terrorist attack or an invasion – we crave information, and we are so hungry for it we will swallow almost anything. We seek out social media while the trusted sources take time to check their facts. And yet our governments are slow to learn from this repeat cycle. Concern fades away as the real truth slowly emerges.

Before shields, we just need more people to be *interested*.

* * *

Darren Jones is the Member of Parliament for Bristol North West, when I speak with him, but a few days later he'll be named Shadow Chief Secretary to the Treasury.

He's interested.

He's also young, sensible, friendly, highly intelligent – and has the manner and tone of a thoughtful politician that fits neatly into any era except perhaps this one, precisely because of that.

Darren thinks the public is ready for government to do as Alice Stollmeyer recommends and make bold moves to regulate AI. 'I think the public are kind of cool with that because we do it in other places. The CE mark, for example: when you buy a fridge you don't want it to blow up, do you?'

He's not against AI itself. He thinks if we use it right, there will be great opportunities for people to do fewer mundane jobs, embrace more fulfilling work and even work for fewer days of the week. He thinks if we don't use it, we will be left behind as a country.

But we have to be very careful with it.

Because he has also admitted, on the record and in Parliament, that he too (like Dr Daniel Jolley and me) thought that the Pope was entering his rap era.

'We have all seen the fake picture of the Pope wearing a white puffer jacket created by artificial intelligence,' he told colleagues, in a sentence never before said in the Houses of Parliament. 'It was an image I saw so quickly whilst scrolling on Twitter that I thought it was real until I stopped to think about it.'

I have a feeling the Pope wearing a puffer jacket will go down in the annals of history. There'll be a statue of it at the Vatican. It'll get its own animated series.

But while it sounds fun, Darren's point was that we are well aware of how we ourselves respond to breaking news cycles on social media – the need to share it, the excitement, the race to discuss it, not wanting to allow verifying it as actually true to slow us down. 'Many of us look at the headlines or the fake images over a split-second, register that something has happened, and most of the time assume it to be true.'

He's been a sometimes lone voice in Parliament when pushing these concerns for some time. He's pointed out the clear and obvious risks. He's worried about 'deepfake videos, photos of politicians saying or doing things that are not true to interfere with elections, or [...] fake hostage recordings of someone's children'.

That's actually happened, by the way. A woman named Jennifer DeStefano in Arizona answered her phone one day to hear her daughter – who was away on a school trip – screaming for help because 'these bad men have me!' It was only when she was already in the process of negotiating with the kidnappers now threatening to pump her daughter full of drugs that she was told about a new scam involving AI voice cloning and ransoms. Imagine if this and worse becomes as much a part of daily lives as emails from Nigerian princes or calls from people pretending to be from our banks or computer companies are. Imagine the dark creativity involved, the relentless terror, the never-ending, uncertain unease. Imagine also the wide-ranging implications for the integrity of every democratic process going.

Darren's seen the beginnings of all this in his own life, at least in the way we're currently used to things. He's met people who've seen dodgy videos. Read blogs. Accused him of things he hasn't done. Formed opinions strong as granite based on cubes of melting ice.

'As a constituency MP,' he says, 'I run lots of events to talk to my constituents and listen to them online and offline. Before the summer I had my annual summer coffee morning in Bristol North West – lovely part of the world – we were in a kind of bowling green, people came to drink tea and coffee. We talked about bus stops and climate change and whatever else you want to talk about. And there were a couple of people that came who were absolutely convinced, *absolutely convinced*, that there was this connection between the World Economic Forum, with whom I've done some work, Bill Gates, Covid, climate change, clean air zones, and ultimately a conspiratorial elite that's trying to control human behaviour and to restrict people's freedom.'

'That's different from bus stops.'

'And it is complete nonsense. Complete and utter *nonsense*. But my constituents that made that case – it wasn't that they were unsure and were asking about it, you could tell that they genuinely believed it. And they weren't unwell, they weren't mad, but for whatever reason they had consumed information from the internet that had led them to deeply believe that this was the truth. And I was like, look, you're perfectly entitled to your views, freedom of speech is important. [But] I don't agree with any of those points and these are the reasons why. And they were very polite about it, but they probably went away thinking, well, he's part of the problem though, isn't he? He did a meeting once at the World Economic Forum. I don't know where people anchor themselves around facts and truth.'

And that's basically just social media we're talking about – something Darren thinks is just an early case study of what is to come in terms of altering public discourse and confidence in information, and a test we've already failed at. 'We're only now trying to regulate it in 2023,' he says. 'And we're not doing that very well either, if I'm honest. And we've seen the implications it can have on public discourse, on people's confidence in information, on the human ability to *discern*, when there's so much information that you consume in such a quick period of time, the validity or the weight of the argument compared to the rubbish that gets pushed out there. Either because you've got people who are purposely trying to breed distrust by putting out disinformation, or you have people who are sharing things without knowing it's not true, or you've got people who just want to get clicks for advertising revenue and, say, write headlines for example that don't actually reflect the real story.'

I ask Darren whether he's seen the recent video of then-presidential hopeful Ron DeSantis. He'd been deepfaked. His face and voice copied incredibly effectively. His mannerisms replicated. He'd been digitally dropped into an episode of the sitcom *The Office: An American Workplace*, standing around with all the usual characters, while desperately trying to prove he is not wearing a pair of lady's trousers.

Things like this – DeSantis in lady slacks, the Pope in a puffer jacket – are the very playful side, though, of a terrifying progression that is already creeping up on every single one of us.

'Do you worry you'll wake up one day to a convincing video,' I ask Darren, 'where you appear to be saying, "Hi, I'm Darren Jones, and I hate Bristol. Also I am working with Bill Gates to make it more convenient to walk to the cinema and thereby lock you up?"'

It's a world which Darren is worried about personally, but more to the point globally.

'My voice is available on the internet all over the place. It'd be very easy to claim my voice and make me sound like I'm saying whatever you want me to say. But I think we've not had that problem in the UK yet so I don't quite know how we respond to it ... but I also worry because it gives bad actors an excuse for things that they *have* done but then can *deny* they've done.'

I'm confused.

'So let's say Trump has said something outlandish, which he is wont to do, maybe he could *then* say, oh no I didn't *actually* say that, that was just a deepfake. And then everyone goes, "Oh yeah, there's loads of deepfakes, I see them all the time. I don't really *care* what's real or not anymore. But I like Trump, so he must be right."'

And though this is a throwaway thought, to me it feels very powerful.

Because it implies that soon, this won't be a world of one shared reality where we all agree on the truth. It won't be two or three shared realities, one of conspiracy theorists versus realists, of propagandist 1 versus propagandist 2, or democratic reality versus populist reality.

Because just to cope with the sheer amount of information we are forced to deal with in any one hour, as we struggle to allow our brains to cope with what is true, what is not, what we can bear and what we can't, there is a real chance we will all end up operating in our own personal realities.

And worse, far worse: there will soon come a time when this new world is so overwhelming and so pervasive and so totally out of our grasp and we are indeed so unutterably screwed ... that we won't even care.

15

The Old Chinese Man

And the Great What If ...?

Books are important.

I mean, I would say that, wouldn't I? But they are.

That highly original thought struck me that day in Professor Rory Cormac's Nottingham office, the one with those floor-to-ceiling shelves, and those thousand or so books, and those millions of words.

After Dad had to leave to attend to business on higher planes than this one, my mum set about carefully and lovingly distributing his own huge collection of very specific academic books on Germany and literature to libraries or archives around the world that might need or want them.

It's only with the benefit of hindsight I realise not just *how* precious they were, but *why*. Why my mum was taking such great care to find them appreciative new homes; I drove some of them to academics myself, like little passengers, these small thoughtful gifts from my dad.

But it's obvious why they were so precious.

No internet back then, no Amazon. No e-books, no email, no Audible.

Bookshops didn't stock the obscure texts you needed, nor the specialist information; they didn't even know how to order from foreign countries or how to sneak things in from communist states.

Dad must have waited months for books to arrive and then hungrily devoured them. Each one must have felt like a sudden revelatory conversation.

I didn't realise the power of those moments for him before writing these paragraphs.

Anyway, Mum set aside some books for me – the ones I might be able to understand. The more mainstream German history ones.

Sadly for me, this meant I suddenly had around 60 books with Adolf Hitler on the cover.

Hitler this, Hitler that, Young Hitler, Old Hitler, Hitler's Spiciest Zingers, Hitler in Space.

When I took all the Hitler books home and left the box out, I am fairly sure the cleaner who spotted my sudden enormous collection of apparently Nazi literature had me immediately put on a list somewhere.

Anyway, Rory's office had a similar vibe. I don't mean it had a Nazi vibe. It didn't have a Nazi vibe. But all those book spines facing out, promising tales of coups, spies, propaganda, Cuba, the Cold War and China …

Information from books he trusts.

* * *

From the day I started writing this one, and thinking more and more about 2020 and the impact it had on the world, I kept reminding myself of that old Chinese saying – *may you live in interesting times* – and how for so many years I had mistakenly thought it such a nice sentiment.

May you live in interesting times! I hope there's plenty going on to entertain and educate you!

But after considering the future, I really do wish sometimes that we could go back to less interesting times. As you start to realise you are living through an absolute revolution in global misinformation and a world in which you're constantly questioning the truth, you could be forgiven for thinking, I didn't want things *this* bloody interesting.

I thought back to that moment in our house in Loughborough in 1989, with that first seismic event I can remember: those East German students staring in disbelief at the BBC as the Wall came down. Them calling it propaganda. It made me think of a box of old slides I found recently. Pictures of Dad in the GDR.

Old blue cars, empty streets. Functional buildings, concrete, no billboards.

There's Dad in Berlin, standing with a group of Russian guys by Checkpoint Charlie. And there he is, somewhere in East Germany, with a man in thick glasses who may or may not have been the friendly Stasi handler Dieter. A man keeping his eye on Dad, the personal way.

The way it happened back then.

* * *

The Cold War might be over, but we've found ourselves in a brand new one; an incredibly complex war that can reach from our screens and drag us in directly, whatever the issue. Trump, Biden, Brexit, Ukraine, Russia, China, Taiwan, Israel, Palestine, Iran. Climate change, Covid, vaccines, net zero, economic inequality, racial injustice, Big Tech, immigration. Local traffic-calming measures in and around Ipswich.

I remembered my intelligence contact telling me his opinions about the old Chinese man: that 'somewhere there is a string attached'.

At least there was only one. After exploring our current world, I feel there are strings everywhere now – *millions* of strings. Attached to every part of us, tugging for our attention and leading us into oncoming traffic. It's no longer just governments dealing with this stuff; it's all of us.

* * *

It had been a while since the old Chinese man had been in touch. I had long written off the idea of spy contact from him as a conspiracy theory, of course, but where's the fun in that? If I'm honest, I still secretly toyed with the idea of what I guess we might call the 'Great *What If*'.

It wouldn't leave me alone.

In some ways the old Chinese man had come to perfectly represent the times.

That the theory he could be a spy even crossed my mind is because we are living in a world in which we know we have to be careful. We're on high alert. Every text from an unknown number could be a scam, every news story a misreporting. We're in a confusing and paranoid fog that hostile states are perfectly happy with. If we're always questioning the truth, even when it's true, then we're constantly looking the wrong way.

'I get suspicious friend requests online,' Rory told me. 'Twitter requests, LinkedIn requests from very attractive young Russian blondes wanting to talk about Syria. I've got a colleague who's been hacked a couple of times because he's critical of China.'

'What did they do when they hacked him?'

'All his colleagues received an email from him with a forged resignation saying "I resign, I'm going to work in Hong Kong and I'm a wanker! I hate you all!"'

I couldn't help but laugh. In some ways being a troll must be quite fun sometimes. Imagine going through your output with your line manager on appraisal day.

'Nobody was really expecting that email,' said Rory. 'But there was a tell-tale sign it was fake. For some reason this particular colleague would always write the date at the end of his emails, which is completely unnecessary. But this resignation didn't have that. So even in my job, even if only for thirty seconds, you can fall for this stuff.'

* * *

Admitting you can fall for 'this stuff' is something we all have to do. Whether it's Darren Jones MP talking about MC Pope-a-lot in the Commons, me, or Rory here.

I've learned our defences in this confusing new world are few: we can keep calm. We can talk to our peers. We can stop sharing things online, just to be first. We can bookmark our verified news sources and ignore the sensationalist ones. We can check in with our friends and family. We can just be actively aware that disinformation, propaganda and conspiracy are constantly at our windows, throwing pebbles for attention. We can stay determined to avoid the traps that so many of our friends, families and colleagues have fallen into by maintaining a keen sense of self-awareness. We can insist our governments and institutions try to protect us from the worst of it. We can tell the truth.

And even though we often blame those who fall for the lies, I had discovered just how easy it is to enter the rabbit hole on your own – and just how many people in the world are actively trying to push you down it.

Many invent the rabbit hole in the first place, then point at it, saying 'have you seen this rabbit hole?!' and as soon as you peer over the edge – wallop – they've pushed you in. Lone actors, roomfuls of trolls, individuals looking to influence you into following their narrative, paranoid loners desperate for others to join their gang, propagandists paid by their bosses to sway your opinions and change your mind, and whole governments.

There are millions of rabbit holes for us to fall down, and somewhere there's one with your name on it. One perfectly tailored to your interests, your biases, your state of mind. One that will appeal entirely to you, and whether you leap into it or fall, it will introduce you to people just like you who want to believe the same.

I'm nowhere near immune. Everything I told you about at the beginning of this story has more in common with some of the people I met along the way than I'm comfortable with.

My story was like a 12-Step Programme for Conspiracy Theorists:

- I'd found the old Chinese man's email at a strange time of my life.
- I'd felt alone, powerless, numbed by grief.
- I'd stumbled across something unusual while feeling that loss and helplessness and vulnerability.
- During a time of great international and national tumult and outright confusion.
- A time of uncertainty when all I craved was certainty.
- I'd sought evidence for my own theory.
- I'd amassed exciting but unprovable clues to support it.
- I'd made assumptions I'd decided were educated guesses.
- I'd done some 'wider reading' and felt I had special knowledge over my friends who just weren't awake to what was *really* going on.
- I sought out expert testimony that said I could well be right, which didn't say I *was* right, but made me *feel* right.
- I considered there might be an 'end game'.
- I was even the one saying strange things down the pub.

And in the end, because of those 12 Steps … I decided that I, Danny Wallace, *might be personally up against the Chinese themselves.*

And *yet* …

And yet despite it all, despite knowing all this, when you don't have a concrete answer or proof, human nature means there will always be that Great *What If.*

What if the old Chinese man really *had* been a member of the Chinese state intelligence services after all? Doing things the old-fashioned way? Writing emails, sending out the official story about how wonderful China is, hoping to influence a Western academic?

In essence, instead of blasting out a quick TikTok vid or trolling, he was doing things the way men my dad's age did.

There was something strangely dignified and still somehow believable about it.

So I figured it'd be silly of me not to at least get Rory's opinion on the old Chinese man. After all, he'd just told me he was the target of something not dissimilar: the strange approaches from young Russian women hoping to engage on topical issues. And his colleague, the victim of some weird Chinese prank in which he apparently emailed all his colleagues, declared himself a wanker and resigned.

So as we sat outside in a bright sun drinking our pot of tea, I propped up my iPad and showed Rory the strange fonts, the cuts-and-pastes, the odd language, the long explanations of how well China was doing in the world. Just one last time.

And the first thing he says is, 'Well, it looks like it's been through Google Translate. It's been cut and pasted from various things.'

'It has, right?' I say, still trying to remind myself I had *finished* with this, it was just my own conspiracy theory. 'But what about how over the top he is, when he's saying how close he was to my dad?'

He *hmms*.

'Well, I've had emails from Chinese students which use very odd fonts. I assume it's because they're cutting and pasting. And some Chinese students and other overseas students do get very over the top. It's always "Dear Professor Sir, I'm so honoured to have even taken your class, it has been life-changing for me." It could be perfectly normal phrase-ology that doesn't work in English. It could be expressions they have that we don't.'

This is all very sensible.

I think back to my friend Mark laughing in that pub in Charing Cross, as I told him about the emails. It's just a dif-ference in language and culture. *Obviously.*

But then Rory pauses.

But.

'But ... I also think it's fishing. Just dangling, seeing what happens. It could be an enthusiastic amateur who's just doing his best? Either with the complicity or the blind eye of the state.'

'A senior government man I told about it said, "It's very possible it's what you think it is, but if it is, Danny, they have *not* got their A-team on it,"' I share.

Rory laughs.

'One would assume they're doing this to other people as well. I would guess it's someone fishing ... wanting to take any opportunity to promote a Chinese narrative? With the Covid references, I would guess that's some sort of set line. Like a talking point.'

'Like in Russia? In the troll farms?'

Uh-oh. I had to be careful not to be pulled back in. I had to remember what I'd learned. I didn't want the Great *What If* to lead to a Step 13.

'Yeah, like Russia, but just very lo-fi and amateurish. So for example, when Covid started, the first line from the Chinese that everybody started pushing was "There is noth-ing to see here". Then it was, "Oh shit, there *is* something to see here, but look how well we are dealing with it!" Then when Covid moved to Italy, the line changed to, "We are the nurse of the world, and we are helping everybody!"'

Government stooges even started doctoring and disseminating videos of genuine Italians clapping on their balconies for Italian hospitals, he tells me, so that they looked like they were clapping to thank the Chinese.

'They never missed a chance to tell us how brilliantly they were doing. And private citizens as well as people working with or for the state would amplify these lines. Some of it is pride: it's believing the doctrine. But then there's also this fear that if you're not doing it, and someone notices, they might report back to the party that you're not joining in. Like, why isn't this person promoting how great we are? Is this person not proud?'

It reminds me again of Dad, and East Germany, and the Stasi. Just before the communist regime turned to dust, it's thought that as many as one in fifty East Germans collaborated with the secret police, offering up information to them on the thoughts and actions of their neighbours, colleagues, close friends ... even their parents and spouses. Many were terrified not to, because the state was very careful to foster that paranoia that the state is much bigger than it is, with eyes everywhere.

It's the 'Stalin syndrome' that Kamaliya and Zahoor were talking about in their Hampstead house. That *truth is what we say it is, and you can trust no one but us*.

'Was your dad ever approached in real life?' asks Rory.

And that's the question I instinctively say yes to, but it feels like an empty yes. I'm still missing that actual anecdote. Though perhaps I won't be for much longer.

'Who else have you shown these to?' asks Rory.

'There's a guy called Nicholas Eftimiades I was thinking about contacting. He annoyed the Chinese state because he wrote a bunch of books.'

'I have those books,' says Rory, because of course he does, because books are important. 'He's former American Intelligence, isn't he?'

* * *

So maybe I could just ask one more person. Just to put my mind at rest. Just to do my own research.

Nicholas Eftimiades is known for his work in Chinese Intelligence Operations. He worked for seven years in the US government's National Security Space Office, and also at the Defense Intelligence Agency.

After his own book detailing the vast scale and scope of Chinese intelligence techniques and operations across the globe was published, China branded him an enemy of the state.

When he picks up his phone to talk to me on Zoom a day or two later, he seems fairly relaxed about all this. He has a huge cigar on the go and a big red mug of coffee. As he wanders around his Pennsylvania house with its double-height ceilings, red walls, Chinese rugs and vases and wall-mounted Japanese swords, I can see it's frosty outside.

I fill him in, tell him I think I'm being paranoid but there are also reasons I might not be. I tell him the old Chinese man has gone quiet on me, and that I've probably invented my own conspiracy, but that I'd talked with Rory and still had a few questions.

He talks urgently, loudly and has many questions to get through in as little time as possible. I feel like I'm contacting a stressed hostage negotiator who needs all the details, and fast, because there's a bomb about to go off somewhere and only I hold the key.

'So first of all, what year did your dad meet this guy? The year is IMPORTANT.'

'I think maybe 2009?'

'I can't attest for the mood that year. If you'd said early 2008, 2007, 2006, it was a carnival atmosphere. All Westerners welcome. Deals being done. Lies being told to make more deals. But China still seen as the promised land. Who PAID for him to go?'

Good question.

'The university might have paid for his flight?' I say. 'He was staying in a cheap little hotel nearby. I mean, he was invited.'

'No question he would have been invited,' says Nicholas. 'No *question* he would have been invited. But who paid for it and how did he get paid? If it was a local association, there's probably an intelligence affiliation. If they gave him a handful of cash, which is almost *always* the case, they say "hey, please take this, you've come all the way here" and they always pay the fee in *cash*, in *person* …'

'I don't think they paid him in cash. I don't think he even got paid. I imagine they covered his economy-class flight and hotel.'

'Money is a great way of getting dirt on someone. You walk in, make a speech, walk out with five thousand in cash. They hope you'll get addicted to the money.'

I remember my civil servant contact telling me the same. That's such a Robin Zhang move!

But if there's one thing I know about my dad, it's that he couldn't give a stuff about money.

(Although once to save money on porridge, he incorrectly filled out a multibuy request at a local health shop and accidentally took delivery of more than twenty 15kg bags. He would never finish them. Actually, *I* will probably never finish them.)

'See, were the intelligence services active back then?' Nicholas asks himself.

'Absolutely,' he answers.

'Was it as tenacious and aggressive as it is nowadays or since 2012?' he asks himself, thinking.

'No,' answers Nicholas.

He takes a puff on his cigar.

'So the question then comes ... in that case, *who was behind the emails and why?*'

He points at me urgently.

'WHAT WAS YOUR FATHER'S RELATIONSHIP WITH CHINA?'

'That was the only time he went,' I say nervously, 'though he liked the food.'

'And he went there to lecture? See, given your father's line of academia, I have a tougher time with that. If you're telling me your father was a nuclear physicist, OK, I *get* that, it makes *sense* to me. But this guy's talking about *EAST GERMAN VOICES OF DISSENT?*'

He spits the words out like he was saying my father's expertise was *SWANS WHO SHIT PEANUTS*. This guy's talking about *LADIES WHO BUY SPEEDBOATS?*

But he makes a good point.

So I guess that stops the idea dead.

'That said,' says Nicholas, slowly, 'you mentioned they used the word "friend"?'

'They said he was their *best* friend.'

He holds up one hand as if to say, 'Wait'.

'The word for friend in China is *pangyo*, but the connotation is very different. You have a society which is hierarchical. There's a pecking order. And academics are at the very top of that hierarchical society. Because in that system a professor is godlike.'

In China, professors and academics are closely aligned with the government. They're involved in government policy. They are at the heart of it all. It's probably second nature to assume the same is true of UK academics, even if they drive 12-year-old Hondas and order too much porridge.

'They wanted to stay in touch *forever* and be best *friends*,' I say. 'But again, I haven't heard back from them lately.'

'You can have the best friend [in that world] … but the day you become useless to them is the last day you'll ever see them.'

Or … what if the old Chinese man just didn't want to write to me anymore?

Anything could have happened!

He could have lost interest when he realised he was no longer talking to the man he met that evening by a lake, but to a boring grieving son instead. Maybe I was a burden to him. Or he could have become ill. Maybe he just tripped and broke his typing fingers.

'So that's that,' I say.

Then Nicholas grins.

'Unless ...'

Unless what?

'Unless you wrote back to them and now you pretend to be a professor. You could say "Hey, it appears I am to be made a professor at my dad's university!"'

We start to laugh.

'So I appear useful again?' I say. 'So that I become a ...'

'*Friend*.'

Ah yes, a *friend*: someone who might be able to propel the opinions of the Chinese state to a new and impressionable audience.

'You see how fast they write you back!' he says. 'Give it a shot. Write an email. I bet they'll say, "Oh, Danny, forgive me for leaving it so long!"'

※ ※ ※

That day in Nottingham with Professor Rory Cormac, by the way, ended unusually.

So we're finishing up, and Rory invites me back to his office so he can sign a copy of his new book for me.

It's a beautiful day and I'd like the walk, so we wander through the dappled light under campus trees and he tells me about his next project – a sort of academic thriller featuring some incredible forgers, which will definitely be a film one day.

We get to his office and he finds me a book.

I fling my backpack onto a tall chair by the shelves, and it's then – right above my bag, like it's meant to be – that I spot a particular spine, almost like it has a spotlight on it. I recognised the book because by complete chance, I had a feeling I also owned it.

I inherited it from Dad.

Don't worry, it's not another Hitler one.

This one was the story of *Die Firma*, the Stasi, the terrifying East German secret police.

The Stasi Files by Anthony Glees.

Published exactly 20 years before.

Almost absent-mindedly, I flicked to the index.

And then …

'*That's my dad*,' I said, finding Wallace, Ian and some page references, and Rory walked over and stood at my side.

Pages 260, 272, 273, 354 …

I flicked through and found a relevant page.

Glees's book says very specifically that on 3 February 1982, some spies gave a list of 'operationally relevant contacts and lists of hostile-negative people' to Markus Wolf, the mysterious man I knew only the name of, but who I know now was dubbed 'the Man Without a Face' during the Cold War for his incredible ability to elude being caught in photographs.

I knew Wolf was one of the most successful espionage chiefs of all time. He was head of the Stasi's ruthless Foreign Intelligence Department and pulled off all sorts of coups, planting agents in foreign governments and infiltrating peace movements.

Did Markus Wolf know who my dad was?

On the list Wolf had in his hands were a small number of dangerous names the Stasi claimed had links to the US embassy, to MI5, and to the British Secret Service – or were simply enemies of the state who wouldn't cooperate. Who told Stasi spy recruiters 'to get lost'.

Ian Wallace, in Leipzig in 1977, was approached by several individuals and walked firmly away from each one.

Dad was on the list. Dad told the Stasi to 'get lost'. Dad was an enemy of the state.

And there it was.

One occasion where I could now say with confidence that my dad had indeed been approached by foreign agents trying to recruit him.

I had my missing anecdote.

One that begins with a retiring academic and an old Chinese man by the West Lake in Hangzhou and ends in the office of an academic called Rory at the start of his career, and a book I had noticed by chance.

But I'd also found something else. I'd found a new, 13th step in my 12-Step Programme for Conspiracy Theorists, as I allowed myself one small step further into my rabbit hole, peering into that Great *What If*, mirroring once again exactly the thought processes of the classic conspiracy theorists ...

- If They could do *that*, They could do *this*. If *this* is true, why can't *that* be? If *East German* spies were after him, why not *Chinese*?

So I emailed Professor Anthony Glees. He's an expert in terrorism and radicalisation, and former head of the University of Buckingham Centre for Security and Intelligence Studies. He remembered my dad well and found his notes from their interview.

'Your father tried and succeeded to garner facts and evidence about East Germany from *inside* East Germany, whilst refusing to be supplied in any way by the Stasi.'

When you put it that way, it's almost like *Dad* was the spy.

'He was approached by seven different individuals, I don't know how many times, in an attempt to "control" his writing by feeding him information.'

Then he warns me: 'My advice, for what it is worth, and it isn't worth very much, would be to *treat any contacts* your late father had with *great care.*'

Does he mean the old Chinese man?

'I must confess, I'd be inclined to be anxious about that Chinese contact. He's unlikely to be one person – and they are *always* on the look-out for people to recruit …'

* * *

A few days later, feeling less anxious than I think Glees would like, I decide to do what Nicholas Eftimiades suggested.

Just a little experiment.

The old Chinese man was still quiet, despite his bold claims of wanting to keep in contact 'forever'.

So I write him – or her, or Them – a further short email, informing him that just recently my life has taken quite the turn for the academic. I tell him I have been travelling up and down the United Kingdom visiting various educational establishments.

(I did not mention that these were primary schools.)

I said I had been making short speeches and guiding the minds of students.

(I did not mention I was talking to them about my children's book series.)

I said they had proved *very* open to my ideas.

(Well, they *were* about nine years old.)

And I signed off as *Dr* Danny Wallace.

(Which is morally allowed, as I have an honorary doctorate from the University of Dundee awarded to me for services to doing things exactly like this.)

And I expected to wait a few days for a response, if a response would ever come at all, if there was still a file of some kind open and waiting for more. Because somewhere ... *somewhere* I believed again there was a string attached.

And the response came within *hours*.

And in among more talk of outstanding achievements in the field of Chinese excellence, and a recent and highly successful visit to a Tulip exhibition, the words:

Before I was your father's very good friend.
I hope now you become my very good friend.

I'll let you know if we keep contact. Forever.

Until then, all I ask is this: may we all soon live in *deeply* uninteresting times.

Acknowledgements

My first thanks are to my editor, Suzanne Connelly, for such calm, clear, smart and enthusiastic suggestions in shaping *Somebody Told Me*.

Second, thanks to the old Chinese man, obviously, wherever and whoever you are.

Thanks to everyone I spoke to while knee-deep in research, including those I can't name.

To Jessica Patel, Laura (W) Nicol, Francis Goncalves, Caitlin Goncalves, Brent Lee Regan, Alistair Coleman, Dr Sophia Moskalenko, Professor Rory Cormac, Dr Daniel Jolley, Dr Nicholas Eftimiades, Professor Anthony Glees, Kamaliya Zahoor, Mohammed Zahoor, Jessikka Aro, Dr Bharat Pankhania, The Secret Senior Civil Servant, The Secret Senior Spy, The Secret International Journalist, Koko the Gorilla, Karl Pilkington, Professor Robin Dunbar, Alice Stollmeyer at Defend Democracy, Dr Giulio Corsi, Darren Jones MP, Sarah Reed, 'Ben', 'Paul', 'Jack', 'Terry', 'Sasha', 'Tom', Conor Gogarty, Sam Delaney and George Monbiot.

Thanks to Robert Kirby at United and Andrew Goodfellow at Ebury and all those at both.

Biggest thanks to Greta. You give me never-ending encouragement.

Thanks Mum, and thank you Dad. Hey – we found that picture of you.

Love you, man.